Ein Sachverhalt ist denkbar heisst:
Wir können uns ein Bild von ihm machen
Ludwig Wittgenstein

Why diagrams?

We use diagrams in order to:

● present facts in a clear and attractive manner

● to visualize relations and matters which are not easily understood

● present things effectively without having to use many words or figures

● to be able to visualize things that by nature are not visual

We might have other reasons for employing diagrams:

● give an impression of thoroughness and show that we have a structured relationship to what we are working with

● draw the audience's attention to what we consider is interesting and important

● keep the audience alert during an oral presentation or a lecture

● be able to break up masses of grey copy in a report or a publication, thus making it more interesting

It would be hypocritical to claim that the last four reasons are more valuable than the first four. All good communicators know that the persuasive part of a presentation is important if one really wants to get information across in a cluttered environment. Diagrams thus become an indispensable tool in a process which aims at creating understanding.

This book investigates the possibilities inherent in the use of diagrams as a vehicle of communication. It will hopefully serve both as a guide and an inspiration.

BIS Publishers
Building Het Sieraad
Postjesweg 1
1057 DT Amsterdam, The Netherlands

T +31 (0)20 515 02 30
F +31 (0)20 515 02 39
bis@bispublishers.nl
www.bispublishers.nl

ISBN 978-90-6369-228-5

Conceived, designed and edited by
Jan Gauguin.

A few words about software
This book was not intended to function
as a software manual. The editor and
the contributors have not attempted to
recommend any one product over
another.
This also applies to the operating
system of your choice, and every effort has been made to ensure that the
methods discussed can be implemented using software available for
both Mac OSX and Windows.

Jan Gauguin

Designing Diagrams

Making Information accessible through Design

BIS Publishers

From our earliest times as human beings, we have recorded visually our attempts to describe and explain the world around us and the world inside us, their past, present, and future. The cave paintings at Lascaux in France, show prehistoric explorations of visible language that encompass descriptions of people, animals, and the natural environment. Egyptian tomb drawings depict elaborate rituals of the afterlife, assemblies of divine beings, forces of nature, and sacred objects. Thousands of years later, Aristotelean, then later Copernican drawings delineate our understanding of the cosmos. Over the centuries drawings of our planet's continents and seas show our understanding of the Earth's geography.

Throughout recorded history, information visualization has enabled us to keep track of, and to discover, structures and processes beyond what our verbal languages could easily express. Different cultures and times have provided numerous variations and startling innovations of form. The lean, rectangular, Mendeleev Periodic Table of the Elements is one way to view the world as a physical combination of the elements of the universe. The Tibetan Hindu Wheel of Life, with its densely illustrated, circular depiction of the cosmos, centered on a rooster, snake, and pig chasing each other's tails, is another rational means of depicting the entire universe. Whether we are looking at a personal nineteenth-century "memory" of a dream-trip through heaven, or we are looking at a Pacific Islander's navigation charts of the nighttime sky made through combination of sticks and bindings, we can be amazed by the creative imagination of human beings who saw a possible way to diagram an entire world.

These "visible languages" of tables, forms, charts, maps, and diagrams have evolved through the centuries. Before William Playfair dreamed up his bar chart and line chart techniques, our means of visualizing numerical relations was less powerful. Charts of various kinds enabled us to see patterns, trends, and outliers, more readily. The latest multidimensional charts enable us to track phenomena in spaces of more than four dimensions. These visualizations depict data from models of the world's most complex, and sometimes ubiquitous circumstances, e.g., social interactions.

Maps of varying dimensions and topologies enabled us to view the surface of the spherical earth on flat sheets of parchment or paper, providing a practical format in which to summarize our geographic knowledge. Map makers once hailed Mercator's projection as a breakthrough, but many others have emerged in the centuries since then, some very specialized, like Buckminster Fuller's Dymaxion globe, which, laid flat, best preserves the shape of the continents. Computer graphics today, combined with global positioning systems and mobile telecommunication, enable maps to have a greater impact on our daily lives than any time previously, as we navigate our daily itinerary.

Thomas Kuhn, the noted scientific historian, described advancement in scientific knowledge, as we lurch forward through changes of fundamental paradigms, from a set of concentric crystalline spheres of the Platonic earth-centered classical universe, to the Copernican heliocentric orbits of the planets in our modern world. The solar visual model was even absorbed into subatomic particle theory in the form of the Bohr atom: electronic "planets" orbiting around a nuclear aggregate of protons and neutrons forming a "sun." Late in his life, Kuhn acknowledged the role and importance of diagrams in summarizing bodies of knowledge and in enabling bold thinkers to formulate new paradigms, especially as they worked out the patterns of coalescing thoughts. For example, he pointed to the image of interlocking rings known to Maxwell that stimulated his contemplating parallel, related mathematical expressions of electromagnetic theory.

Millennia ago, Plato drew mathematical-geometric diagrams in the sand with a stick. In modern times, we have drawn them with pen or pencil on paper, or chalk on a board.

For centuries, such diagramming was often merely mono-chromatic, but occasionally ornamented with or semantically assisted by color, typography, signs, and illustrations. The most potent of our information visualization techniques were, for the most part, static, two-dimensional depictions. They might be abstract, or elaborate pictorial depictions with much adornment, or something in between. However, they were painstakingly constructed, and for the most part two-dimensional objects, even if they depicted elaborate three-dimensional structures. Only in the last century has diagramming taken on new capabilities with the rise of computers graphics.

Today, computer-based techniques offer startlingly fresh, unconventional, novel techniques for displaying all forms of information visualization: tables, forms, charts, maps, and diagrams. Because diagrams are the most "free-form" of these visible languages, allowing for flexible topologies, structures, and visual formalisms, diagrams offer the most dramatic example of new capabilities:

• Three-dimensional diagrams of perceptual or conceptual spaces
• Dynamic, changing, real-time diagrammatic displays based on current states of evolving data
• Abilities to "run" diagrams forward and backward in time
• Abilities to zoom in and out of spatial constructions and to view them from any desired perspective
• Diagrams themselves as user interfaces connected to models of data and functions
• Diagrams as virtual realities, which we can inhabit
• Diagrams combined with music, speech, sound and video to become multimedia constructs
• Diagrams used as a means to reason
• Diagrams that computers as well as human beings can read (so-called machine-readable diagramming techniques)

With the rise of augmented reality displays and augmented cognition techniques, diagrams stand poised to become part of our daily life and a constant companion to our thinking things through. The role that diagrams can play in our communication becomes amplified through effective computer graphics techniques, through semi-automatic depictions, through global telecommunication, and to social interaction networks combined telecommunication with diagramming.

Our future communication may become much more visual (diagrammatic) than verbal, as millions, eventually billions, of people around the world recognize that diagramming has become a visual *lingua franca* by which we can express our facts, concepts, and, yes, even emotions effectively to anyone, anywhere, at any time. The tools at last have evolved that can enable almost anyone with a computer to make, and view, these constructs.

In 1943, Herman Hesse, in one of his last major works, *The Glass Bead Game* (aka *Magister Ludi*), envisioned a future society in which all knowledge was transformed into music. Perhaps a more likely, audiovisual solution, is to imagine all future knowledge transformed into a multimedia experience in which a widely understood and "writable" diagrammatic representation of all knowledge provides us with a display, and a "handle," by which to understand and manage all of reality, all of what we perceive and what we conceive.

On a more down-to-earth, current-timeframe level, this book by Jan Gauguin provides a welcome focus for professional designers and the interested lay audience in all matters of designing effective diagrams. Our professional book shelf is surprisingly bare in regard to primers and instruction manuals for good diagramming. This book begins with the basics, but then moves on to a gallery of diagram-types and sophisticated, articulate, and complex solutions. This present volume will add to the usable, useful, and appealing studies that focus on this topic providing both how-to-do-it insights and an appreciation for good design.

Aaron Marcus

Aaron Marcus is president and founder of
Aaron Marcus, Inc. (AM+A) in Berkeley, California, USA
(www.AMandA.com)

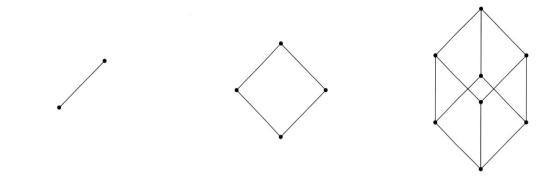

According to Paul Klee we get a line by taking the point for a walk. Pursuing this train of thought, we will investigate some of the possibilities resulting from putting basic shapes together, thereby discovering interesting combinations.

Like many other visual occurrences in our culture, diagrams are a field that suffers from a certain degree of poverty and stereotype thinking: Not all angles have to be 90 degrees. Lines do not always have to be straight. Curves can be employed to good effect. The polygons and the volumes stem from classic geometry and might be well known to many. Not so many are aware of the possibilities inherent in combining them.

Creating grids and proportional systems can be fun. Besides, they can add discipline and continuity to your presentations. Hierarchies and balance can be expressed through design.

What has this to do with diagrams?
The exercises shown can be viewed as syntactic manipulations, devoid of any "contents". I must therefore ask the readers to use their imagination and "read" something into what is shown. Relations can be revealed and communicated through design. The shapes and the colours are useful in order to emphasize both affinities and differences. A shape has many possibilities of graphic presentation. Colours can appear active or passive. A spatial presentation is useful if we want to approach a complex from several viewpoints.

As this is a book about visual communication any further verbal elaboration on the themes mentioned above seems out of place. We shall have to employ Klee's "thinking eye".

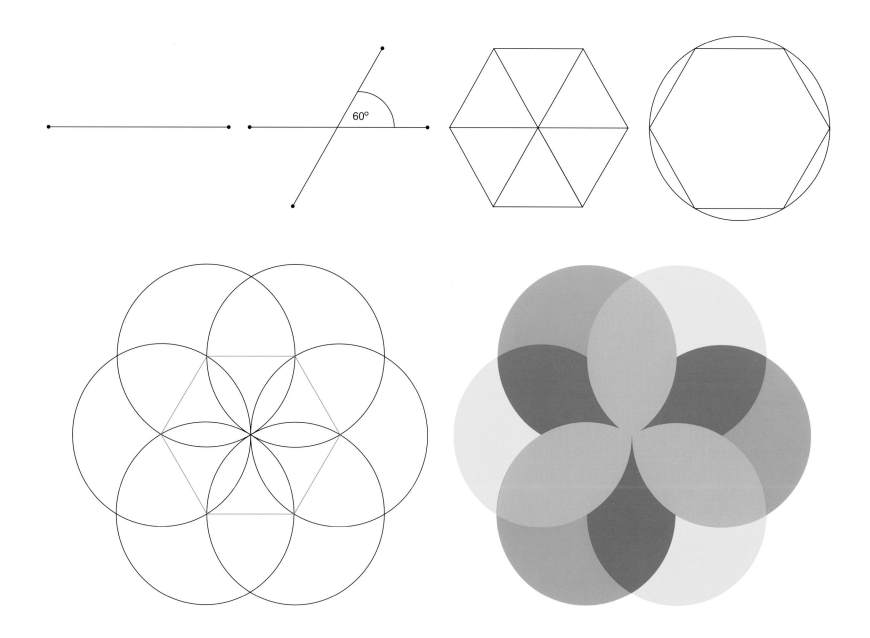

Group of circles using the hexagon as coordinator.

Diagrams which aim at showing complex relationships, or how things affect each other can be designed this way. This is only one example. There are numbers of combinations using different polygons and colour overlapping.

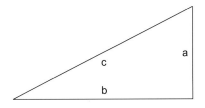

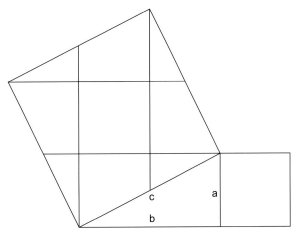

The Pythagorean triangle is a construction where one of the angles is ninety degrees. Line b is twice as long as line a. The hypotenuse (c) is then $a^2+b^2=c^2$. (This sets the size of the large square).

In our construction (on the right) straight lines have been drawn from the four corners of the large square.

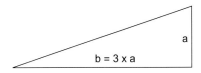

On this triangle we have given the catheter (line b) three times the length of a. This creates a "wrong" square but can produce some new and interesting results.

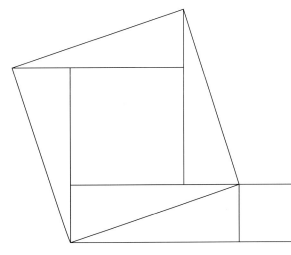

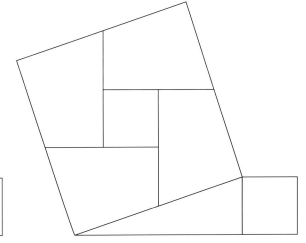

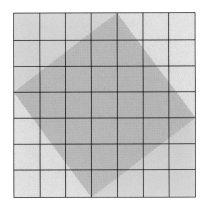

The Pythagorean puzzle games
Draw a grid of 7 by 7 small squares. We have drawn in four triangles in each of the corners with a right angle between the two sides. The red area which is left when the four triangles have been removed is a square made up of 49 minus 24, which makes 25 small squares in our grid.
This reveals and visualizes the "secret" of the Pythagorean axiom.
Historians claim that the Babylonians knew about this proof long before Phytagoras.

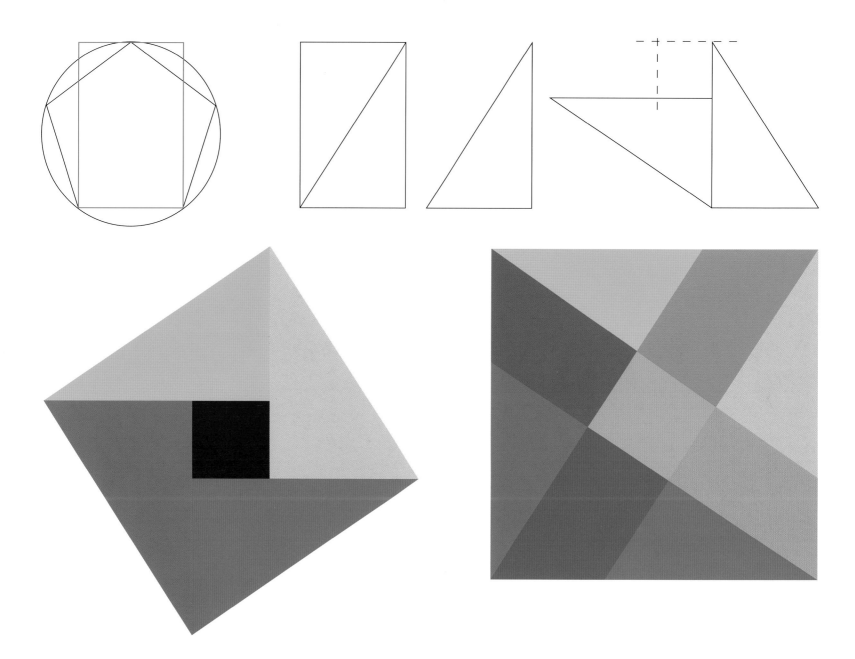

The starting point of this construction is a rectangle with the Pythagorean proportions (3:4:5). (Top left drawing). Dividing the rectangle gives two triangles with a right angle. The square that divides the rectangles is equal to the difference between the catheters of the two congruent triangles. Four triangles are needed to form a square. The construction has a number of possibilities for divisions and subdivisions.

This can be useful in diagrams expressing differences and divisions. Besides, playing the Pythagorean puzzle game can be an educational and entertaining activity in itself.

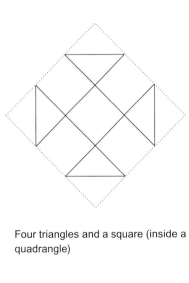

Four triangles and a square (inside a quadrangle)

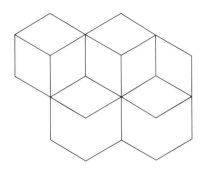

Six overlapping hexagons which produce nine (oblique) squares

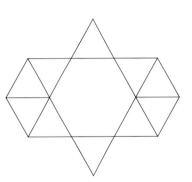

One hexagon and ten triangles

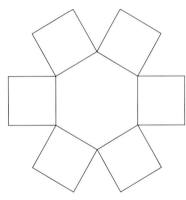

One hexagon and six squares

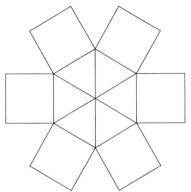

One hexagon, six triangles and six squares

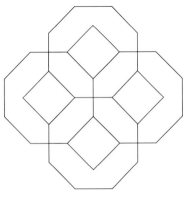

Four overlapping hexagons and four squares

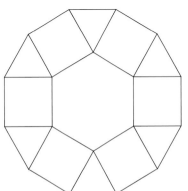

One hexagon, six triangles and six squares

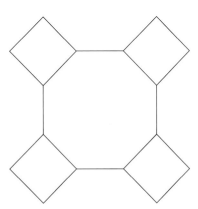

One octagon and four squares

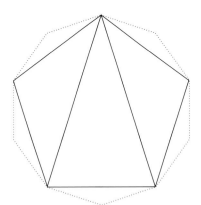

One pentagon, three triangles (inside a decagon)

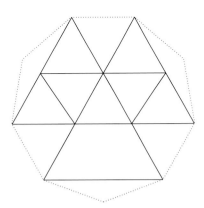

Three plus three triangles (inside a nonagon)

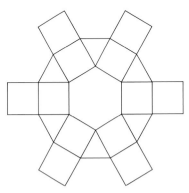

A dodecagon, a hexagon, six triangles and twelve squares

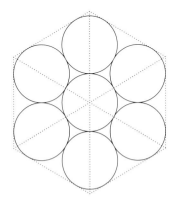

Seven circles organized in a hexagon

13

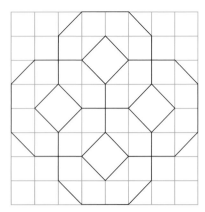

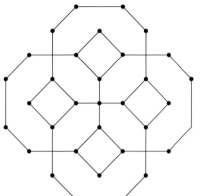

Lines to points

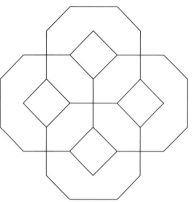

Contour as lines

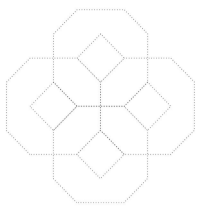

Contour as points

The motif (or figure) is made up of horizontal, diagonal and vertical lines. These are assembled in a grid consisting of 8 by 8 squares.

The figure which evolves from this arrangement will be axis/mirror symmetrical. This means that it will remain unchanged when rotated 90 degrees or shown mirror reversed. We will investigate possibilities of presenting this figure employing different (known) techniques. There are, of course, many more possibilities in employing textures and structures but the aim of this exercise is to develop a catalogue of possibilities. This will hopefully prevent us from finding "solutions" too early in the process. These illustrations were produced in a vector-based program. Unlike pixel-based programs where a grid defines the resolution of the image, vector illustrations can be blown up indefinitily.

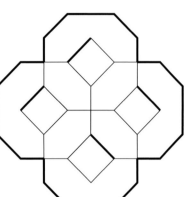

Contour as thick and thin lines

Surface hatched

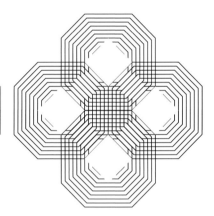

Surface as overlapping lines

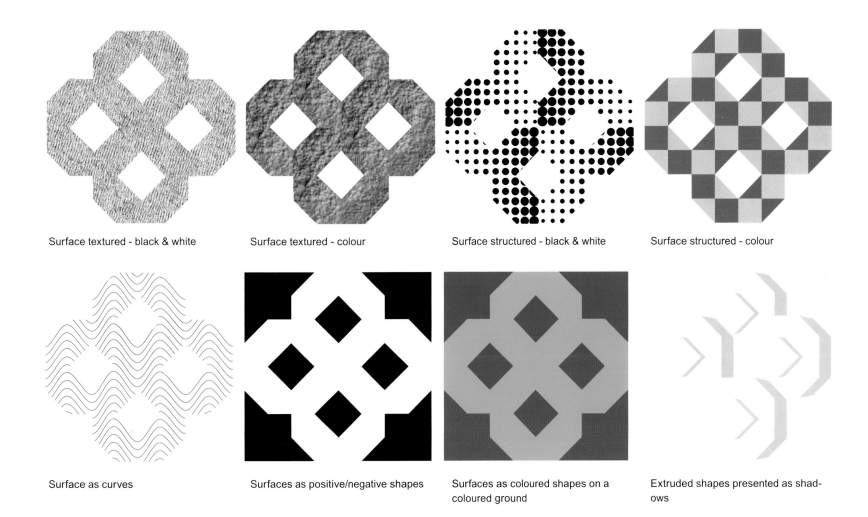

Surface textured - black & white

Surface textured - colour

Surface structured - black & white

Surface structured - colour

Surface as curves

Surfaces as positive/negative shapes

Surfaces as coloured shapes on a coloured ground

Extruded shapes presented as shadows

We are in debt to Buckminster Fuller (1965-1983) who investigated the design possibilities in combining Platonic and Archimedean solids. His work had a profound influence on 20th Century architecture and principles of construction.

On a more mundane, two-dimensional level, many of the combinations of shapes that make up these solids lend themselves to diagram constructions. They have an inherent logic and (mostly) a symmetrical makeup.

They can be "manipulated" to serve our needs in many situations: Explaining the flow of information; Mapping out organizational patterns; Make to/from situations visible to the viewer. A further investigation into this area might bear fruit.

The use of colour and typography is not shown here, but are natural ingredients in the process of creating meaningful designs.

(see page 196 **Crichlow**)

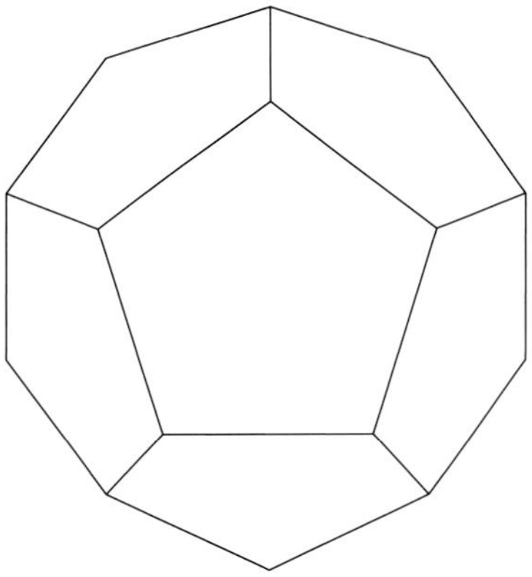

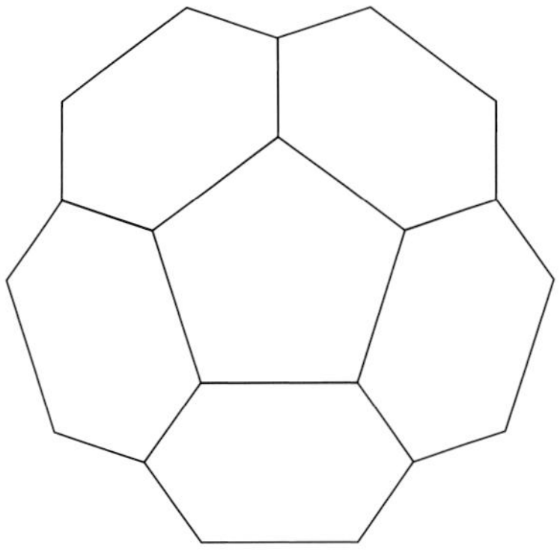

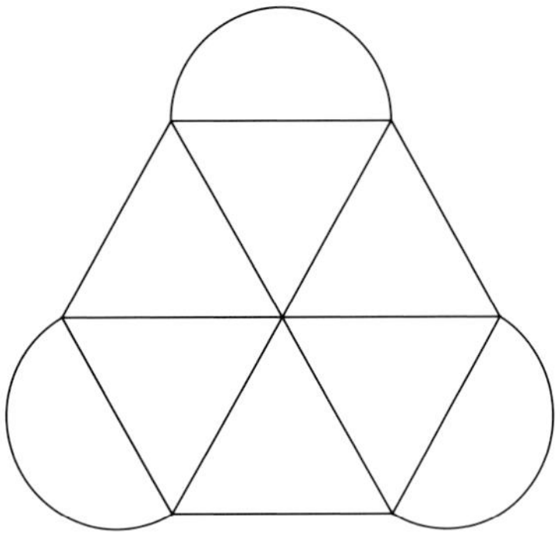

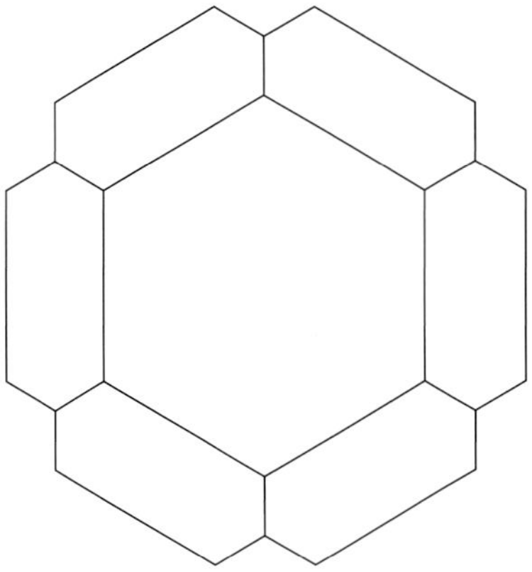

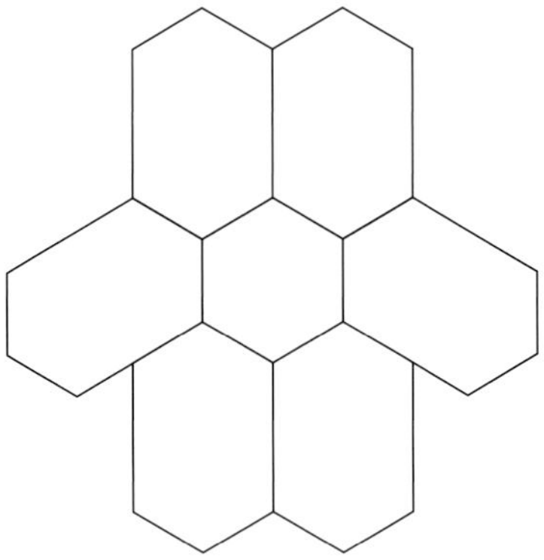

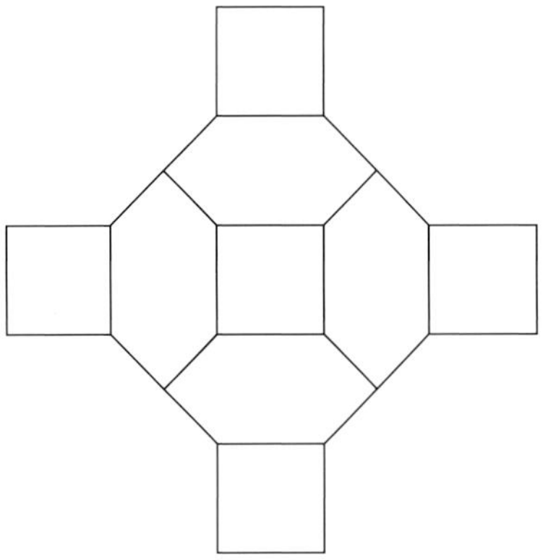

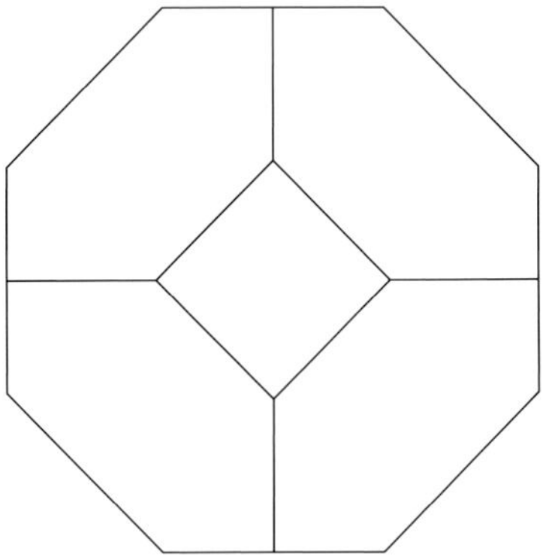

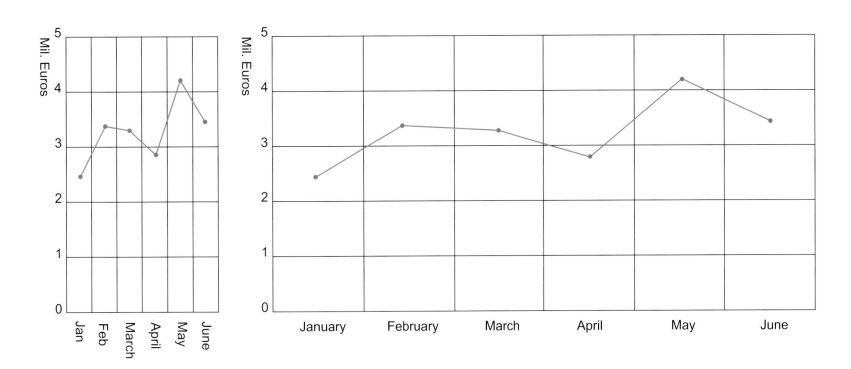

These two diagrams are made from the same data but they are perceived differently. If they are supposed to show the sales from a motor company over a six months period they produce different impressions in our mind.

The narrow design on the left looks as if seasonal variations have been fairly dramatic. The one on the right might make us believe that the variations have been small (with only May as the "peak" month).

Our choice of width and height will depend on which message we want to send. Our choices will be governed by practical considerations applied to each case. Still, there are some governing principles:

Diagrams shown on a screen must conform to a "landscape" proportion. (Screens in the "portrait" format do not exist)

Designs are either square or rectangle. (Sizes that are somewhere in between should be avoided.)

Too many proportions in one and the same job leave an arbitrary impression.

This chapter deals with some of the methods at our disposal.

The theories of the proportions derive from ancient geometry and were rediscovered and refined during the Renaissance. They are concerned with numeric and geometric relations between parts (in a work of art, in a building or in the human body.)

The oldest we have been able to record stems from the Greek sculptor Polyklet (Polykleitos) and is from app. 400 B.C

Euclid from Alexandria (b. app. 315 B.C) and his associates also made attempts at geometric analysis of proportions. Euclid is credited with having revealed the mystique surrounding the Golden Section. The harmonies the Greeks sought are given a geometric explanation. (See page 20).

The Roman architect Vitruv (31 B.C. – 14 A.D) devised a numerical system by dividing the human body into parts. The face should be 1/10 of the total length of the body, the head should be 1/8 and the chest 1/4 and so on. Vitruv built his theories on what the Greeks had left behind and produced "About Architecture". His writings were rediscovered in 1413. Both Albrecht Dürer and Leonardo da Vinci used Vitruv as a basis for their own studies. Dürer's "Four books on Human Proportions" appeared in 1528.

Leonardo Fibonacci's numerical system is explained on page 21.

During the Renaissance, the proportions were given a metaphysical dimension: The principles reflected a harmony that God had bestowed on the Universe. ("Divina Proportione").

In more recent times, Le Corbusier (1887-1963) devised a system based on the average height of men (183 centimetres) and called it "Le Modulor".

American industrial designer Henry Dreifuss (1962-1972) produced "The Measurements of Man" where he explored the relationships between the body and the objects man uses.

Myths about the aesthetical superiority of the proportions derive from the fact that the parts and the totality form an inextricable alliance.

Interest in using proportioning as a guideline in architecture and design has varied throughout history: We can find many examples from the Renaissance but the interest seems to wane as we move into the Baroque period.
Architects who received their training before 1920 mostly worked in a neoclassical tradition and had proportioning as part of their curriculum. This generation is long gone, and it appears that much of their knowledge disappeared with them.

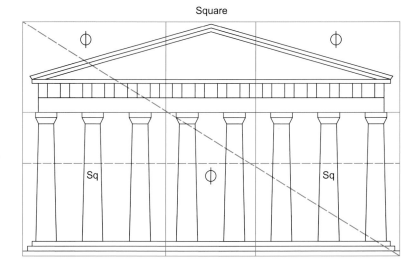

Square

Sq   Sq

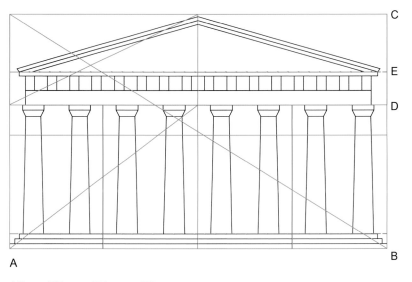

C
E
D

A   B

$$\frac{AB}{BC} = \frac{BC}{BD} = \frac{BD}{CD} = \frac{CD}{CE} = \phi$$

Parthenon (Athens)
Designed by Iktinos & Callicrates
447 - 432 B.C

This remarkable building has been a favoured object for analysis.
It can be measured in different ways, but the proportions conforming to the Golden Section are omnipresent. (The circle with the vertical line in it is the sign for "Golden Section")

Since 1970, Modernism has been under constant debate. Many have questioned the axioms propagated by Corbusier, Gropius, Mies, Rietveld and others. Their detractors often claim that their proportioning was used in order to prove that their solutions represented "objective truths".

The international design scene today is fractionalized and shows a multitude of expressions hardly to be found in any other epoch in history: Traditionalists, revivalists, modernists, postmodernists, deconstructivists and techno freaks are competing for our attention. In my teaching on this subject I try to make it clear that proportioning is a matter of *design*, not style. In my opinion, proportions override aesthetical directions and schools. They simply appear whenever we start putting two or more shapes together. Many undergraduates seem surprised when I show them examples of proportioning applied to designed objects: "Oh, are they *that* old?"

Working with proportioning is not a mechanical process: It can be compared with that of a piano tuner trying to find the right relationships between sounds. (See page 196 **Elam** and **Frandsen**.)

Some historians claim that it was Phytagoras wife *Theano* who found the measurements of The Golden Section.

AB : AC = AC : CB

There is a mention of her in some Greek writings but at that time it was considered inappropriate to publizize the name of "honorable women" in the public realm.

One may assume that sticks like those shown above were employed in the building process in ancient times. The (official) constructions which help us find the Golden Section is shown on the next page.

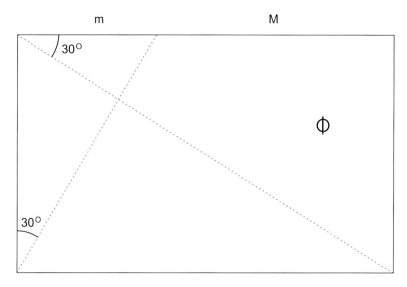

If we know the width of an object we can easily find out how it relates to a golden rectangle. Note that the deciding angles are 30 degrees.

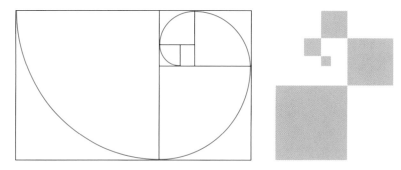

Arrangements in accordance with the progressions in the Golden Section

Methods for finding the Golden Section

In any division of a line or an area the smallest part will have the same proportional relationship to the largest part as the largest part has to the whole line or area.

Figure 1:
A line AB is divided in two and determins the height AB:2. A diagonal starting at point A is drawn to the top point of AB:2.
We then draw a circle with AB:2 as radius which crosses the diagonal at a point we call D. We make another circle with radius AD. Where this meets AB we have found the dividing point E, which divides AB in a "Major" and a "minor" part.
There are other methods of construction, but this is the most commonly used today.

Figure 2:
We can find similar measurements by dividing AB in 13 parts (using our calculator). We can create a 5 x 8 golden rectangle with the measurements we have arrived at.
Beware that this method is not as accurate as the triangular method shown in Figure 1.

Figure 3:
We can let minor (m) in one construction become Major (M) in the following. This way we can produce an "endless chain" where the progression conforms to the relationships in the Golden Section.

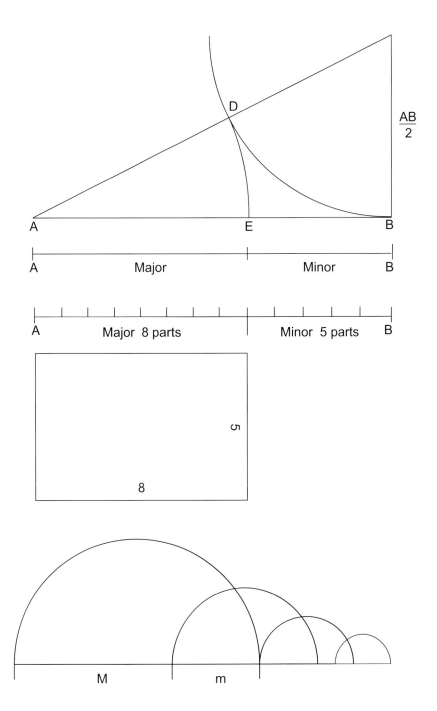

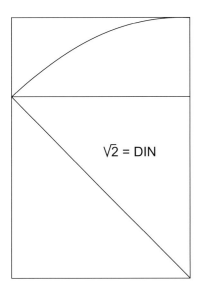

$$\sqrt{2} = DIN$$

We find the square root in second by using the diagonal in the square as radius.

This proportion was known by Renaissance painters as "The Golden Gate" (Must not be confused with the Golden Section). Irrespective of size it created one standard for landscapes and another for portraits.

If a size is divided in two parts, the new size will retain the same proportions as the predecessor. The width of one size will be the height of the next one.

The DIN paper sizes were established in 1922 and became the official United Nations document format in 1975. It has obvious advantages with respect to economy, handling and storage. Britain adopted the DIN paper sizes in the 1960s. In North America other sizes are used.

$1 : \sqrt{2} = 1,414$

The DIN A paper sizes.
The measurements are in millimetres
A0 841 x 1196 (app.1m²)
A1 594 x 841
A2 420 x 594
A3 297 x 420
A4 210 x 297
A5 148 x 210
A6 105 x 148
A7 74 x 105

DIN = Deutsche Industrie Normen

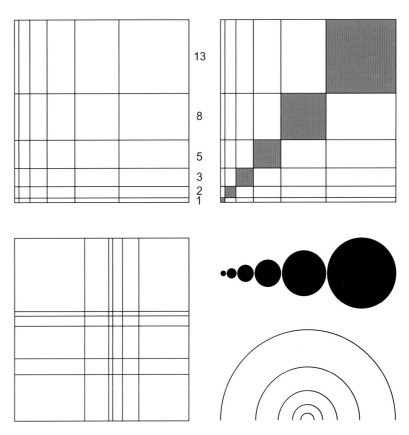

Leonardo Fibonacci (also called Leonardo from Pisa) claimed that he had found the coordinator C (expressed numerically as 1,6) and a "dynamic" chain of numbers: 1,2,3,5,8,13,21,34 and so on.

New figures are included in the chain by adding the two predecessors.

If the new number is divided by the preceding number we get these results: 8:5 = 1,6, 13:8 = 1,625, 21:13 = 1,615, 34:21 = 1,619

We see that the variations are only in the hundreds — 1,6 is constant.

After having reached the fifth number in the chain (8) the proportional pattern is very close to the proportions in The Golden Section. You can divide a line with 1,618 and find a minor to major division of the line.

Fibonacci's written account of this discovery was to be found in his "Liber Abaci" of 1206.

We can take a chosen amount of Fibonacci-numbers and divide their sum with the length of a rectangle or a square. We then have a unit to work from. (In the examples above millimetres were used). We can arrange the proportions in regular or irregular sequence.

The progression can also be applied to curves. The "dynamics" can easily be visualized.

One can also find the square root in second by using the method shown here.

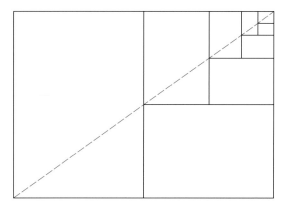

The DIN sizes can be divided in two equal parts. The proportions remain constant.

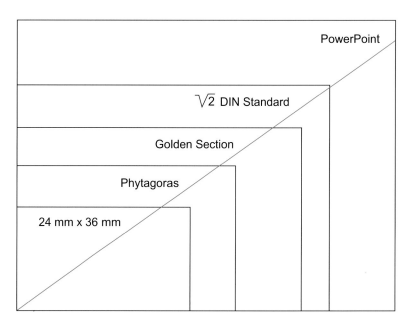

PowerPoint

$\sqrt{2}$ DIN Standard

Golden Section

Phytagoras

24 mm x 36 mm

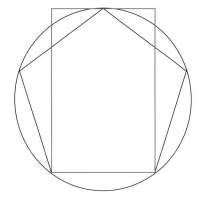

Rectangle according to the Pythagoreian proportions (3:4:5) designed by using the pentagram.
The proportion is 1:1,538
The Pythagorean rectangle is favoured by many book designers.
Jan Tschichold (1904-1974) argued that this was a more elegant way of presenting single column text matter (compared to paper sizes that conformed to the DIN standard). More about Tschichold on the next page.

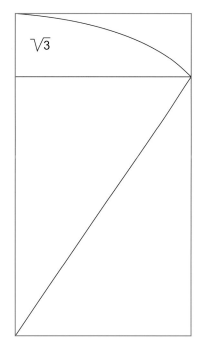

$\sqrt{3}$

We can use the square root in second (see previous page) and use it as a base for making a narrower rectangle as square root in third. (1:1,732)
If we continue this process till we reach the square root in fourth we shall have a rectangle of double square proportion. (1:2)

Which is the "right" rectangle?
We see that the DIN standard paper is not at all congruent with other known proportions.
The American photographic industry established their sizes with no considerations to DIN standardization or U.S paper sizes. This has been a headache for designers and art directors as long as anyone can remember: Nothing seems to fit and photographic illustrations often need extensive cropping.
The only ways to get around this is by careful planning and have the illustrations tailor made to the medium you are using.

Jan Tschichold and the proportions in book design

Tschichold did extensive studies of old books and scripts. He managed to disclose harmonies between paper sizes, type areas and margins and expressed them in diagrams. He called these relationships "unwillkürlich" (non-arbitrary) as they were well known to printers and scribes long before the metric system was established in 1791. In other words: No millimeters (or inches) were needed.
"Although not easy to explain, most people find a geometrically well proportioned book more beautiful than a book that has arbitrary proportions".
It is hard to argue against this statement.

The illustration shows the rectangular proportions he recommends for choosing page formats. These are:

A 1: 2,236 (1:√5)
B 1: 2 (1:√4) A double square
C 1:1,732 (1:√5)
D 3:5
E 1:1,618 The Golden Section
F 1:1,538 The Pythagorean Proportions
G 2:3
H 1:1,414 (1:√2) The DIN Standard
K 3:4

Tschichold, Jan "Willkürfreie Mass-verhaltnisse der Buchseite und des Satzspiegel" Basel 1962

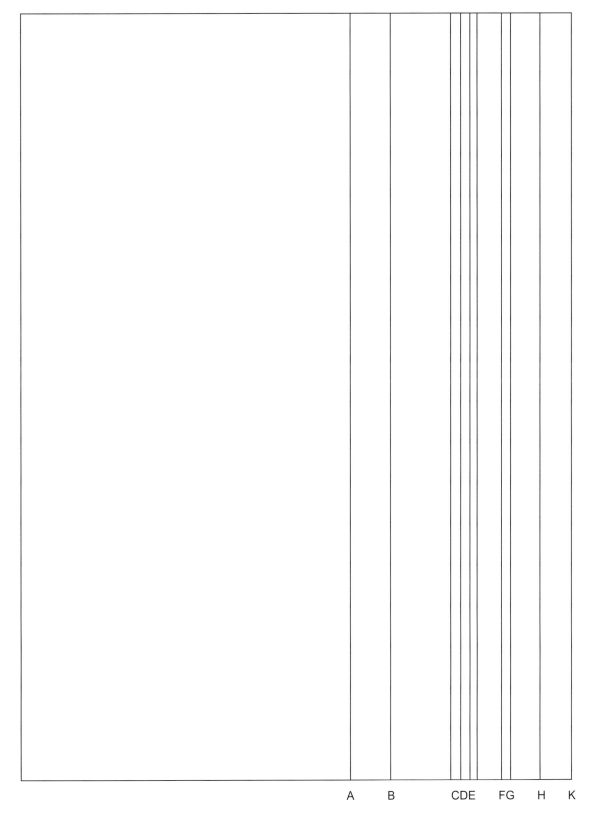

A   B   CDE   FG   H   K

This is a spread from a collection of essays designed by the author. The page size and the type areaes are in accordance with root three rectangles (1:1,732). The margins are determined by letting the diagonals intersect with an equillateral triangle that covers the entire spread.

I have had the privilege of knowing Halina Dunin-Woyseth for more than twenty years. It has also been a great pleasure doing different kinds of professional work together.

During these twenty years I have been working in different places and in different positions. I was a manager in SINTEF doing research within architecture and building technology in the late 80s, and the directing manager of the research foundation of ALLFORSK from 1990 until 1995. Both being located in Trondheim.

For the last ten years. I have been a full time professor in spatial planning at the Department of Landscape Architecture and Space Planning at the Agricultural University of Norway, located 30 kilometers south of Oslo. In January 2005 the department was renamed, and is now called the Norwegian University of Life Sciences. Throughout all these years, Professor Dunin-Woyseth has remained a very competent and hard working planning professional, very much dedicated to developing the PhD education at the Oslo School of Architecture AHO.

I have also been aware of how actively Halina Dunin-Woyseth has worked in the international academic arena, partly through the Nordic network via the Nordic Journal of Architecture, and in a more European perspective through the Association of European Schools of Planning, AESOP. It is very easy to stick the label, not a prophet in her own country, on the work of Halina Dunin-Woyseth. Her name and work are very often referred to in these significant international networks. And her work within the area of developing curricula for PhD studies, is much respected and often commented on in very positive ways.

Over the years, she has also developed an impressive professional network in other parts of the world, such as Japan and USA. By chance I followed her as a visiting scholar to the University of California, Berkeley during the autumn 1987, at the Institute of Urban and Regional Development, IURD, lead by the famous planning professor *Mel Webber.*

My most important professional co-operation with professor Dunin-Woyseth was during the years1992-2001 when I was a part-

time professor at the department of Geography at NTNU in Trondheim, and where Halina was an external examiner. I found this collaboration very creative and inspiring. I think this was partly due to the fact that Dunin-Woyseth, in this period, was already developing her concept for making a PhDs program for other "making professions" at AHO in addition to architects.

In my position, as a part time professor, at the department of geography, I tried to develop a course in spatial planning for theoretically-oriented geographers in a way that would give them some understanding of how planning works in practice. Dunin-Woyseth, in some ways, was working on a similar issue, but from the opposite direction, trying to teach practitioners a more theoretical approach to their field. These courses were based on some very basic principles on which we both agreed. One central theme was learning by practical experience from concrete cases.

In 1993 we wrote a paper together for the 7th AESOP CONGRESS Lodz in Poland with the title, *Learning by practical experience from concrete cases.* The following text is from our common paper from this conference: Modern planning, which emerged in the second half of the nineteenth century has its foundation in the "design professions" of architecture, landscape architecture and engineering. After the Second World War, the planning discipline has expanded to include sociology, psychology, social science, and last, but not least, economics. But entering the 1990`s there are indications that the architects way of learning and practicing planning is on its way back.

The focus of this paper is on one aspect of architectural practice, the architectural way of teaching/ learning. We are of the opinion that the design-based, problem-oriented and experience-based model is an appropriate future model for the teaching of planning to architects. A central reference is made to the Dreyfus model, a theory of step-by-step learning. According to this model, we can observe levels in man´s way of learning and managing a certain skill. We distinguish between accumulated and assimilated knowledge, the first category being general knowledge, which can be taught independently of the context, while the second is very much upon the context.

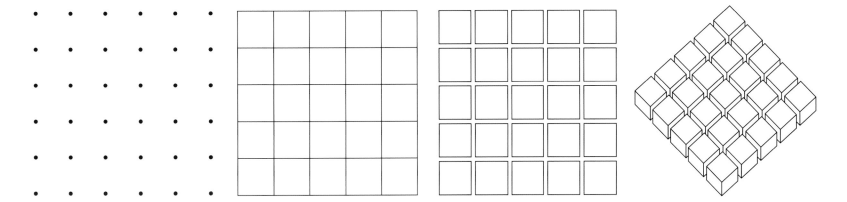

We get a grid by drawing lines between points that are positioned in a regular, topological position to one another.

On layout- and drawing programs a square grid can easily be brought to view on the screen. These are useful as drawing tools but are rather on the simple side.

We can make grids that are tailor made for our specific purposes. The grid is a kind of discipline the designer imposes on the work at hand. The aim is to create order and a better view of possible choices. A universal grid that can be applied to all kinds of tasks does not exist.

Grids have proved to be useful when working with bar charts, flow charts, process diagrams and as an aid to map out organizational structures and visualize connections. They can easily be stored as templates in the program you are using and come in handy when making several charts in a series (or when a similar new job crops up).

Grids can create rigid and monotonous structures. They function at their best when they are made invisible. You can use them as a tool, but need not show them on the finished result.

It is possible to introduce variations in a grid structure. The topological positions of the points remain unaltered. (See previous page)

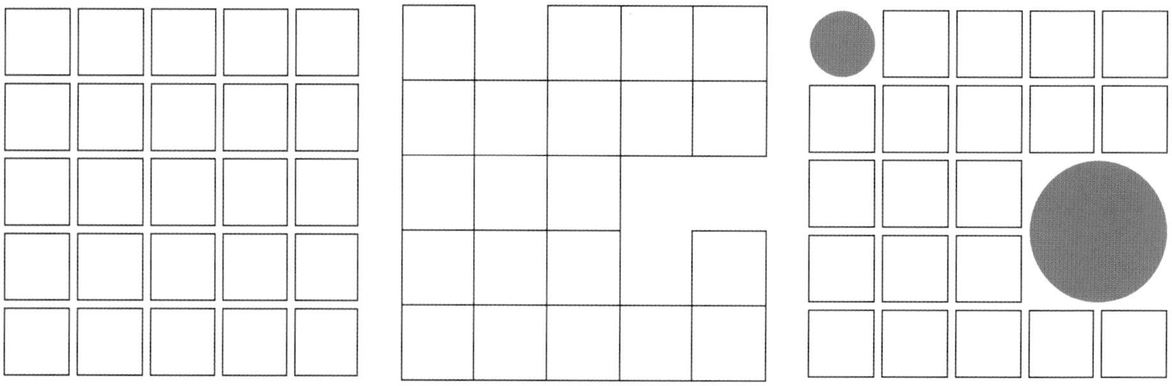

In addition to squares and rectangles, triangles and hexagons can also be combined.
The third on the right is one of several combinations that become operative by combining straight lines with lines at 60 degrees angle.

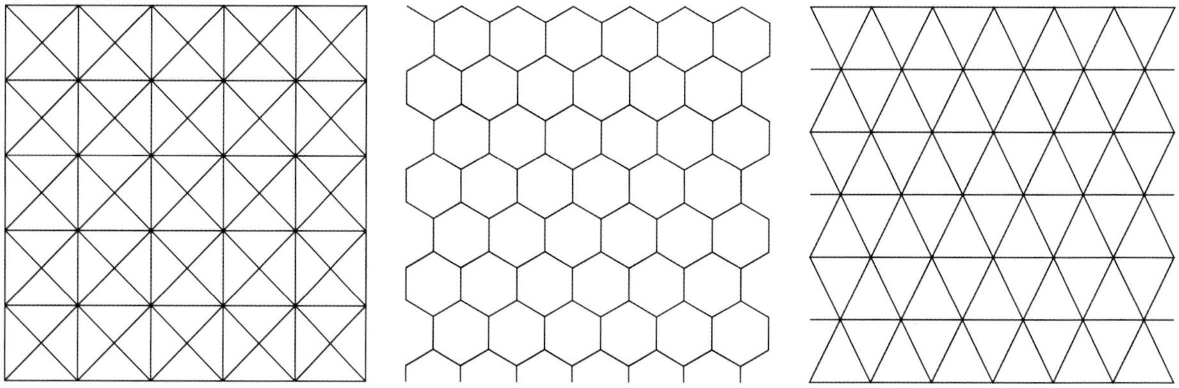

In these networks the "irregularities" of the measures are programmed. From left to right the formulas are:
1/3 net (1;2) : (1;2)
2/4 net (1;1;2) : (1;1;2)
2/6 net (1;1;2;2) : (1;1;2;2)

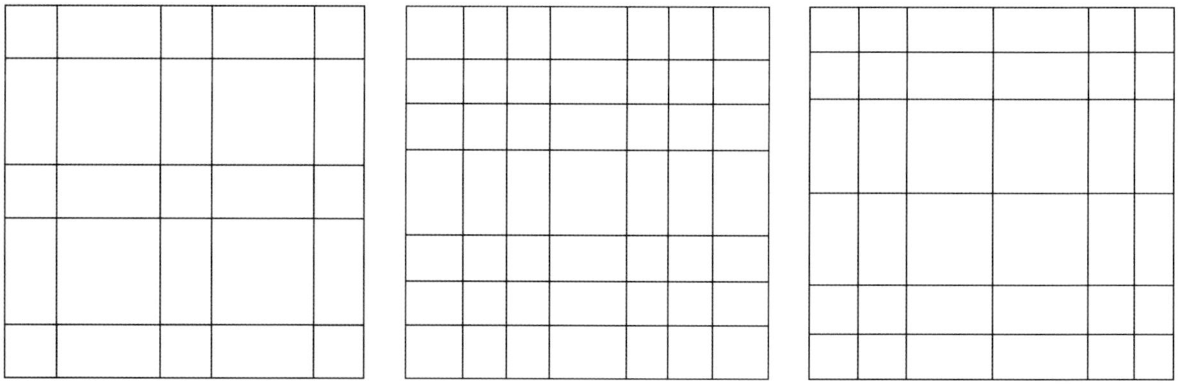

The first on the left is a simple square grid but with a square root in second extension placed on the top of the square. (The construction is shown on page 21)
The second has the extension on the right side of the square.
The third has extensions on all four sides of the square.

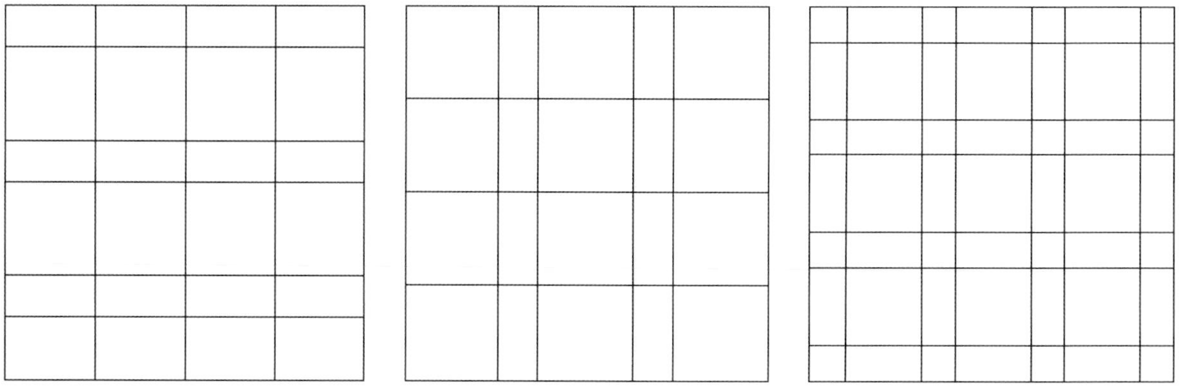

Bauhütten

Bauhütten were used by builders and architects in the 14th century. Similar designs can also be detected in Islamic ornaments.

The model above can be interpreted as a grid, as all the divisions derive from a square. All possible constellations of lines and shapes will have an inbuilt symmetry in them.

The geometry should be easy to handle and there are almost innumerable variations to be extracted from the scheme. These examples (designed by the author) show only a few that could be workable models for diagrams.

There are many aspects of colour: Physical, chemical, physiological, cultural, and symbolic, as well as those connected with fashions and trends. We cannot deal with such a mammoth theme in one sweep. Here we must concentrate on the practical sides of producing diagrams.

Since the introduction of the Internet and the widespread use of colour printers, diagrams in colour now appear more frequently than they do in black and white. Unfortunately, this increase does not seem to have been matched by knowledge and skill in the handling and management of colour. Josef Albers' famous axiom "Too much colour is no colour at all" is relevant in this connection. In many instances, uncritical use of colour can "beautify" and draw attention away from the matter.

When one designs diagrams, one thinks in terms of lines, volumes and general composition. The colours often come as an afterthought. It need not be like this: Colours can give body and presence to your presentation. Colours can appear active or passive. Colours can help to draw the viewers' attention to what you consider to be important. In addition there are the possibilities of overlaps, gradation and the creation of (illusory) spatial situations when appropriate. Whether you are working on paper or screen, it would be wise to have a few thoughts about colour application before you go ahead with the diagrams to be presented. A colour palette could be timesaving and secure consistency in your presentation. (See page 33)

I have spent much time teaching undergraduates the differences between RGB, CMYK and PMS. Colours produced with light behave differently from colours that are reproduced with pigments on paper. It should therefore not come as a surprise that what you get from your printer does not match what you see on your computer screen. There are methods for getting things under control and I hope that the following advice may prove useful:

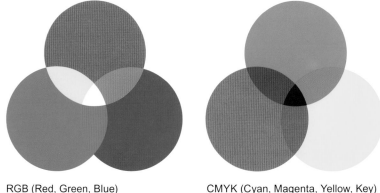

RGB (Red, Green, Blue)
Additive colour mixture

CMYK (Cyan, Magenta, Yellow, Key)
Substractive colour mixture

Colours on screen and for projectors

Programs for drawing and bitmap handling aimed at professionals, now have good facilities for file handling and colour management. The same can be said for monitors and screens which come in different sizes, constructions and with different price tags. If you show one and the same colour picture on different monitors you will see that the colours are presented differently. If the differences are dramatic it is an indication that the monitors need adjustment. One service bureau I sometimes work with have a test program they run through their equipment every day. (The most widely used is ISO 3664 Viewing conditions – Graphic technology and photography). The most reliable values are measured by using a densitometer. This is an instrument that measures the optical properties of colour and light. There is also a handy little device called Pantone Colour Cue which costs (roughly) $ 400. It is hand held and battery driven and can measure CMYK, RGB, LAB and Hexachrome with fair accuracy by pointing at the tinted areas. For most practitioners an "eye-test" is usually sufficient. A photographic full colour motif that you are well acquainted with could serve as the testing object.

Whilst files for print are in CMYK, projectors always work in RGB. Projectors come with different optics and different luminosity and can play havoc with your files if you have not tested them out beforehand. In many cases there is no other way of getting around this than to go back to the files and make the necessary adjustments.

Remember that WHITE does not exist in RGB. The white you see comes from mixing RGB and is often projected to the audience in an unpleasant, harsh way. A light grey or yellow background can soften this light.

Colour management in web communication is more difficult, compared to presenting your work on a single, calibrated beamer. Although you can produce millions of colours on most screens, many browsers do not support colour management yet. Fortunately, this is improving: Do not forget that that until recently, all browsers were limited to the use of 216 web-safe colours.

Colours for printing

The first thing to be done is to make sure that all your files are in the CMYK mode. (You might have imported RGB bitmaps into your layout program.) Standard resolution for bitmaps is 300 dpi.

Colour printers can produce unwanted variations: From time to time you should run a test file through whatever equipment you have at your disposal. To make such a test file is easy: Make six squares, each containing the CMYK colours plus green (100% cyan and 100% yellow) and red (100% magenta and 100% yellow). In addition put in a strip with gradations of greys. Some layout programs have these test strips attached to them.

What comes out of the printer should be viewed in natural light. (Lamps usually have an overdose of yellow in their tubes or bulbs).Another way of testing colours is to run the entire job through a colour laser copier. If you do not have access to one, there are service bureaus that do this for you without charging the earth. These machines are not foolproof, but they give a reasonably accurate picture of what the job is going to look like in print. Printing something in thousands of copies is a serious business and such a pretest might be well worth the expenditure. If you have OK'ed these prints you can use them as guidelines for the printer who is later going to handle the job. Most printing works now want your files to be in PDF (Portable Document Format). It is wise to consult your printer and ask for instructions on how to use Acrobat before you store the files and send them off. It is important that the various devises and equipment used in the production chain, such as scanners, monitors, imagesetters and printing presses conform to a consistent set of measures in order to achieve true colour fidelity. There are different parameters to be used. As an example, there is one for printing on coated stock and another for rotation newsprint. To complicate things even further, there are American, Japanese and European prepress standards to conform to. You should consult your printer and ask which ICC profile is going to be used and adjust your files accordingly. What is "standard" practice varies from printer to printer and from one country to another.

Measured in bytes, PDF files only weigh a fraction of what is contained in the original postscript file. It can be tempting to send them to the supplier over the Internet. Beware that this is not always a safe "road". The risk of having them infected or arriving incomplete is always there. To be on the safe side: Have one set stored on your hard disc and make two CDs (or DVDs) one for the printer and one as backup for yourself. Use "no compression" for both bitmap and vector files if they have not been been conveted to PDFs

As for reproducing colour images, there are different levels of fidelity. Some art books are now done in Hexachrome, so-called Hi-Fi printing. In the Hexachrome range there are two colours in addition to CMYK, orange and green. This needs six colour machines with extremely accurate proofing and colour management programs attached to them. Needless to say, they are not common and it looks as if we shall have to live with the far from perfect CMYK system for a while to come.

Certain colours are practically impossible to get right in CMYK and need to be printed separately as spot colours using PMS (Pantone Matching System). It is hard to get a warm yellow and several tertiary colours can appear muddy in print. The tertiary colours can, however, be made palatable provided we find percentage values and combinations that have proved to be successful. Some light colours might look OK when viewed in RGB on a screen but will appear muted when printed in CMYK colours. Most diagrams come from vector graphics. Those that contain photographic images are relatively rare and are subject to more accurate proofing methods than described here. In the final analysis it is our eyes that decide what things should look like, — not the technology.

Most publishers of design literature have a book out that deals with colour and digital colour management. A search on amazon.com will probably help you find one suitable for your needs and level of knowledge. There are some suggestions on "Literature" pages 196-197. Also websites that can help you to hit the right Hex values for the web. See page 197 – About colour.

It does not harm anyone to acquaint oneself with the various colour theories that exists: Goethe, Hölzel, Ostwald, Munsell, Klee, Itten, RAL and NCS. (The list is in chronological order.) Literature and sample collections are plentiful and easily available from your nearest colour institute. The approaches and methods employed vary from pure physics to artistic/humanistic viewpoints.

The swatches used in the various models have the same shape and the same quantities throughout. The descriptions employed are numerical or alphanumerical. This has obviously been inspired by music. Music has clear and unambiguous denotations for scales, harmonies and chord progressions. It is doubtful that they apply to colours in the same way. You can pick 100 test persons and ask them to identify "CocaCola Red" and "Van Dyck Brown". The answers you will get are likely to show considerable variations.

One assumes that roughly 5-8 percent of the male population has impaired colour vision or are completely colour blind. Women score much higher in colour tests than men do. Our perception of colour is also determined by the climate and the environment we live in.

Josef Albers (1888-1976) seriously questioned the validity of these colour theories. The complexities of colour combinations are well illustrated in his major work from 1963 "Interaction of Color".

To Albers colours reflect movement, energy, change and dynamic experiences. Like life itself. Many designers will agree with this.

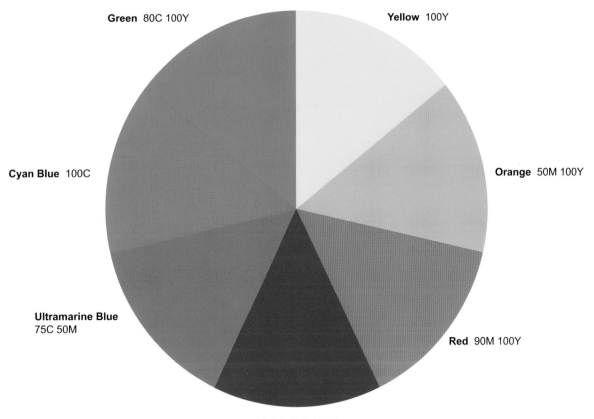

Sir Isaac Newton (1643-1727) managed to break light down into seven different colours by letting daylight through a glass prism. The different colours appear on different wavelengths. He named these colours violet, indigo, blue, green, yellow, orange and red. (Since then other names have been employed. Today's equipment can identify 130 colours.)

He arranged these colours in a circle so that violet touched red. In the middle of his diagram he put in a circular area of white to symbolize that the sum of the spectral colours produced white. Newton did not mix his colours with black.

In today's practice it is possible to reproduce a large sector of the visible colour gamut on a monitor through RGB. With process inks (CMYK) the gamut is limited. The illustration above is a reproduction of Newton's circle (by using today's software). Each of the seven colours are given names and (approximate) CMYK values.

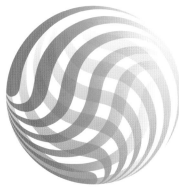

100% Magenta overprints transparent Cyan

Transparent Magenta overprints 100% Cyan

Transparent Magenta overprints 100% yellow

Transparent Magenta overprints transparent Cyan

Transparent Cyan overprints 100% Yellow

Transparent Magenta overprints transparent Cyan

The use of transparency
If you print two colours on top of each other a new, third and darker colour will emerge. In the CMYK printing process the colours will be applied to the paper in this succession: Yellow, Cyan, Magenta and Black (Key). When working in RGB this is not a consideration.

It is possible to control degrees of transparancy or overprint and make gradations. Transparancy can be used to good effect, but it can lead to unexpected printing results.

100% Yellow, transparent Cyan and Magenta

Process colours (Europe ISO Coated FOGRA 27)

Hereafter the colours will be signified by their initials: C70 M60 means 70% cyan and 60% magenta.

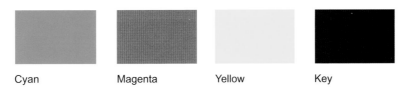

Cyan   Magenta   Yellow   Key

Primary and secondary colours

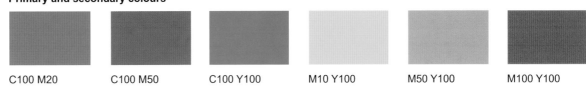

C100 M20   C100 M50   C100 Y100   M10 Y100   M50 Y100   M100 Y100

Tertiary colours

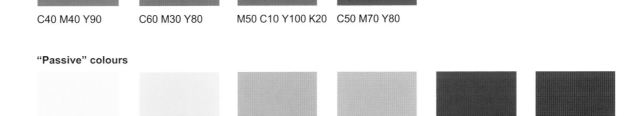

C40 M40 Y90   C60 M30 Y80   M50 C10 Y100 K20   C50 M70 Y80

"Passive" colours

Y20   C20   C20 M20 Y20   C10 K20   C80 M50 K30   C50 M80 K20

These colours can serve as backgrounds to the "active" parts of a diagram. They are chosen so that they can easily carry black or white (negative) type and lines.

In addition to those shown above there is black, white and percentages of black. Large areas of black might sometimes come out a bit thin and grey in printing. You can then apply a rich black (C30 M30 Y30 K100). You must, however, never apply this combination to thin lines or type.
The chosen colours with their CMYK values is not a universal system, but the author's chosen preferences when designing this book.

Drawing programs come with libraries of colour swatches and "colour pickers". Adobe's programs also have a "Live colour" function which gives you chosen harmonies and combinations. You can modify these by turning the handles around the RGB colour wheel. This way it is possible to arrive at combinations using a minimum of time. Combinations that seem plausible can then be stored in a library. In any case, designing one's own palette and using the eyedropper tool is timesaving and secures an efficient workflow.

In screen communication everything will have to be in RGB. Converting RGBs to CMYK for printing should not be too difficult. You must use your eyes, make a printout and determine the percentage values.
If you want to show your work on the web, you must search out the appropriate Hex values. (See recommended websites on page 197)

Axiometric presentations

Axiometric

means deciding dimensions along an axis. This is a method of presentation often used by architects to visualize rooms inside a building.

An object which is described axiometrically will have three dimensions related to the picture plane. The horizontal and the vertical distance will be in accordance with the scale one works in. Diagonal and curved lines will be subject to some modifications.

The presentation is orthographic. There is no perspective.

This method of presentation is also called "oblique drawing" (as opposed to "flat" two-dimensional rendering of plans).

Within axonometry there are the following main categories:

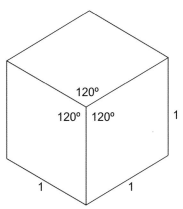

Isometric

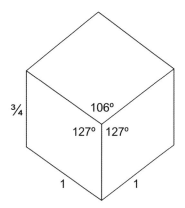

Dimetric

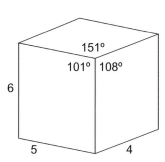

Trimetric

Isometric

means equal measures. The object is positioned so that the three axises have the same angle.

The object need not be a cube (as shown here) but the visible angles will be 120 degrees in relation to another. The lines in an isometric rendering will be parallel and always 30 degrees in relation to a straight, horizontal line. In an isometric presentation all three planes will have the same dimesion. How to use an isometric grid is explained on the next page.

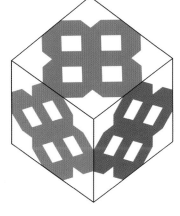

Dimetry

Here the object is turned so that two of the axsises are equal (as opposed to three in isometry). In many instances it is practical to emphasize one of the planes and give it prominence.

Trimetry

presents the object with three different planes and angles in relation to the picture plane. The area fronting us will dominate and we get the impression that the cube "stands" in (an illusory) three-dimensional space.

Our figure behaves differently on the three variations of the cube. There will be shortenings when the figure has to conform to the different planes. We used the same figure as described on page 14. It is mirror/axis symmetrical and the distortions will be equal on both sides of a middle line. CorelDraw was the program used (See page 197 **Uddin**)

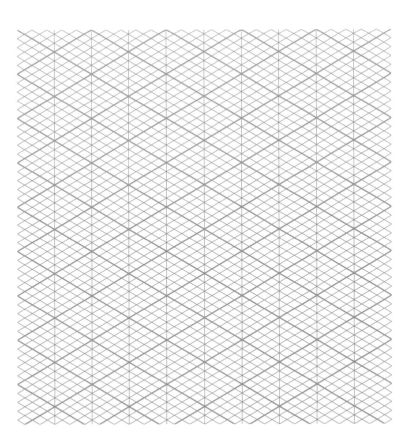

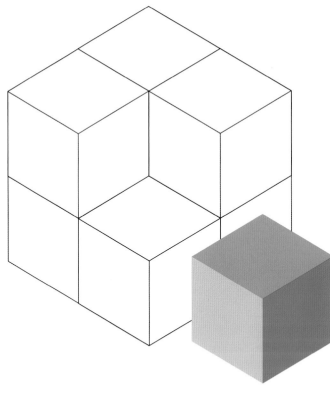

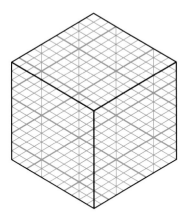

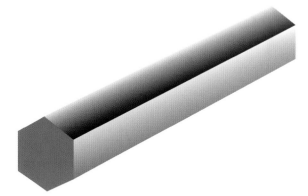

Shown above is a part of an isometric grid. These were previously to be bought on printed sheets but in our "digital times" we shall have to create our own in a drawing program. This way we can design them to suit our specific purposes. In this instance we have put 2 mm between each line and tilted them 30 degrees. The thick vertical lines are guidelines only. (They are put between every fifth element, which makes "counting" easier.) An isometric rendering of an object will show three sides of that object. There is no perspective, but we have a feeling that we are operating in space.

Employed in diagrams these presentations can be useful if one wants to show that a complex has more than one side to it or that a piece is part of a whole. (See diagram on page 34) Isometric lettering requires a bit of work: Each of the letters in a line must be adjusted in order to comply with the grid. This is achieved by converting the letters into curves.

Take a look at Hitchcock's 1958 production of "North by Northwest" next time it is shown or available on DVD. Saul Bass used isometric lettering in all the credit titles for the film. The effect was stunning!

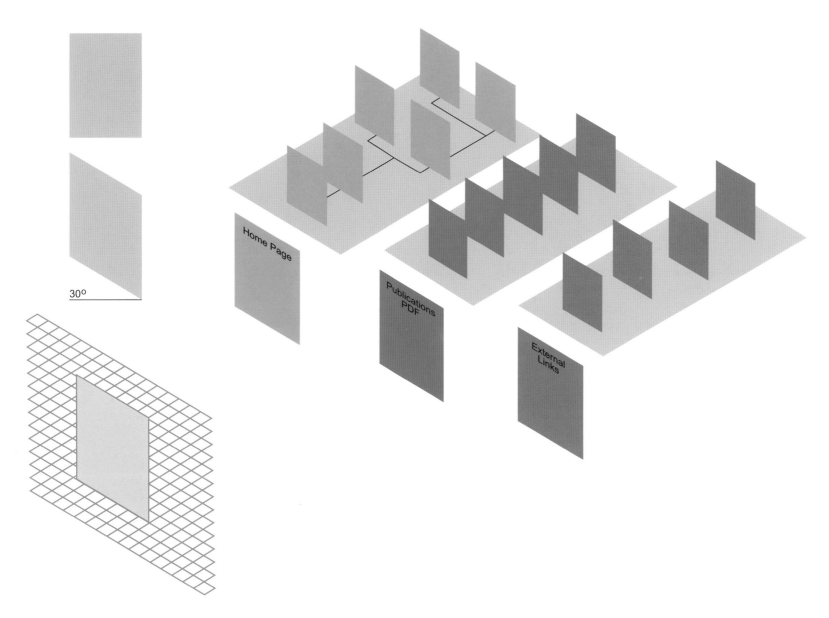

30°

Home Page

Publications PDF

External Links

Navigation through a large and complex web site can sometimes be cumbersome. By introducing an "architecture" as modelled here, we can create levels, sequences and hierarchies. We place the cards (read: *links*) on an isometric grid. Colour coding helps, too. (See page 196 **Uddin**)

This (and the illustrations on the preceding page) were done using Illustrator. Some distortion of the type must be tolerated when it is set at an angle.

Those who enter a school of architecture or an art academy usually go through an obligatory course in perspective drawing and construction. Most of this activity has moved from the drawing board to the computer. There has been a continuous development in programs like Archicad, 3D Studio, Solid Works and others. One can easily move from orthogonal rendering to axiometry, isometry and transmetry by using keyboard combinations and menus. The same applies to light sources and the application of shades and shadows.

It is possible to develop diagrams along these methods if one wants to show the information in a three-dimensional context. The rendering of cubes, spheres and solids can be done more accurately in a 3D program than in programs intended for statistics and "business graphics".

CATIA (Computer Aided Three-dimensional Interactive Applications) is a program package which, amongst other facilities, can transfer physical (handcrafted) models into computer data. It has found its way into architectural offices, but can hardly be called common software for graphic designers. It is expensive to buy and requires considerable training. Still, it is worth looking into if more complex renderings are required.

As for showing diagrams based on statistical material, one must exercise a certain degree of sobriety. Programs intended for architecture, building construction and product development are not necessarily functional when it comes to diagrams. (Organizational diagrams are a different matter). This "sophistication" can sometimes cloud the intentions and complicate the perception of factual information. This author is neither "for" nor "against" using such equipment, but will leave to the readers to decide which technique to choose for the job to be done. Here are some examples where both 2D and 3D software has been used.

From B.Taylor "New Principles of Linear Perspective" London 1715

There is basically nothing wrong about showing that there has been growth. These two bar charts are based on the same figures, but are they similar in expression?

An introduction of perspective can add some drama to the presentation, but will inevitably introduce an element of distortion. Here the x-axis gives the history from right to left.

As children we learned to read from left to right. Without the gridlines most people will encounter difficulties in understanding this.

This example was done with CorelDraw software, using a 2-point perspective.

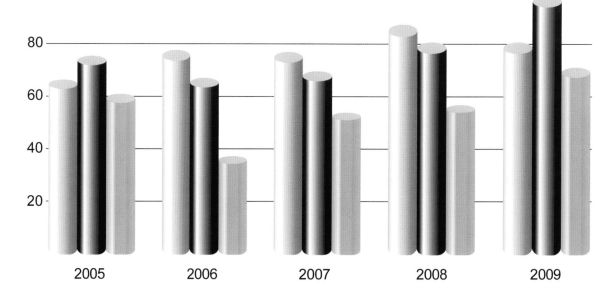

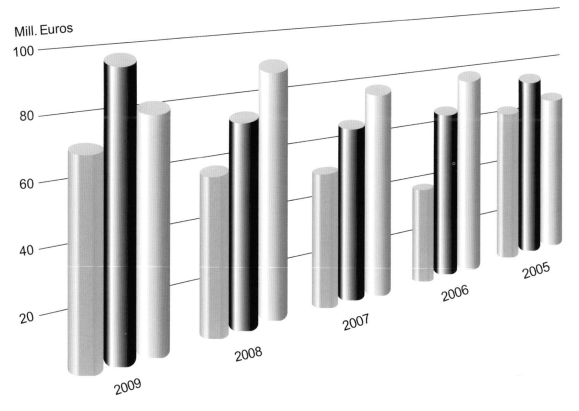

The same diagram as shown on the preceding page using 3D software. The program used was Alias Wavefront Design Studio, employing a 3-point perspective in the second version.

3D applications usually have a facility for cylindrical and cubical mapping. In this example a "chessboard" pattern has been used to good effect.

Adding type to a 3D design can produce unwanted distortions. It is better to add it "straight" on a separate layer when everything is ready.

Mill. Euros

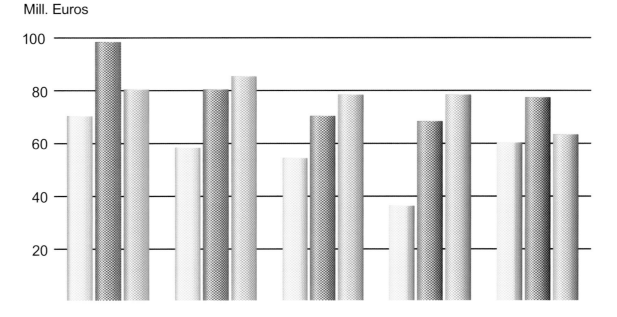

Mill. Euros

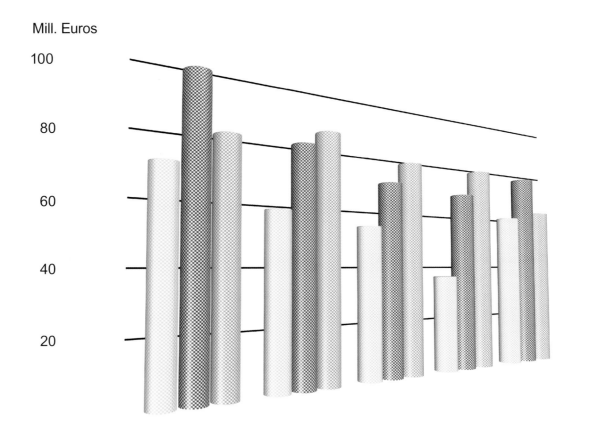

60 pt. Times New Roman

60 pt. Verdana

Are the two types shown above of equal size? If the point size is an indicator, they are. Optically they behave differently.

Times New Roman was launched in 1932 as an attempt to find a traditional serif face that could cope with fast-moving rotation printing on newsprint. It is still popular and widely used. It has high character count and performs well in large areas of text.

The same can not be said about Verdana, a typeface made primarily for titles and signage. (Matthew Carter, 1996). The high x-height accounts for good visibility when viewed from a distance. It performs well in screen display.

Thousands of type faces can now be downloaded from the Internet or are available on CD ROMs. Many are remakes of old favourites from the days of lead and photocomposition. Some have survived the digital transition, some have not.

As a general guideline, fonts designed and marketed by software manufacturers for digital reproduction are generally of a higher standard than those that have only been subject to "adjustments".

The Open Type Font-definition is the new standard. These fonts are relatively expensive to buy but offer a variety weights, optical kerning and alternative signs (ligatures, small caps, fractions). The face used for titles is sometimes different from the one used for body copy. Compared to TrueType and Type 1 fonts they perform well on both the PC and MAC platforms. A Unicode character set can contain 65 535 signs and accommodates most "unusual" languages one would care to mention. All recent layout programs now support Unicode and the Opentype format.

Microsoft's new ClearFace collection shows promise and might offer further advance in type-on-screen technology.

In many cases it is feasible to use the same typeface on the diagrams as for the rest of the publication or presentation. (Like in the book you are reading now: Everything set in Arial). In some cases, like illustrated essays and annual reports, one would prefer a serif face for lengthy body copy. In such instances, a sans serif face (Myriad, Verdana, Tahoma) can help to make the diagrams stand out without making them too obtrusive. Choosing a typeface is a personal thing. It can be compared to choosing one's friends: After a while, you know how they are going to behave. In any case, diagrams should function with as few words as possible.

More about OpenType on www.microsoft.com/OpenType/OTSpec/ and https://istore.adobe.com/type/browser/C/C_otfpro.html.

The typographic measurement system was established by Francois A. Didot and divides a Cicero in 12 points. Didot's Cicero dates back to 1784 and has no relationship to the metric system established by the French Academy of Science ten years later. The meter and the Cicero were adapted by practically all European countries, but not Britain and her overseas possessions.

The English-speaking world uses Pica which is app. seven percent smaller than the Cicero. The Pica does not relate to the Inch-system. As most software programs and fonts come from the USA, the Cicero is now a thing of the past.

It might appear inconsistent that we use inches and centimetres when measuring paper sizes, margins, column widths and illustrations horizontally, but use picas and points when deciding measurements vertically.

In all layout and drawing programs we can adjust measurements by right-clicking on the vertical ruler. There should be no problems attached to having our diagrams in picas and points and make them align with a chosen number of typographic lines (the type size + leading). A menu will tell us how correct the size is. In many cases it would be practical to store the standard measurements as vector rectangles in the library attached to the program you are using. This could save time and labour.

The development and application of grids is a large subject and cannot be dealt with adequately in this book. Other authors have done admirable work in this area. (See page 196 **Roberts/Thrift** and **Tamara**.)

For the record: A Cicero measures 4,5108 mm and the Pica is 4,233 mm. In Postscript one inch is six picas (72 pt.).

abcdefghijklmnopqrs
abcdefghijklmnopqrs
abcdefghijklmnopqrs
abcdefghijklmnopqrs
abcdefghijklmnopqrs
abcdefghijklmnopqrs
abcdefghijklmnopqrs
abcdefghijklmnopqrs

The type is 11 pt. on a 14 pt. body.
The box has 6 lines of 11/14 pt
6 x 14 = 84 points (7 picas)

This will be the intervals

The illustration shows (in reduced size) the grid used for this book. It is a multiple grid which can accommodate two different type sizes: 11/13 pt. Arial for essays and 8/12 pt. Arial for captions. There is considerable variety in the illustrations used in the book. Although the illustrations provided by the author are kept at a minimum with regard to sizes and proportions, imported material from other sources does not conform to any "standards". The four column layout is flexible enough to cope with this.

The two-columns and the four columns do not align completely (measured in points). There is a discrepancy of four points. This must be considered tolerable.

The gutter between the columns is set at 5 mm (not as one pica). This in order to avoid fractions in the metric measurements of illustrations.

The inside and the top margin is set. The measure of the bottom margin is determined by how many typographic lines the column will take.

Trimmed paper size: 250 mm x 250 mm

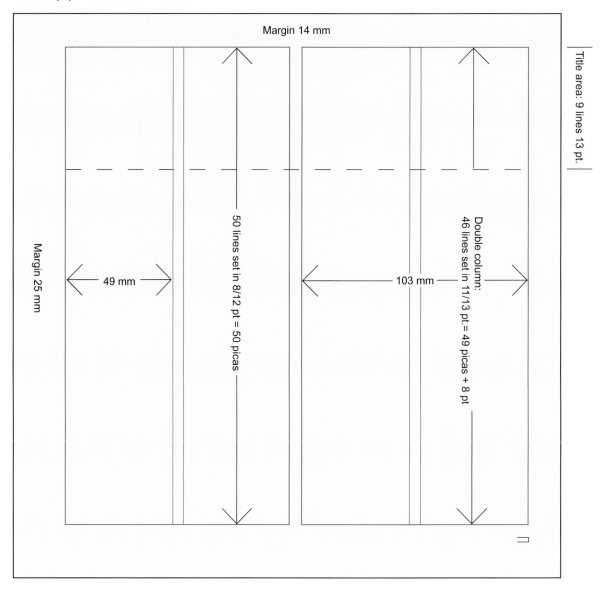

Margin 14 mm

Title area: 9 lines 13 pt.

Margin 25 mm

49 mm

50 lines set in 8/12 pt = 50 picas

103 mm

Double column: 46 lines set in 11/13 pt.= 49 picas + 8 pt

A clear head and a sharp pencil are still the prerequisites for producing a diagram. In many instances one could sometimes wish that both designers and students spent more time thinking and using simple tools before they went to their computers.

In a fast-changing digitized world one must be prepared to spend time keeping track of developments through the IT press, websites, manuals and other sources of information. There are excellent tuition programs containing instruction videos that can be downloaded from the web for modest sums of money. (See page 197).

The subject of this book is not bits and bytes, but as practitioners we must be allowed to air some views. We are at the mercy of an industry which does not always comply with our needs.

In the design community, Apple's products have a strong position. However, the majority of data users are connected to PC networks and although the communication between the two "communities" is improving rapidly, things are far from perfect: Some files are not exchangeable and printers may complain about incompatibility or missing fonts.

The fact that we have had three different font technologies has caused havoc in many situations. The current development within OpenType is a step in the right direction but things are not yet perfect. (See page 40 about choosing type).

The software industry is dominated by four giants: Microsoft, Adobe, Apple and Google. These companies are so much bigger than the others that they more or less decide what the standards should be. Unfortunately, the "war" between these is far from being over. Our daily working lives would have been easier if programs and file formats were more compatible.

Equally irritating are the frequent "updates" which not only cost money, but are mere attempts to rectify weaknesses in the previous program version. In most industries it is the practice not to launch new models until they are near

perfect. This thinking does not seem to apply to the software industry. The new version of Adobe Acrobat Professional is a major improvement and has made many things easier and file management more accurate. Both Apple and PC manufacturers have launched machines with 64-bits processors in them. This will increase capacity compared to the 32-bits especially when fast performances are needed. (Video editing, animations etc). Adobe is working with manufacturers who produce add-on programs which speeds up the information flow from web to print. The change in computer use, from a work tool to a complete entertainment machine, is already noticeable. A lot of things might be different in five years time.

Programs to make diagrams with

Microsoft's Office package has conquered a large share of the market but they now have to compete with newcomers like OpenOffice and Google docs.

Both Lotus and Sun's StarOffice have diagram modules attached to their worksheets, but the most commonly used program for diagram-making is Microsoft Excel. There is a good collection of standard designs to choose from and it is possible to make amendments to these and store them in the menu as "Custom Types – User defined". By adding Visio 2007 to the office package there are the possibilities of making flow charts, time lines and graphs relevant to engineering activities to the repertoire. On pages 92-95 you see a case where a furniture manufacturer keeps track of its use of materials for production. With limited time and money at one's disposal diagrams in Excel can be produced quickly both for documents and screen display.

In a more professional situation, there are obvious limitations: Excel can easily show the development of exports from Britain to France over a five year's period, but it cannot show the development from France to Britain in the same diagram.

The program has no rulers, which means haphazardly sizing and scaling. One cannot break up vector objects into parts (like in a drawing programs). One cannot modify or adjust curves. Colour management in Office programs is poor and sometimes non-existing. (No CMYK menu). Many publisers do not accept office files for printing. They have to be redrawn in Illustrator. (Or, if you prefer another drawing program, delivered in the EPS format). Still, for the price you pay, MS Excel has many satisfied users and is a good, workable program.

There is an offering of cheap software intended for "Business Graphics" but they have little to recommend them. Some have worksheet-like setups, but they do not function as worksheets. Amongst the more serious offerings, one should mention Harvard Graphics and SPSS Inc. They have a good assortment of types and can import data from most office programs. (More details from www.harvardgraphics.com and www.spss.com). ConceptDraw Professional is now available for both Windows and MAC users (www.conceptdraw.com).

Within GIS (Geographic Information Systems) there are several software packages where it is possible to develop information based on cartographic data.
(See chapter about GIS on page 115)

Most of the 2D illustrations shown in this book were made in Illustrator, CorelDraw and Freehand. In the CS5 version of Illustrator it is possible to draw shapes into a predetermined 3-point perspective grid. Adobe's Creative Suite allows for quicker and easier import of vector graphics into animation software and the conversion of layout files to web programs.

In my experience, programs are gradually getting better and more functional and can meet most of my needs. (See page 197 for interesting websites)

In this connection, one must be allowed to raise a few unpleasant but pertinent questions: It is true that one can save time by using programs that draw everything for you. Is speed the only parameter for producing good diagrams? I believe one should turn one's attention to producing diagrams that are innovative, intelligent and informative. This is where the challenges are.

The use of clipart and photo archives
Many design professionals sneeze at the employment of "used" material. They view it as something inferior and not in line with their creative integrity. These attitudes are about to change. We now have access to an abundance of material easily found and purchased from Internet sources. It is hard to justify the time spent drawing a car if the same car is available as both bitmap and vector drawings from a professional stock agency costing $40 or less.

No one draws electronic symbols, flags, traffic signs or trees by hand or with mouse anymore. There is also 3D clipart to be bought. This saves one from building cubes, cylinders and other standard volumes from scratch.

The quality of clip art collections can vary enormously and one must be aware of the licensing requirements before one makes a purchase. Images are often advertised as "copyright free" which only means that you pay for the use of them. The copyrights remain with the publisher.

Photographs that are not digital can easily be scanned and prepared for printing in Photoshop. Searching in archives may take time, but in many cases it is cheaper and more convenient to pay a royalty fee than to have a photographer do the job from scratch. Designers should build themselves a library of symbols, boxes, buttons, textures and similar material. This should not hamper inventiveness. It should rather be complementary to what we can produce ourselves. We have more choices and a wider field to play on.

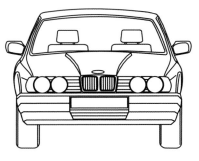

Original clipart drawing. It is failrly detailed, but does not take reduction in size too well.

The same drawing, but in line only.

We have now abandoned colours but kept the details. The appearance is lighter.

This was made for reduction in size. Many details have been brutally taken away. The illustration can now serve as an icon for "personal vehicle " rather than as a rendering of a specific model.

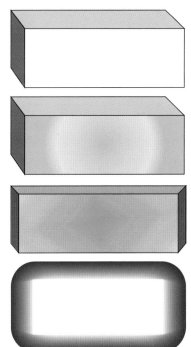

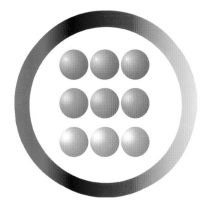

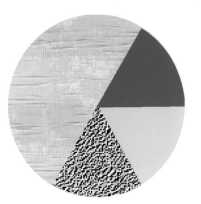

Samples from the authors own (tailor made) gallery.

Most of what is shown here comes from CorelDraw and Illustrator. Corel offers a good selection of textures, patterns, objects and other accessories as part of the program package. One must, however, exercise some taste when using these offerings. On some of these examples the vector images have been subject to modifications that are available in the programs.

Experienced digital designers are probably well acquainted with a multitude of file formats that can be found in programs on both the MAC and the Windows platforms. For the benefit of the not-so-experienced and those who believe that all design jobs have to be done on a MAC it is important to point out that there are some "open standards" that work well on both platforms. Here are the strengths and the limitations:

PSD

Adobe Photoshop files are generally written and read by Photoshop, however, there are several other Adobe applications that will read this format. A Photoshop file will retain all of the original file attributes. Saved file characteristics include the following:
• Resolution
• Color space (CMYK, RGB, grayscale)
• Spot color channels
• Image bit depth

In order to use Photoshop files in programs outside the Adobe software family, you must first convert them to a TIFF.

TIFF (Tagged Image File Format)

This is the most widely used file format in desktop publishing today. It is a raster-based file that supports the following:
• RGB
• CMYK
• Grayscale
• Lab
• Indexed color
• Layers of separate images

When placing a TIFF file on a page, any clipping path that has been defined can be retained and applied. However, Photoshop's Alpha channel information will not be translated when placing a TIFF. Files for printing should be in 300 dpi. The files have a tendency to be on the heavy side and one can encounter difficulties when sending them over the Internet or having them printed on colour laser copiers and other kinds of office printers. There are other options:

JPEG (Joint Photographic Experts Group)

Uses of the JPEG file format are far and wide. Initially, the file format was intended for use in Web applications, but has found a home in the high-end print production markets, as well. The JPEG file format can be your best friend if used properly, or your worst enemy if implemented incorrectly. A JPEG file is encoded by using adjustable compression. (Small file, Medium file or Large file). This means that to achieve smaller file sizes, image data is actually thrown away. JPEG is fine for making photo archives but be very careful when using it in a print production workflow.

The JPEG format will support the RGB, CMYK, and gray-scale color spaces. The use of JPEG images is supported in HTML and Web applications. There is no support for transparency in a JPEG file.

PNG (Portable Network Graphics)

A PNG file (often pronounced "ping") is a pixel based image that can be used to display 24-bit images on the Web. It is ideal for on-screen presentations.

Unlike JPEG, PNG compresses its data lossless. This way the file will be smaller but retain the characteristics of the original image. Also it has an alpha-channel, which means that it allows a full range of transparancy values. However, because of the lack of support for the CMYK colour space, and the fact that there can be no color separations, PNG files should not be used for printing.

EPS (Encapsulated PostScript)
is an image file that can contain either vector or bitmap information. An EPS file can be created using any color space and any image bit depth. An EPS is really a collection of several other image files all in one. EPS files are generated from several sources and are structured to published code constraints. An EPS file has two main parts:

• The preview
• The high resolution image data

The preview of an EPS file is necessary to display the image in a page layout application, and the high-resolution portions of the file are necessary for imaging to a particular output device.

These files are particularly useful if you do not know which programs the recipient is using. Files done in CorelDraw for Windows can be sent to someone who is working with Illustrator on the MAC platform. EPS files can easily be placed in presentation programs (like PowerPoint). When designing diagrams, text is often placed inside images. For this purpose EPS is the right choice.

Files should be scaled in a size as close to the actual size as possible. Enlargements should be avoided, as this can cause a blurred image. Modifications and corrections are best done in the program where the file originated. Many publishers prefer to have illustrations delivered in EPS to files done in the original drawing program. EPS files have been built specifically for the print production world, and are not supported by Web browsers.

PDF (Portable Document Format)
is not only a file format but a technology which was invented by Adobe in 1991 and released in 1993. It has grown into the ISO standard for trusted electronic documents and forms. Its range of applications is growing and cannot be described fully here.

Many printers prefer PDF files to documents done in PostScript. PDF also makes the communication between Windows and MAC users easier.

PDF can store extended font information. (A facility not found in EPS).

Before delivering your PDF files to a printer or a service agency you must consult them first. Different ICC profiles and different output devices are used. A PDF intended for newsprint will be different from a file made for printing on coated paper. There are differences in colour standards used in Europe, USA and Japan.

PDF users and developers have their own website at www.pdfzone.com.

Geography and cartography is outside the scope of this book. Geographic maps give information about the size and position of rivers, lakes, mountains, cities and other natural features through the means of points, lines, texture and colours. These elements are classified and ordered in a code system.

To add information to maps that is not purely geographical is not a new idea. There are maps from the 17th century that contain fanciful and imaginative illustrations of various topics. C.J. Minard (1781-1870) tried to visualize Napoleon's march to Moscow. His famous timeline diagram (from 1838) shows us not only what a vast country Russia is, but also the losses the French army suffered as they moved forward and then retreated.

Airlines give us maps which show us their network and destinations. Usually these maps only show the outline of countries and continents. Other kinds of surface information are deleted. We can call this a generalization where the loss of details is compensated for by giving the user easy access to essential information. By putting such information on the Internet one can use links to guide the user from the general to the specific.

An example of the application of statistical information to maps is dealt with in a special section starting on page 116. The use of interactive electronic guides is another expanding area which will need attention and design considerations. Several museums have already been using these to lead their visitors through the different sections.

GPS (Global Positioning Systems) gives geographic information from satellite sources. (See page 118)

Here we shall look at ways of revealing information by using maps and (relatively unsophisticated) software as starting points.

From Harry Beck's 1933 diagram of the London Underground. Beck started his innovative work in 1931. The "map" he designed was made up of horizontal, diagonal, vertical and (a few) curved lines. The only surface information he included was the River Thames.
The proposal was at first opposed for being too radical and not in accordance with the surface geography. Beck argued that surface information was uninteresting as long as you were riding a train many yards below the surface of the earth.
The principles of his pioneering effort have been adapted to similar transport systems around the world.
(See page 196 **Garland**)

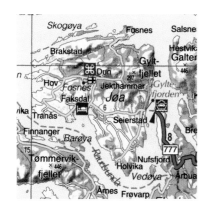   

   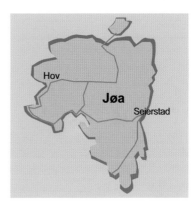

Adaptation and redesign of geographic material

An island off the northwestern coast of Norway is the basis for this exercise. A map usually gives a generalized picture of reality. In this case we have a strategy for what this "reality" should contain: We have made considerable amendments to the map of the island. Still, the main characteristics have been retained and the total shape is recognizable. Furthermore, we considered size and the reproduction situation we had to adhere to.

The result would probably not please the geographers who have spent hours getting the map "right". We, on the other hand, have tailored the map to what could be of interest to the viewers and the information requirements of a specific situation. Consequently, a tourist on four wheels needs a map different to that used by the local authorities.

To start with, we must have a strategy where the communication goals are clearly defined. The illustrations show some of the possibilities when one employs bitmap and vector graphics (or uses a combination of both). In these examples: Photoshop + CorelDraw.

Norway's population

is divided into 19 counties and it was necessary to use five colour codes to explain the regional differences.

The country is so long that there was no way of getting it into a square paper size. There is considerable perspective shortening applied to the northern section. This was done by employing two-points perspective in CorelDraw. The county borders have been simplified and the absolute minimum of black lines have been used.

These geographic inaccuracies were introduced in order to make the diagram comprehensible.

Troms
151.673
6 pr.km2

Finnmark
73.732
2 pr.km2

Nordland
237.503
7 pr.km2

Sør-Trøndelag
266.323
16 pr.km2

Nord-Trøndelag
127.457
6 pr.km2

Møre og Romsdal
243.855
17 pr.km2

Sogn og Fjordane
107.280
6 pr.km2

Hedmark
187.965
7 pr.km2

Oppland
183.235
8 pr.km2

Hordaland
438.253
30 pr.km2

Buskerud
239.793
17 pr.km2

Akershus
477.325
104 pr.km2

Oslo
512.589
1200 pr.km2

Rogaland
381.375
44 pr.km2

Østfold
252.746
65 pr.km2

Vestfold
216.456
101 pr.km2

Vest-Agder
157.851
23 pr.km2

Aust-Agder
102.945
12 pr.km2

Telemark
165.710
12 pr.km2

Under 100.000

Between 100.000 og 200.000

Over 200.000

Over 200.000
Over 100 per km^2

Over 500.000
Over 1000 per.km^2

Source: Statistisk sentralbyrå

50

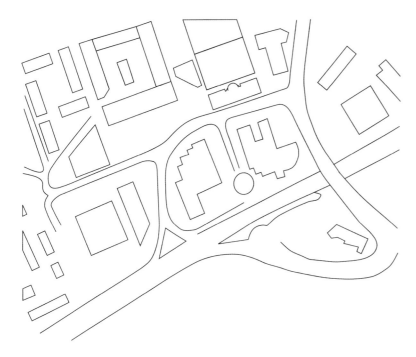

Detailed maps of selected areas are usually available from the planning authorities in the city in which you live. They are correct with respect to details and measurements. On the other hand, they show absolute *everything* there is in the chosen area.

This tracing (in Illustrator) was done from such a map and only contains elements necessary for the wayfinding process. It is the skeleton of the map you see on the next page.
In the final version the hard edges and the rectangled were rounded off. The appearance became "smoother".

The map on the next page was made by the author for an invitation to an international ergonomics conference held in Oslo.

In this instance, seventy percent of the participants came from other countries or other parts of Norway. The conference lasted three days and it was therefore necessary to present the facilities the area could offer. The standard city maps handed out by tourist offices are usually inadequate and of limited value.

One important innovation in this area was Richard Saul Wurman's ACCESS guidebooks which covered several large American and European cities. They emphasize the user's actual information needs, often leaving out "irrelevant" geographic details. Wurman's own standpoint was that they "were guided by my own ignorance and not relying too much on local expertise".

A special mention should be made of a research project initiated by Danish Design Center in the late 1990s. Tactile maps were developed for the visually impaired or totally blind. Such "noncommercial" projects should be encouraged. The findings were documented in both the Danish and English language and published in the book "Finding the Way". (See page 196 **Dansk.**)

The modernist axioms "less is more", "maximum effect with minimum means" are in this context not always valid. On the contrary, details can enrich a map and make the process of finding things easier. A set of traffic lights, a sculpture, a shopfront or even a billboard advertising sign can serve as a "landmark".

The selected area has good train and bus connections and can cater for most immediate shopping needs. From the point of architectural and environmental planning, the area cannot claim to be of any outstanding merit. Any attempts to make the map look "prettier" or "tidier" than what it depicted seemed futile.

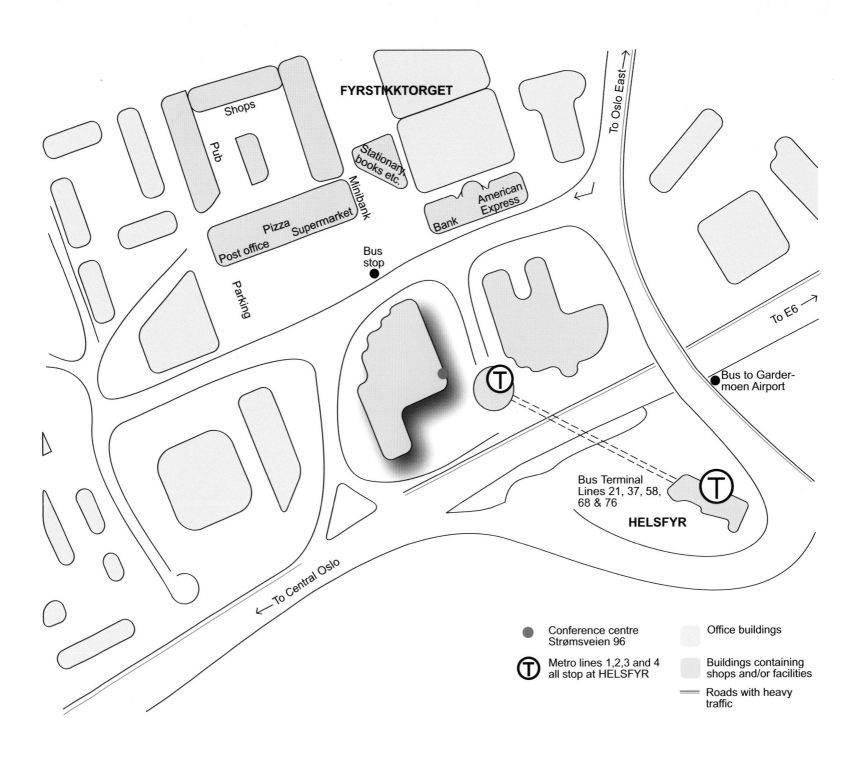

FYRSTIKKTORGET

Shops

Pub

Stationary books etc.

Minibank

Pizza Supermarket

Post office

American Express

Bank

Parking

Bus stop

To Oslo East →

To E6 →

Bus to Garder-moen Airport

Bus Terminal Lines 21, 37, 58, 68 & 76

(T)

HELSFYR

← To Central Oslo

● Conference centre Strømsveien 96

(T) Metro lines 1,2,3 and 4 all stop at HELSFYR

Office buildings

Buildings containing shops and/or facilities

Roads with heavy traffic

The visualization of statistical and operational data

A business enterprise does not need to be big before it generates a substantial amount of figures. These are usually stored in worksheets and data bases and are accessible to those who wish to see them and/or have access to them.
We can envisage the following scenario:
We have the management of a company that operates in a fluctuating market. These fluctuations are not easy to foresee, but it is possible to develop rational strategies based on past experience. This "experience" is usually stored in previous year's accounts in columns and rows. These figures are not only numbers but perception units. They have to be read, memorized and interpreted. Furthermore, they must be organized in a new pattern in order to serve as tools for decisionmaking. This is a daunting task which (in most cases) is beyond the intellectual capacity of those who are responsible for a company's further development. The problem is not the absence of reliable data. There is too much of it.
We are trying to find paths in a wilderness and cannot see the wood for the trees.

The growth of the computer industry, which started with the invention of the micro processor, has not been matched with a corresponding capacity to understand numbers and figures. A lot of the information we receive or have access to we cannot understand or it does not concern us. In many instances we cannot relate it to a contextual framework we are comfortable with. This is where diagrams have proved to be of indispensable value.

Attempts to visualize data and statistical information go back more that 200 years: One early pioneer is *William Playfair* (1759-1823) who published his "The Commercial and Political Atlas" in London in 1785. He later followed it up with "The Statistical Breviary" (1800).

Using ruling pen and hand lettering he produced descriptive diagrams and put on paper interesting thoughts about their usage. These writings appear surprisingly "modern": Playfair warns us about "creative" accounting and the abuse of diagrams for political purposes.

In the German-speaking world *Johann H. Lambert* appeared even before Playfair with his "Beiträge zum Gebrauch der Mathematik und deren Anwendung" (Berlin 1765). Still, Playfair is regarded by many as the father of statistical diagrams.

Recent research has shed light on the remarkable achievements of *Charles Joseph Minard* (1781-1870). His best-known and widely publicized graph showing the disastrous results of Napoleon's 1812 Russian campaign is a remarkable piece of work. So far, one has been able to find fifty-one *cartes figuratives* produced by his fertile mind. Minard was trained as an engineer and worked as a field engineer and railroad constructor for ENPC until his retirement in 1851. In his "second career" starting in 1844 he worked with his graphs dealing with costs for the transport of goods and people and other statistical matter. He often combined a stylised map with dramatic flowing lines in order "to convey promptly to the eye, the relation not given quickly by numbers…" In 1865, the city of Paris needed a new central post office. Naturally, there was a discussion about where to place such an institution. Minard's solution was a map showing the population of each arrondisement by squares with areas proportional to population (not geographic outlines). In that way it was possible to find the ideal location by pointing out the visual and geometric centre of gravity.

Minard would probably have become a brilliant graphic designer had he been born 130 years later.
(See page 196 **Friendly**)

By the end of the nineteenth century pictorial graphic statistics were beginning to be widely used. They can be found in newspapers and journals as well as academic publications. *Willard Cope Brinton* (b.1880) is supposed to have lectured to his students at Harvard in 1914 about "Graphic methods for presenting facts". Presenting "a small number of brief and simple rules which may be used as a sort of grammar by persons who have graphic presentations to prepare and interpret". Needless to say, the world has grown considerably in complexity since 1914. Still, Brinton's initiative might have triggered off an awareness from which we can benefit today.

From the 1960s onwards there has been a tremendous growth in the production of annual reports and other corporate communication publications. This has been most noticeable in USA where companies usually have a large number of shareholders. This accounts for large print runs and generous budgets. European and Asian companies have caught up, but Americans are still in the lead.

Recently, a former professor of statistics at Yale University, *Edward R. Tufte* has been extremely active. His first edition of "The visual display of quantitative information" was ready in 1982. He had problems finding a publisher for it and had to mortgage his house and start a publishing company of his own. The aforementioned book must now be regarded as a classic and has (counting revisions and reprints) sold more than a million copies. (See page 196 **Tufte**).

Tufte has also been successful with his "road shows". These are one day seminars held in various cities in USA. He claims that if you think statistics is boring, it might be that you have not been able to get to the right figures.

Tufte admits that the skills of a graphic designer are needed in order to get a good, printable result. He is otherwise critical of overworked layouts, irrelevant illustrations and what he has aptly named "graph junk". You might like to know more about this indefatigable man on www.edwardtufte.com (See page 196 **Tufte**)

Your choice of diagram type is governed by the communication situation you are in at any given time. Where will the recipient focus his/her interest: A historical development? A comparison? Developments in a market? National or regional variations? A probable development?

Regardless of what the situation happens to be, one has to assemble, group and interpret the available data and try to find a pattern which can make a presentation feasible. This makes the design of diagrams a challenging task.

In some instances one does not have concrete data to rely on and must base some of it on foresight. This situation occurs often when one deals with areas like demography and economic forecasts. One must be honest enough to tell the readers that the graphic presentation of these figures are not 100% real.

This chapter intends to give a brief overview of the standard diagrams and their application. Some types, like the radar- and scatter diagrams, are used by certain professional groups, but not presented here.

Mathematicians use Venn and phase diagrams to express their models. These remain in areas that are outside the scope of this book.

Animated diagrams like those you see on TV during elections can (for obvious reasons) not be presented in a book. Touch screen presentations are also a method not dealt with here, but you can see an example of their use on page 132.

We must keep in mind that there are limits to what an audience can absorb in one go. We learn something new in relation to something we are already familiar with. Too much "creativity" in this area is not necessarily a good thing. Still, there is a lot of uncovered ground and room for innovations.

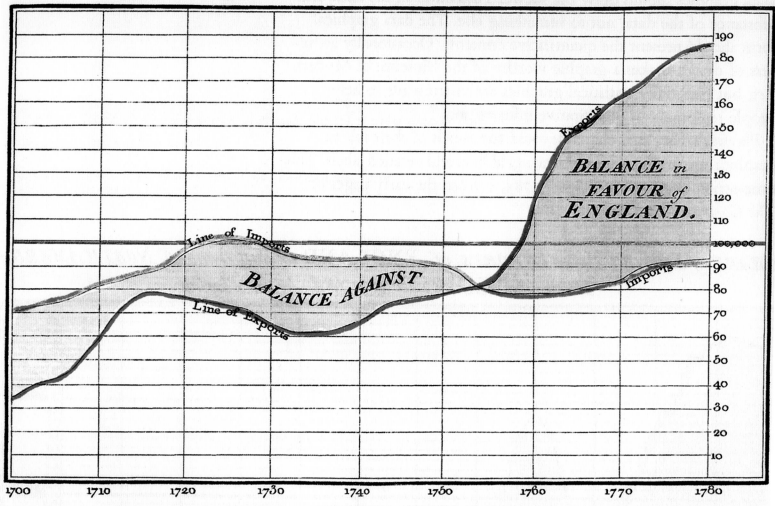

BALANCE in FAVOUR of ENGLAND.

Line of Imports

BALANCE AGAINST

Line of Exports

Imports

Exports

The Bottom line is divided into Years, the Right hand line into L10,000 each.

Published as the Act directs, 1st May 1786, by Wm. Playfair

Neele sculpt 352, Strand, London.

One of the 44 illustrations to be found in William Playfair's "The commercial and political Atlas" (London 1785) Playfair's work has previously only been available from archives but was published by Cambridge University Press in 2005. (See page 196 **Playfair**)

It is interesting to note the correlations of the expansion of Britain's exports with the effects of the Industrial Revolution. Still, Brits buy Danish pork and Norwegian wood products.

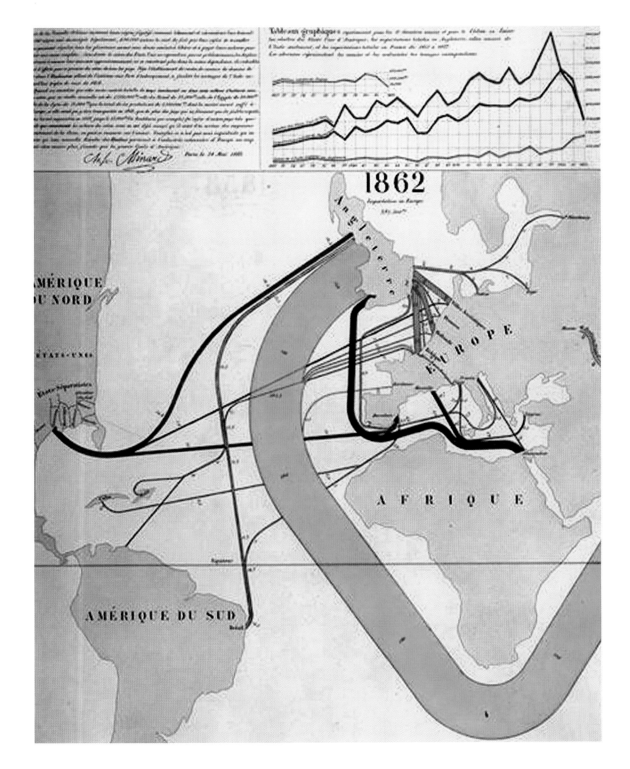

C.J. Minard
Flow map showing the trade of cotton in Europe in 1862. After the outbreak of the American civil war, exports of raw cotton from the south of the USA declined. At a glance, it is clear that this has stimulated the trade with India.

This is one of several diagrams from "Geigy heute" (Birkhäuser 1958), The book was to celebrate the chemical-pharmaceutical company's 200th anniversary. This particular diagram shows how a section of the company's operation was organized.

The designer, Karl Gersner (b.1930) was one of the innovators in Swiss graphic design in the late 1950's and early 1960's. His own book "Designing Programmes/Programme entwerfen" was, and still is, inspiring reading for anyone interested in rational, corporate graphics. A new edition of this book (originally from 1964) appeared in 2007. (See page 196 **Gerstner**)

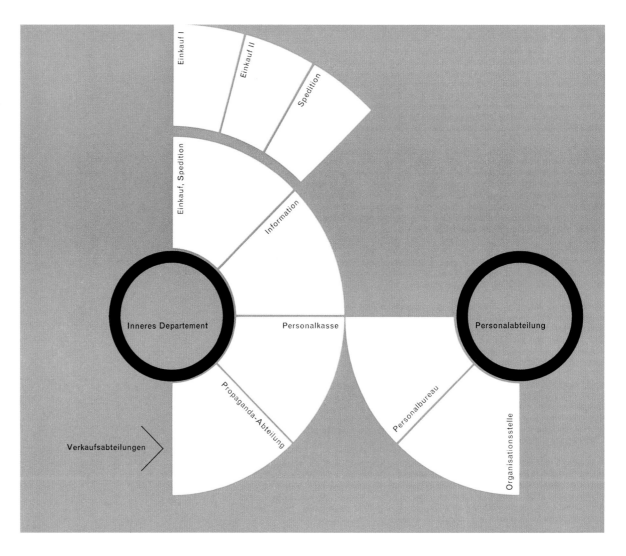

One of a series of illustrations to be found in the book "Nobrium: Towards True Precision in the Control of Excessive Anxiety" This is entitled "Anxiety: A physical profile"

Client: Roche Pharmaceuticals

Pentagram, London, UK 1971
Design and Art direction: Mervyn Kurlansky
Designer: Madeleine Bennett

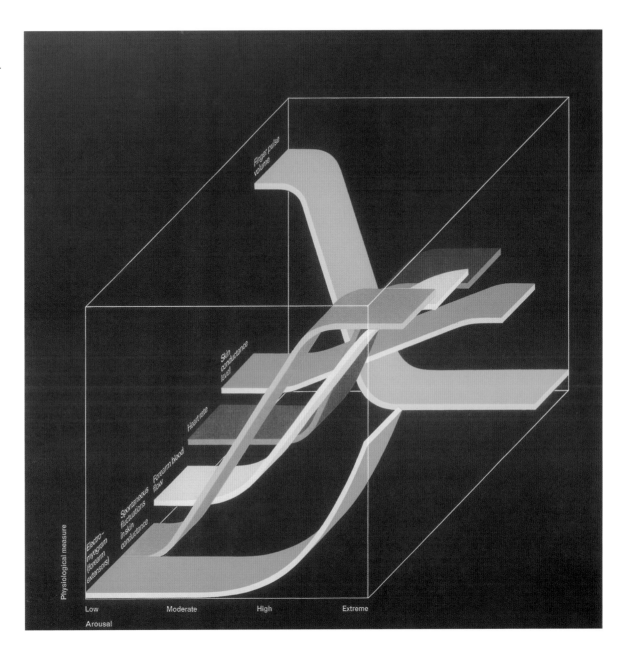

Cover of monograph Soft Where Inc, Volume 1, 1975. It is about computer graphics, conceptual and visible language. It shows "Genesis 1 and 2" a 1973 score for a ritual chant performed in 1974 by groups of men and women where earth, air, fire, and water meet: at sundown by the ocean.

Client: Rhode Island School of Design, Art and Design Festival, 1974.
Designer/Artist: Aaron Marcus

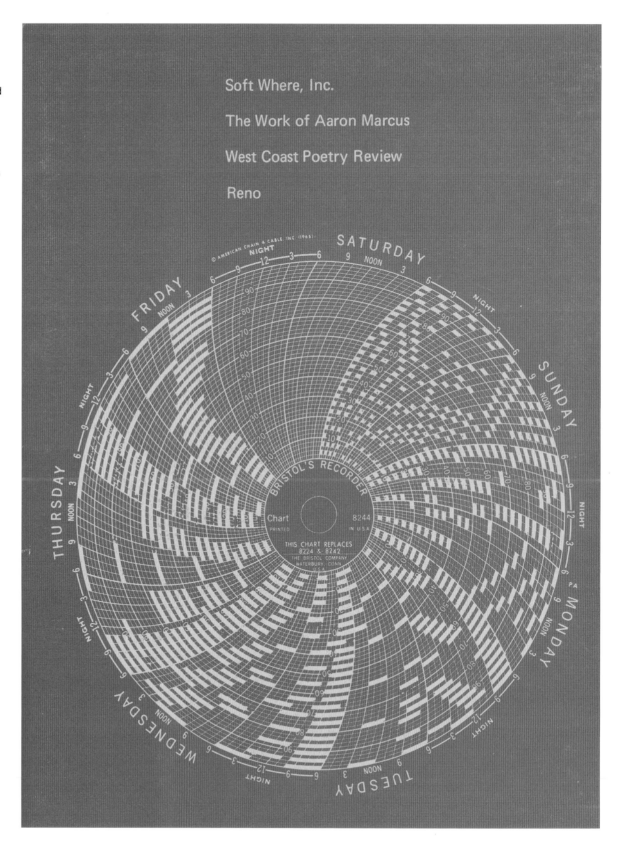

The key people in the development of a picture language

Otto Neurath (b.Vienna 1882 d.Oxford 1945) is not easy to classify as a scientist, nor can he be earmarked as belonging to any political fraction. His life runs parallel to that of many German-speaking scientists in the 1930s. In spite of this, he expressed a fate in mankind and took an optimistic view of society.

Marie Reidemeister (1968-1986) joined Neurath as an assistant at Gesellshafts- und Wirtshaftsmuseum in 1925. After the closing of the museum there was a period when they worked together in The Hague. They moved to England in 1940. She married Neurath in 1941 and has since been known as Marie *Neurath*. She carried on with her picture education in England into the 1970s.

Gerd Arntz (1900-1988) was the designer/illustrator responsible for most of the graphs and the exhibition material in Vienna and The Hague. Arntz often used lino-cutting to finish his figures.
He did not follow Otto and Marie to England, but remained in The Netherlands until his passing. (His large body of work can be viewed on www.gerdarntz.org)

The Otto & Marie Neurath ISOTYPE Collection is now in The Department of Typography & Graphic Communication, University of Reading, England

Transforming information

Transforming (from German "Transformator") is the process of selecting, analysing, ordering and then visualizing information, data, ideas and connections.

Otto Neurath founded Vienna's social and economic museum (Gesellshafts- und Wirtshaftsmuseum) in 1925 and was instrumental in putting transforming into practice through exhibitions and publications. His idea was to bridge the gaps between the sciences and make "difficult" economic, social and technological information comprehensible to the layman.

The work was carried out by a small staff to begin with, but after a while academics and specialists from different fields contributed to the various projects. They became confident in the belief that every kind of scientific statement is open to a visual treatment.

Political events terminated the activities in Vienna in 1934 however by the end of the 1930s Neurath's work had attracted international attention. The term ISOTYPE (**I**nternational **S**ystem **o**f **TY**pographic **P**icture **E**ducation) evolved. ISOTYPE was intended as a helping language: Some words of explanation are necessary in any chart. Still, languages can create unnecessary barriers between nations and groups of people. These can be reduced without detaching graphs and illustrations from the text. The graphs were not meant to be in competition with normal language, but as a help inside its narrow limits. To create a language of signs (like Chinese script) was never the intention.

"International Picture Language" was published in London in 1936, "Modern Man in the Making" in New York three years later. The present-day interest in the pioneering efforts of Neurath is remarkable.

The permanent exhibition of the
Gesellshafts- und Wirtschaftsmuseum
in the new town hall in Vienna (Opened
in December 1927).

The inherent weakness of ISOTYPE

Although Neurath envisaged a pictorial system of education, we still depend on words. Images can only help to get across existing contextual information. "Images" is not something that can be created from nothing (like an artist does it) but must represent something.

Images can be drawing, paintings, photographs and films. Neurath's and Arntz's system is made up of simplified, but easily comprehensable forms drawn by hand.

A pictorial code does not possess the same characteristics as the alphabet and the numbers. To make a pictorial code work it must be free of any ambiguity. This is not always easy to achieve. ISOTYPE can work well with target groups that are familiar with their context. They are easy to comprehend if the viewers can relate them to their own life and work situation. There are doubts as to this method's ability to represent new information and new processes.

The use of simplified figures can easily degenerate from prototypes to caricatures. Not all Asians wear turbans. Frenchmen do not go to work in striped shirts or wear berets. When a barrel of oil is depicted it must be made clear that the barrel represents a set quantity, not the entire year's OPEC production. The "Man" symbol can only be approximately correct. In order to show a figure like 875 one would have to chop off an arm or a leg. (If one man represents 1000 people).

Comparative statistics may often have an ideological or political twist to them, even though the statistical information might be accurate and reliable. (Beware!)
The drawings must be updated in order to keep up with technological developments and aesthetical trends.

The illustration shows a (relatively late) example of Neurath's work.

The horizontal arrangement represents changes in quantities, while vertical arrangements show passages of time, or like in this example, a comparison between various data.

The low coverage of motor cars in Germany can be explained by the fact that the nationalized car industry had not yet got their mass production of Volkswagen going.

Television was still at an experimental stage in 1937. Hence, "audio" is synonymous with "radio".

The telephone must (today) be considered out of date.

The typeface used is Futura.

This was redrawn in CorelDraw by the author from an old print and stayed as close to the original as (digitally) possible.

Motor Cars, Telephones, Radio Sets 1937 per 50 population

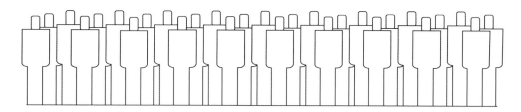

United States

Great Britain

France

Germany

This appeared in Michael Young and Theodor Prager's "There is work for all" and shows the distribution of wealth in prewar Britain. Published in 1941.

Ownership of Wealth in Great Britain

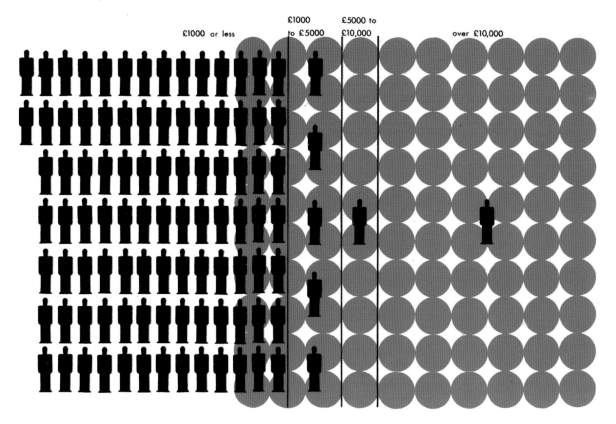

£1000 or less   £1000 to £5000   £5000 to £10,000   over £10,000

Each red circle represent one percent of total capital held.

Each man symbol represent one percent of total population aged 25 and over

The inherent possibilities of ISOTYPE

Signage systems that transcend language barriers have improved and can be found at airports and train stations many places in the world. Some of them are internationalized; some have a more local flavour. The set of pictograms used to make drivers aware of tourist attractions along French roads precede the verbal signs giving the place names. They are restricted to France only.

Tourism is a growing industry, and is a field where ISOTYPE can work well. The AIGA Symbol Signs, as shown on page 66, are not strictly in accordance with the way Arntz did them, but are certainly influenced by those found in ISOTYPE. The Symbol Signs are perhaps more adaptable now than when they were designed thirty years ago. They have the advantage of being well known, are graphically consistent and can be used in other areas than "transport". (For which they were originally intended). Many of them lend themselves well to statistical diagrams.

Data programs, World Wide Web, smartphones and iPods are areas where ISOTYPE can thrive and can be employed for both educational and entertainment purposes.

An apple can be an iconic sign. In order to be iconic it must have a physical resemblance to what it wants to depict. The illustration above shows different degrees of iconic presentation. The word "apple" is, irrespective of language, an index-linked sign. Such a sign must go through a code system (the phonetical alphabet) in order to be perceived and interpreted. As we can see, it is hard to find a universal icon for "telecommunication". The sign must be seen in a historic, social and technological context.

(See page 196 **Hartmann** & **Bauer**, **Neurath** & **Kinross**)

AIGA Symbol signs

The complete set of 50 passenger/ pedestrian symbols developed by AIGA (American Institute of Graphic Art) is now available on the web, free of charge. There is a complete range both with and without a black background. (from www.aiga.org)

Produced through a collaboration between the AIGA and the U.S. Department of Transportation, they are an example of how public-minded designers can address a universal communication need.

This system of 50 symbol signs was designed for use at the crossroads of modern life: in airports and other transportation hubs and at large international events.

Prior to this effort, numerous international, national and local organizations had devised symbols to guide passengers and pedestrians through transportation facilities and other sites of international exchange.

While effective individual symbols had been designed, there was no system of signs that communicated the required range of complex messages, addressed people of different ages and cultures and were clearly legible at a distance.

To develop such a system, AIGA and D.O.T. compiled an inventory of symbol systems that had been used in various locations worldwide, from airports and train stations to the Olympic Games. These copyright-free symbols have become the standard for off-the-shelf symbols in the catalogues of U.S. sign companies.

AIGA Signs and Symbols Committee members:
Thomas Geismar, Seymour Chwast, Rudolph de Harak, John Lees and Massimo Vignelli
Production designers:
Roger Cook and Don Shanosky Page, Arbitrio and Resen, Ltd.

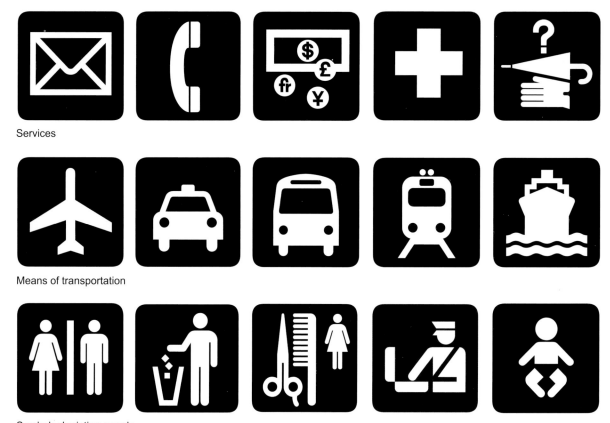

Services

Means of transportation

Symbols depicting people

Project coordinators:
Don Moyer and Karen Moyer Mark Ackley and Juanita Dugdale
(From AIGAs website april 2004 www.aiga.org)

Otto Neurath would probably have been pleased to see the outcome of this project if he had been allowed to live long enough. It is hard to image this kind of "pictorial education" without Neurath's pioneering efforts as background.

The AIGA Design Committee handled this in an exemplary manner and left behind a thorough report giving detailed descriptions of their work. ("Symbol Signs"). The various design suggestions submitted by Cook & Shanoski were evaluated according to three categories of criteria: Semantic (the relationship of a signs to its meaning), Syntactic (the relationship of one visual sign to other signs) and Pragmatic (the relationship between the signs and their users).

Since its launch in 1974 travel and cross-cultural communication has expanded tremendously and tourism now counts as one of the biggest industries in the world. The present day use of mobile telephones and multimedia guides was an unknown phenomenon in 1974. They are therefore more "topical" today than they were thirty years ago. The fact that they can be used without paying any royalty fees should not harm anyone.

Although they were primarily designed for signage to view at a distance, most of them perform well in smaller sizes. That makes them adaptable to many graphic jobs.

The French cartographer and scientist Jacques Bertin developed a system for graphic organisation of maps, which was first published in 1967.

Bertin's starting point was statistics that dealt with demographic and economic matters. This information was transformed through a sign system into readable maps. (See illustration). The circles and the rectangles indicate quantities or percentage values that, grouped together, can give valuable information about population density, agricultural production, income per family and other themes. The system has three hierarchies: Qualitative, sequential and quantitative. (See page 196 **Bertin**)

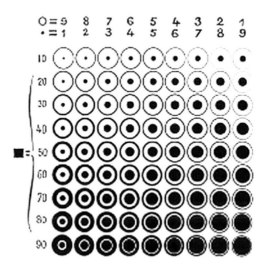

After close to forty years, Bertin's pioneering effort still has many valuable principles to follow, but conditions have changed. Statistical information is more exact and easier to obtain today than it was when Bertin did his initial work. GIS (Geographic Information Systems) has made huge strides in later years. Colour printing was still considered a luxury in 1967 and usually confined to large circulation magazines.

Bertin uses the shape of his homeland (France). France has a pleasant, firm outline which makes visual organisation of the elements (relatively) easy. This situation does not apply to all geographical areas.

There are also inbuilt problems of perception: As soon as you combine two patterns, a third pattern will inevitably emerge. It is possible to make a map of Rebublicans and Democrats by counting the votes in the state of Missouri after an election. It can also show how the density of each group is distributed throughout the state's territory. The Netherlands is more complex as there are more political parties competing for votes on a small territory. One can easily end up with a patchwork which is difficult to perceive. On the other hand, if one wants a "at a glance" view of what an area contains, a well designed Bertin-map can work quite well.

The different (standard) diagrams

The sector diagrams

We have these figures to relate to:

Matter A 6179
Matter B 4830
Matter C 1987
Matter D 610

The sum of these (100%) is 13.606.
One percent is 136.
There are 360 degrees to divide up in a circle. One percent is 3,6

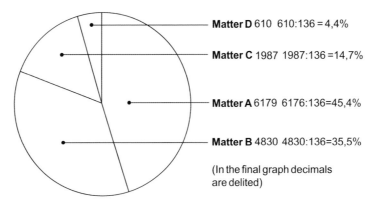

Matter D 610 610:136 = 4,4%

Matter C 1987 1987:136 = 14,7%

Matter A 6179 6176:136=45,4%

Matter B 4830 4830:136=35,5%

(In the final graph decimals are delited)

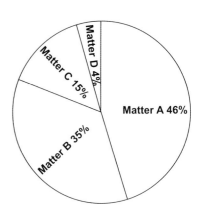

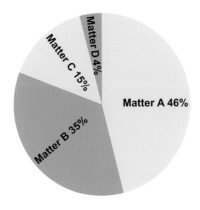

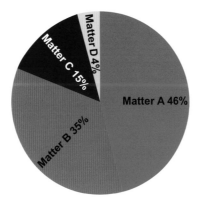

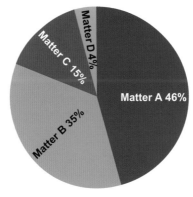

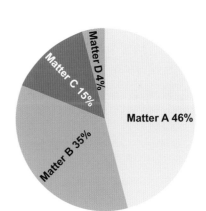

Monochrome colouring. We need only a 20% difference between the values in order to keep them apart.

Here we have used samples from the colour circle and ganged them up with no consideration to percent/saturation ratio. A bit on the violent side, perhaps.

In this sample we have attempted to strike a balance between dark and light, saturated and passive colours. No single element is allowed to stand out as "primadonna".

There is no doubt that it is Matter C we want the viewers to focus upon.

The label "Matter" is only to be understood in a model context: It could be tonnage, dollars or people. The sum of the parts will always be 100%
As for making pie charts it is handy to use the worksheets in programs like Excel or Lotus and have the diagram maker to do the arithmetic for you.

All you have to worry about is stacking the numbers up correctly on the worksheet. In these examples, the pie charts were done as finished art in Corel Draw, whilst the dividing up of the pie was done in MS Excel. The percentages given on the labels are only approximately correct.

When designing pie charts it is important that the viewers get the total picture in one gaze. Consequently they work best if the labels are put on top of each pie. In some instances this can be hard to achieve and one has to find other solutions. It is possible to combine the chart with a table giving the exact

amounts in dollars, tonnage etc. The colour codes can be attached to each section of the table. This author has not been able to find any useful theories about colour combinations and harmonies in this area of work. Everything is circumstantial.

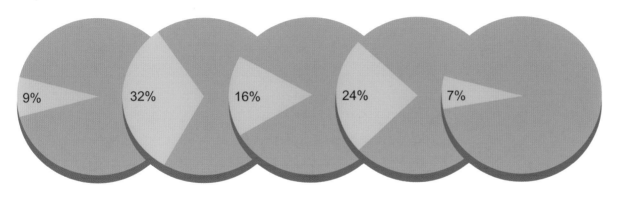

Sector diagrams can be arranged on a time axis (the x-axis) or used as comparisons between countries, regions, socio-economic groups and markets.
By stacking them on top of each other we can save space and get a coherent picture.

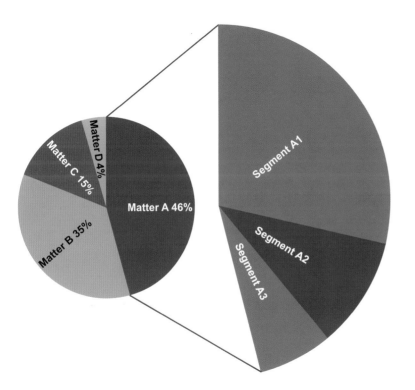

It sometimes happens that we want to break one of the pies into segments to get a fuller picture.

The doughnut is another variation of the pie chart. It tells us what made up the total. It is surprising how little these are used. We can envisage a situation where a product manager has to report to his board and explain the expenditure on one of his projects. In the public sector, school and hospital managers are under constant attacks for exceeding budgets.
Household expenses can be explained in a similar way.

69

These are the most common ways of visualizing quantitative developments historically. That they move from left to right is not only a question of habit, but has something to do with how we perceive information. (We read from left to right).

The horizontal axis which shows the development in time is called the x-axis. Quantities are arranged vertically on the left of the diagram and called the y-axis. This is a standard one must adhere to, and is also a question of habit.

Our choice of graphic techniques in this area depends entirely on what we want the readers to understand: Do we want to emphasise accurate readings of quantities, or do we want to show a tendency? We can also use them to good effect as comparisons.

Remember that comparisons in money value must be inflation-adjusted in a graph covering a time sequence of five years or more. Too many graphic presentations showing "growth" have a tendency to ignore this.

There are many possibilities and hopefully you will get some input by looking at the examples shown here. Some of them are common; others are not so frequently used. Other publications like annual reports and sections of the business press are worth studying.

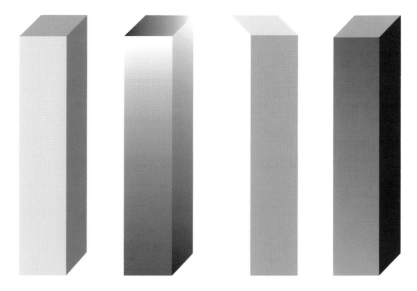

The shapes of the bars need not be flat and two-dimensional. One can add both visual "presence" and a bit of drama to them.

The examples here are made in 2D software (CorelDraw). Attention is paid to positions, colour and lighting.

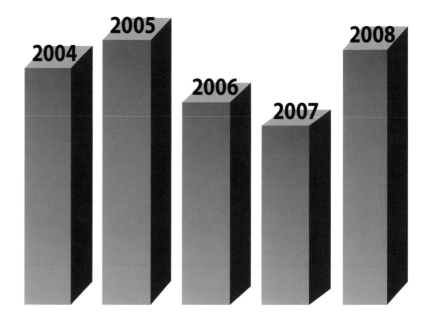

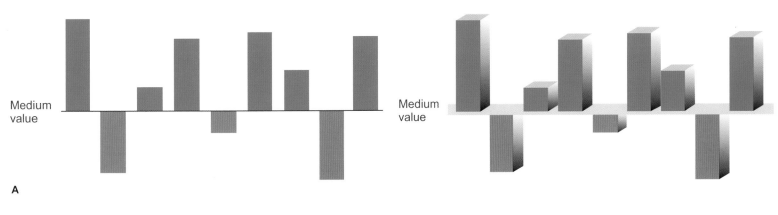

A

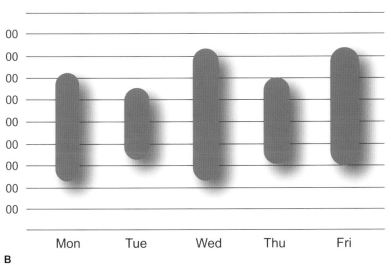

B

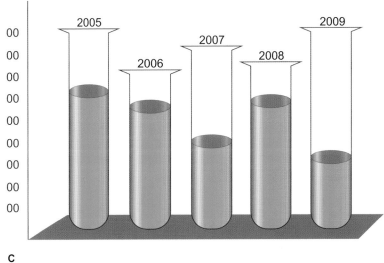

C

D

A There are bar charts that do not start at zero on the Y-axis. (The axis that gives the quantities). In this instance all measures relate to a medium value. Consequently, some values fall below this established medium.
Adding some isometric depth does not seem to do the diagram any harm.

B The variation diagram is another category of bar charts. The bars are not tied to a zero point or a medium value, but "float" between a maximum and a minimum value.
Examples are swings in temperature or the ratings on the stock exchange.

C If we are working for a company in the chemical/pharmaceutical area it can be tempting to combine the chart with a relevant illustration.
In this instant we emphasize a part of the whole and make the total into "transparent glass".

D The clock is in reality a diagram that gives you the time of day. Combining it with a bar chart it can give valuable information about variations within a time sequence.

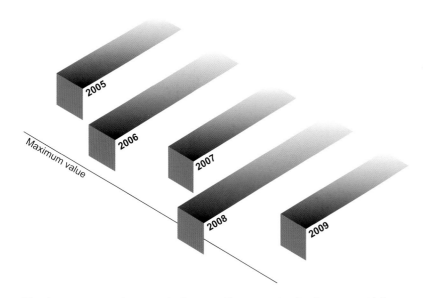

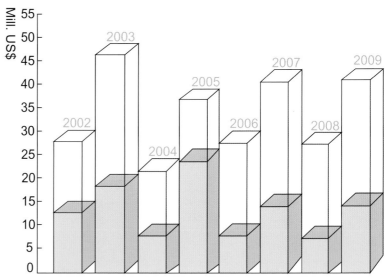

Year-by-year comparisons can be interesting enough, but in this instance we are more interested in how volumes relate to a maximum value and estimated expectations.

Governments often impose restrictions on how much banks are allowed to lend out. Airlines and train companies are interested in running at their highest capacities.

In this case we are clearly interested in emphasizing the parts. We simply make the total look like "transparent glass".

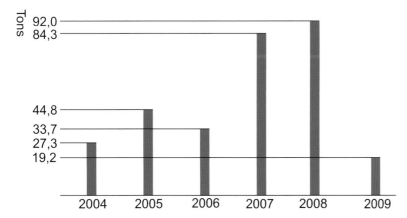

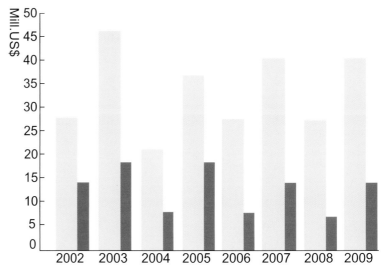

In this instance we have reduced the width of the bars in order to include the relevant quantities. In other words, we have managed to get the best of both worlds, without sacrificing legibility and graphic quality.

This diagram is based on the same figures as the one above. The bars are different in both width and colour. The red bars can be profit after tax or how much a single product represents compared to the total turnover.

Such a dual bar chart can also be useful when comparing something which in its essence is impossible to compare: One cannot compare a nation's consumption of beer with its intake of 40% pure liquor.

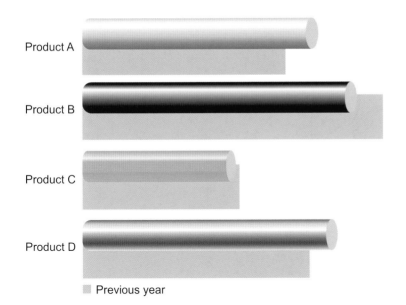

Product A

Product B

Product C

Product D

▢ Previous year

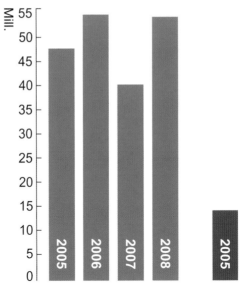
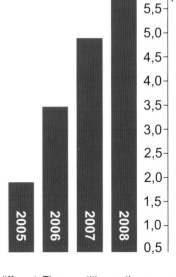

Bar charts can also be horizontal. In this case there is no time sequence to consider. Company shareholders are sometimes interested in knowing how the various sectors of the company or the different products have been doing. (Not only the net total). In this model the difference between the reported year and the previous year should be easy to grasp.

It is permissible to have two y-axes in one and the same chart; provided there is no doubt in the reader's mind as to what is what. Here, the time sequence is the same, but the two colours indicate that the charts are different. The quantities on the y-axes are very different.

From this we can read, that although the total turnover may vary from year to year, there has been continuous growth in exports.

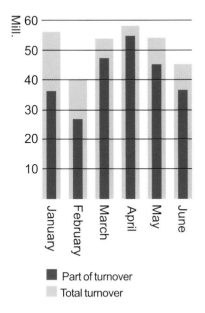

▢ Part of turnover
▢ Total turnover

Here we have combined the total and parts of the total in the same chart. In newspapers we sometimes have to confine ourselves to narrow column measures.

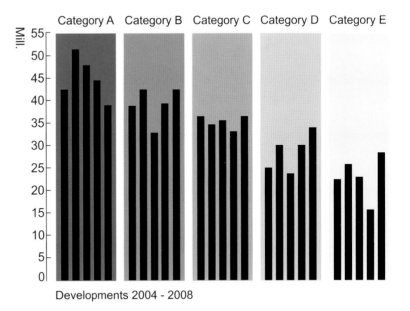

Category A   Category B   Category C   Category D   Category E

Developments 2004 - 2008

Comparative line graphs can easily become crowded or contain too many colour codes. This is one way of avoiding the "salad syndrome".

Most people equate a dark colour with "most".
(Adobe Illustrator was the software used in this chapter))

Whilst bar charts can give a good view of historic develop-ment along a time axis, the line graphs can record small and large movements and variations within smaller spaces of time. These visualizations are aptly called "fever diagrams".

They are used in areas like medicine, GIS (Geographic Information Systems) and electronics, just to mention a few. We have only to open the economy pages in a newspaper to be exposed to variations on the stock exchange, currencies, oil prices and the value of properties. There does not seem to be much to gain by showing examples of these in this book as they appear everywhere. On the other hand, there are vari-ations of the line graph that deserve more attention and could be put to good use.

We shall have a closer look at how these categories of diagrams are designed in order to give maximum legibility, and good presentation of quantities and developments. To begin with, we must make up our minds as to what is relevant from the readers' point of view: Should we show developments over a year, a month, a week, a day or an hour? Is there enough data available to produce a reliable presentation?

There are optical and graphic matters to be considered: How many guides do we need to make readings accurate, without making the graph look cluttered? Do we need colour coding of the lines and how many? We must always keep in mind that there are limits to what the readers can keep track of in one go. In the worse case, the end result might look more like a salad than a comprehensible piece of information.

Even if many of these diagrams are well known and often used, there is room for improvement. Line graphs can easily be connected to illustrations in order to add some drama to them. A bit of visual punch added to our presentation should do no harm, as long as we do not sacrifice legibility.

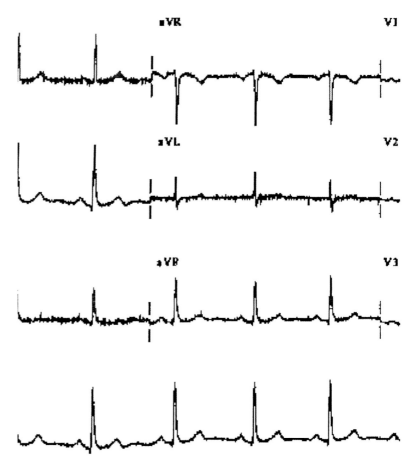

Section from electrocardiogram (ECG)
Healthy, adult person

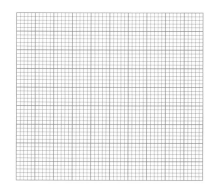

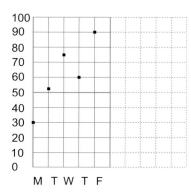

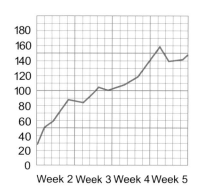

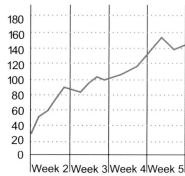

We start with something that resembles old fashioned graph paper. We can easily make something similar digitally by using the grid function in our program.
As there are five working days in a week, it suits us fine to have 5 x 5 subdivisions in each square indicated by a thicker rule.

Having established a time sequence and the y-axis we can plot in the quantities as small dots where they belong.

Depending on the time span the graph is supposed to cover, we repeat this operation. We can now draw a connecting line from point to point. Once completed, we can delete the dots.

We now have to find a balance between details, perception, and the accuracy needed to "read" the graph. Is this a good solution?

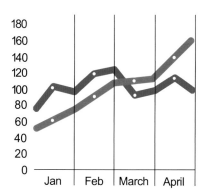

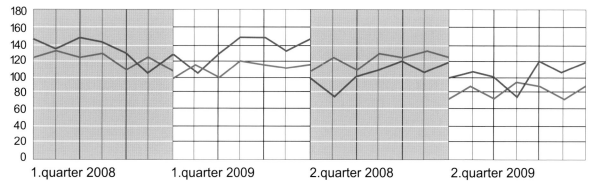

We have now made a big leap: From days in the week (top row, number two from left) to months.
A new set of data has been added so that we now have a comparative graph.
The white dots indicate average figures per month. Hopefully these dots will also help the reader in extracting data efficiently from the y-axis.

To anticipate seasonal changes can often cause headaches for many business leaders. To reduce guesswork it is possible to make decisions based on past experience.

In comparative diagrams like these, accurate readings of figures are not as important as showing *tendencies* in the given periods.

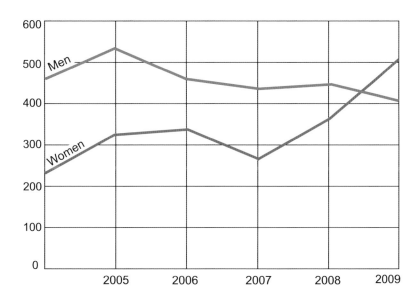

Applicants to faculty 2003-2008 — Women — Men

○ 1st half of 2008   ● 1st half of 2009

These two diagrams tell the same story but we may assume that the top one attracts more attention and possesses more visual "punch" than a simple line graph. On the other hand, the bottom one makes accurate reading of the statistical data easier.

On the photograph of the girls and the boys, reduction of the colours cyan and yellow was necessary. Without this reduction of saturation, the lines in the graph would have become almost unreadable.

Line graphs lend themselves easily to illustration and dramatization. If one only wants to illustrate a trend or a tendency, accurate reading of quantities might not be necessary. Again: It all depends on the communication goals and the situation you are in.

These images were first treated in Photoshop. Then mounted together with the vectors in Illustrator.

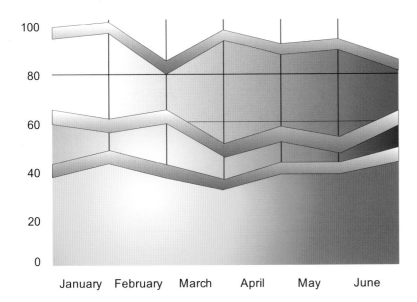

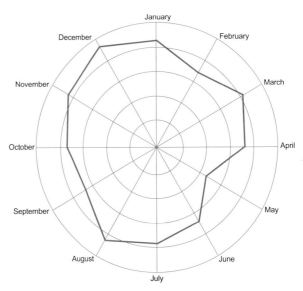

The mountain diagram makes it possible to compare quantities, as each "mountain" has a colour and/or a texture code. In this sample there are three sets of values. The effect can easily diminish if there are too many mountains or not enough difference between them.

The mountain diagrams can also serve as histograms and show developments over longer periods. (Months/years).

Cyclic line graphs give a good overall picture of developments without going too much into details. The values are indicated by circular, radial steps. (Shown here without figures). They have proved to be applicable to many fields: The number of travellers and seasonal variations in various means of transportation. Patients needing attention in hospitals at night. It is surprising how little these charts are used, taken into account how useful they can be.

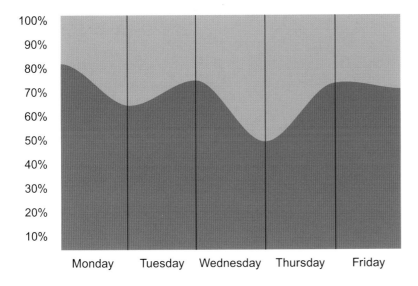

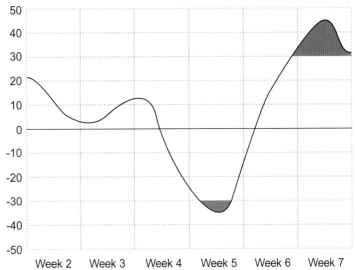

The area diagram is a line chart that emphasises the parts against a maximum value.

The tolerance diagrams (also known as "crisis diagrams") have both positive and negative measures related to a zero point on the y-axis. The "intolerable" values are indicated by a red zone.

Medical personnel are acquainted with these renderings which often come to them electronically. It may be suggested that they could also be useful for financial controllers in companies.

Combination of diagrams

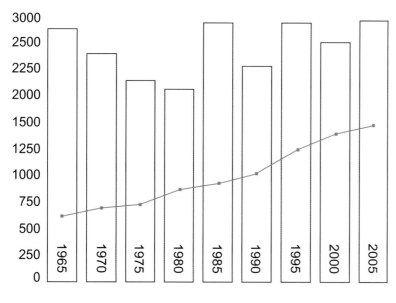

It is permissible to mix bar and line in the same diagrams. On the left the bar chart shows variations in volume over several decades. The line graph shows a tendency. This tendency is a percentage of the total at any given period.

Examples:

The number of applicants to a field of study may have varied over the years. The line indicates that the number of female applicants has been on a steady rise.

The percentage of exports to a company's total turnover can be shown in a similar manner.

Below are two line graphs that can be shown together. They are both based on the same statistical data, but have different "messages" and employ different scales. (Norway's export of salmon over a 6-month period in 2006). The black and red points indicate medium values in a month or in a week. The one on the right focuses on two months only (April-June). The way this information is presented it appears that the variations have been more dramatic than the 6-months diagram on the left would indicate.

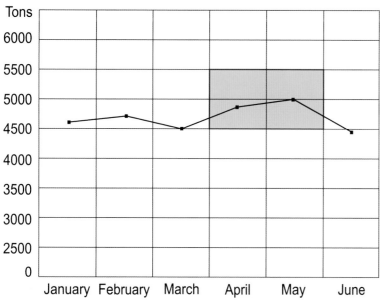

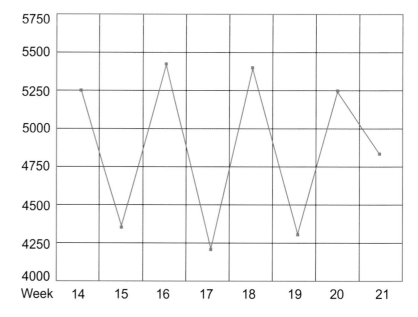

These are useful in order to explain *tendencies*. They are often based on factual measurements and statistical data, but need not show this information on the diagram itself. They can be informative and effective in communicating "the way the wind is blowing" and have a multitude of applications:

So far, they have been widely used in literature dealing with geography, seismology, meteorology and related areas. Good illustrations are to be found in atlases.

There are areas where economists, market analysts and town planners could use spread diagrams to good advantage. The example on this page shows a *centrifugal* arrangement of progressive coloured steps. A *centripetal* diagram would lead the eye in a direction towards a centre or an axis. (Which, in many cases could be just as relevant).

In the 1990s many department stores in big cities suffered loss of trade. Difficulties in finding parking space in the vicinity of the stores combined with lower rents in out-of-town buildings might have been two important factors. To foresee such developments is not always easy, but it possible to plan according to existing tendencies. Not all roads lead to Rome. On page 175 you can see spread and growth diagrams employed on the presentation for the Songdo City Project.

Using the inherent possibilities in available software, there are many ways of producing gradations and "spread" effects. Experimentation relevant to the task at hand should be encouraged.

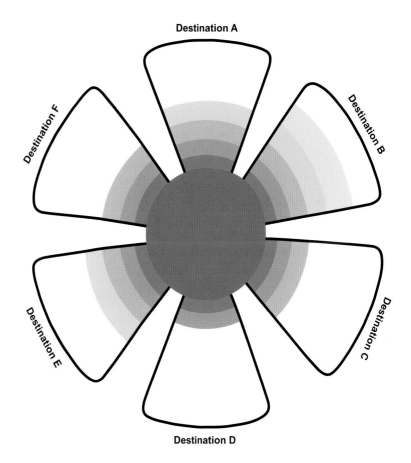

These were made in Adobe Illustrator using the Blend Tool to good effect.

Sector A

A percentage of the
total volume

Sector B

A percentage of the
total volume

Sector C

A percentage of the
total volume

Volume diagrams can display quantitative measures and relations in both an efficient and impressive manner: A bar in a bar chart measuring 10 cm against a value scale can only show a limited quantity. A cube measuring 10cm x 10cm x 10 cm will contain 1000 square centimetres and can contain larger quantities occupying less space.

The models shown here were done with 2D software (CorelDraw) but in this area there could be advantages of doing measuring and modelling employing 3D equipment. It is recommended to use (relatively) simple and recognizable shapes and avoid (unnecessary) perspective. Again: There is no obvious need for making things more complicated than they are.

The application of volume diagrams are many: A bank's investments in different areas. The progressive increments in volumes over a period of time. The percentage of available land measured against a total area. A comparison between the exports from three countries is shown on page 103.

One should not hide the fact that volume diagrams require considerably more work compared to sector and bar charts. One must try to get the planes, cylinders, cubes and other shapes right with respect to the readers eye point and need for information. On the other hand, they are not so common and could hence attract more attention than "ordinary" graphs. They have a "physical" appearance which other types do not possess.

This comes from an EPS file that contained both vector and bitmaps. The modelling of the cylinders was achieved by employing fountain fills to be found in the fill toolbox in Corel Draw. (More about the file formats on page 46)

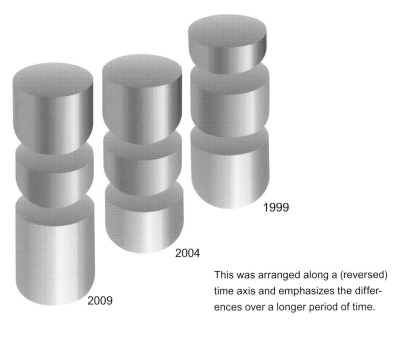

1999

2004

2009

This was arranged along a (reversed) time axis and emphasizes the differences over a longer period of time.

This model for comparisons was made up of trimetric cubes. In a trimetric cube the front is the dominant side. This makes it possible to use this plane for trademarks, icons or titles.

In this example the two groups are set up mirror reversed against each other. In these renderings it is important that one gets the impression that the cubes "stand on something".

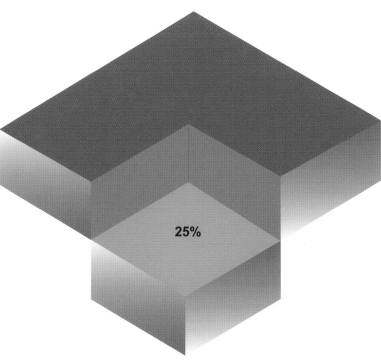

25%

This was made with isometric cubes with only half of the cube's height showing.
(See page 34 about axiometry)

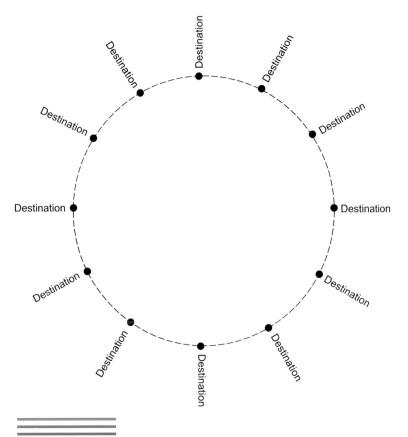

Most of the designs shown in this chapter are based on the assumption that we read from left to right. This does not apply to Networks: Here the lines can connect, disconnect, intertwine, cross each other, overlap in a multitude of directions.

Network diagrams often have the elements shown in the illustration on the left: A circular wheel with a predetermined number of "stops". In this case there are twelve, but there can be fewer or more. The word "Destination" is put in for the sake of convenience but the wheel can have different wording for each stop. Colour coding helps the reader to keep the lines apart.

Network diagrams can help to reveal information about:
Transportation systems
Business relations
Computer systems
Political alliances
World Wide Web structures

There are some interesting examples to be viewed on www.visualcomplexity.com

Matrixes are usually organized the same way as tables with columns and rows. The difference between a table and a matrix is that a matrix gives qualitative information, not figures.

Matrixes are useful in many areas:
You can be guided towards what to switch on and what to switch off when handling an electronic product. If something happens to your car, it is possible to list the symptoms along one axis and suggest actions to remedy the situation in another. One can evaluate products or service on a scale good/ indifferent/bad and get a useful comparison without wasting too much time.

Within market research and opinion polls matrixes have proved to be useful tools: Subjective information can be gathered and then treated numerically into statistics. These can vary from simple "yes/no" and "for/against" answers to measurements with subtle distinctions and gradations.

The challenges lie in designing intelligent structures and finding suitable questions to which there are no simple answers. The arrangements can be alphanumerical or be organized as hierarchies. Three examples are shown here: One is based on facts, the other two give answers to questions of a more subjective nature.

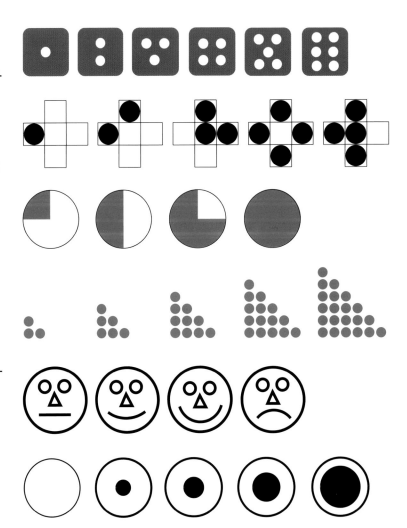

In a matrix arrangement one often uses signs in addition to crosses and zeros. These can indicate good/indifferent/bad, full/half full/empty, often/now and again/seldom according to a predetermined scale. The second from the top has been used for product evaluation. Each of the five squares represents a criterion from which the product can be assessed.

Anyone who has done a fair amount of travelling knows that the standard of hotels can vary. The rates and scales can be an indicator, but they are not the only indicators. There are, of course, variations in requirements: If one is only passing through and need a bed to sleep in, many accommodations can easily meet one's needs.

For working people on the move who need a place to work and want to entertain people, requirements are different. It is useful to know beforehand what facilities the various hotels can offer. Travel agencies give out very sparse information about this. This matrix lists six (fictitious) London hotels. I feel certain that many travel agency customers would find such a listing useful.

I am therefore handing this over to the agencies (free of charge).

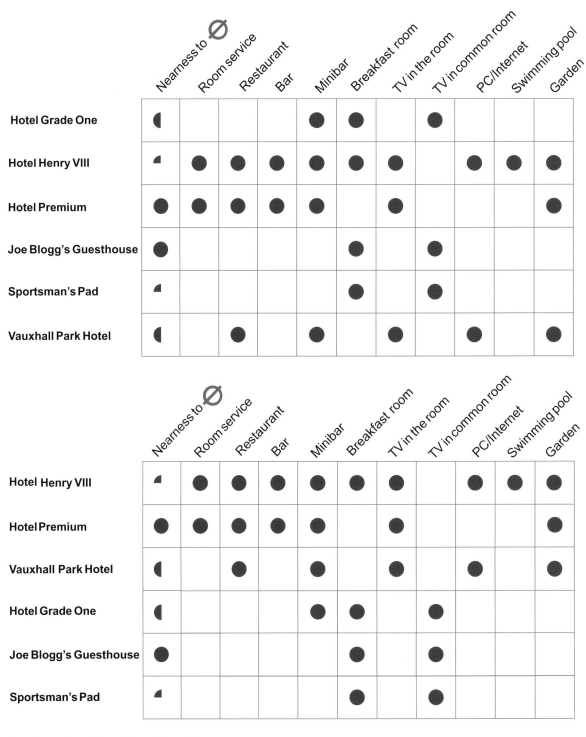

As above but with a hierarchic rating

84

The semantic differential

is often used in market research and behavioural psychology. It has proved to be a good instrument for measuring attitudes to companies, organizations, products and (in a more limited way) to people.

Assessments are made from a vertical, zero axis and there are polar adjectives on either end of a horizontal axis. The test person is supposed to tick off "what you think" on a scale from one to five in either direction. These assessments are collected and treated numerically so that a "profile" can be drawn on a graph.

One must avoid measurable quantities like "expensive/cheap", "high/low" etc. Adjectives must be carefully chosen. In some instances, one must assume that the target group is in possession of a certain knowledge and experience in order to give meaningful assessments. In other situations, a more spontaneous approach is requested.

This is subjective information, measured objectively.

Our image of self does not always correspond with how others see us. The example shows considerable disparity in how the two groups assess the company. This image analysis was carried out as a platform for a corporate identity project. (The company shall remain anonymous). The aim of the exercise was to correct misrepresentation or faulty assessments of the company profile and recommend actions.

This method is known as "The Semantic Differential" or "The Osgood Scale". It was first published in "The Measurement of Meaning" in 1957. (Osgood, Charles E., Suci, George J. & Tannenbaum, Percy H.)

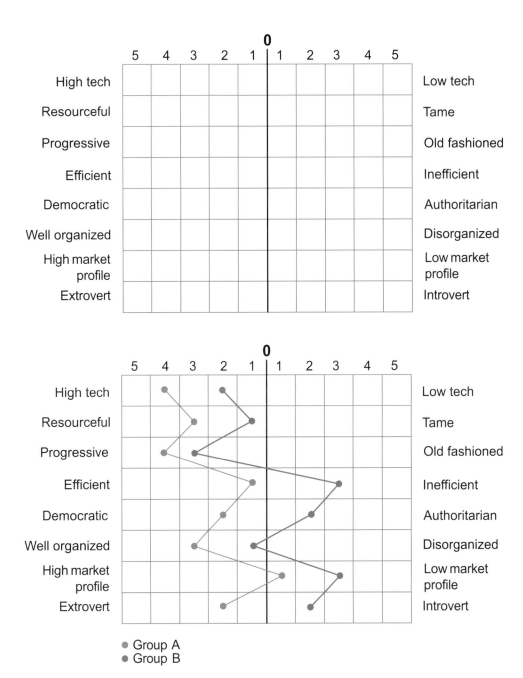

● Group A
● Group B

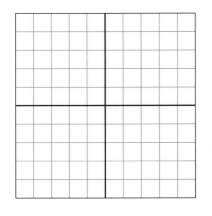

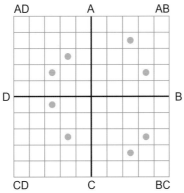

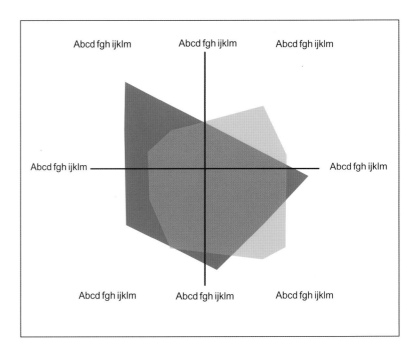

Group A   Group B

In this model one uses a 4 x 5 square grid, where the cross represents the zero point. Again, we get a scale from one to five, but there are four directions, not two. We add words and put in points to indicate values. A,B,C and D are answers to questions of a concrete nature. AB, BC, CD and AD are

questions regarding "softer" values. The test person has to give his/her answers to both categories.

When all the participants have been tested, we can draw lines between the points and get a group profile. (The points indicate median values from the group assembled from the test matrial.) From this we can read that there are more differences in the answers given by Group A than those given in Group B. The overprinted (green) area indicates the test field where the two group's answers overlap.

This is a type of profile diagrams that do not give as accurate answers as those shown on the previous page. We must assume that one will get different answers and find different attitudes when testing people under 25 years of age compared to those who are 50 plus. This goes from attitudes to society as well as habits and preferences.

Experience from referenda has taught us that many Europeans are divided in their attitude to EU and its administration. This is not just a "yes/no" or "for/against" situation, there are different degrees of loyalty to EU to be measured.

For marketers of trend-sensitive products it is important to know if their products are in line with the wishes and expectations of their target groups.

Question one

Group A

Group B

Group C

Question two

Group A

Group B

Group C

Question three

Group A

Group B

Group C

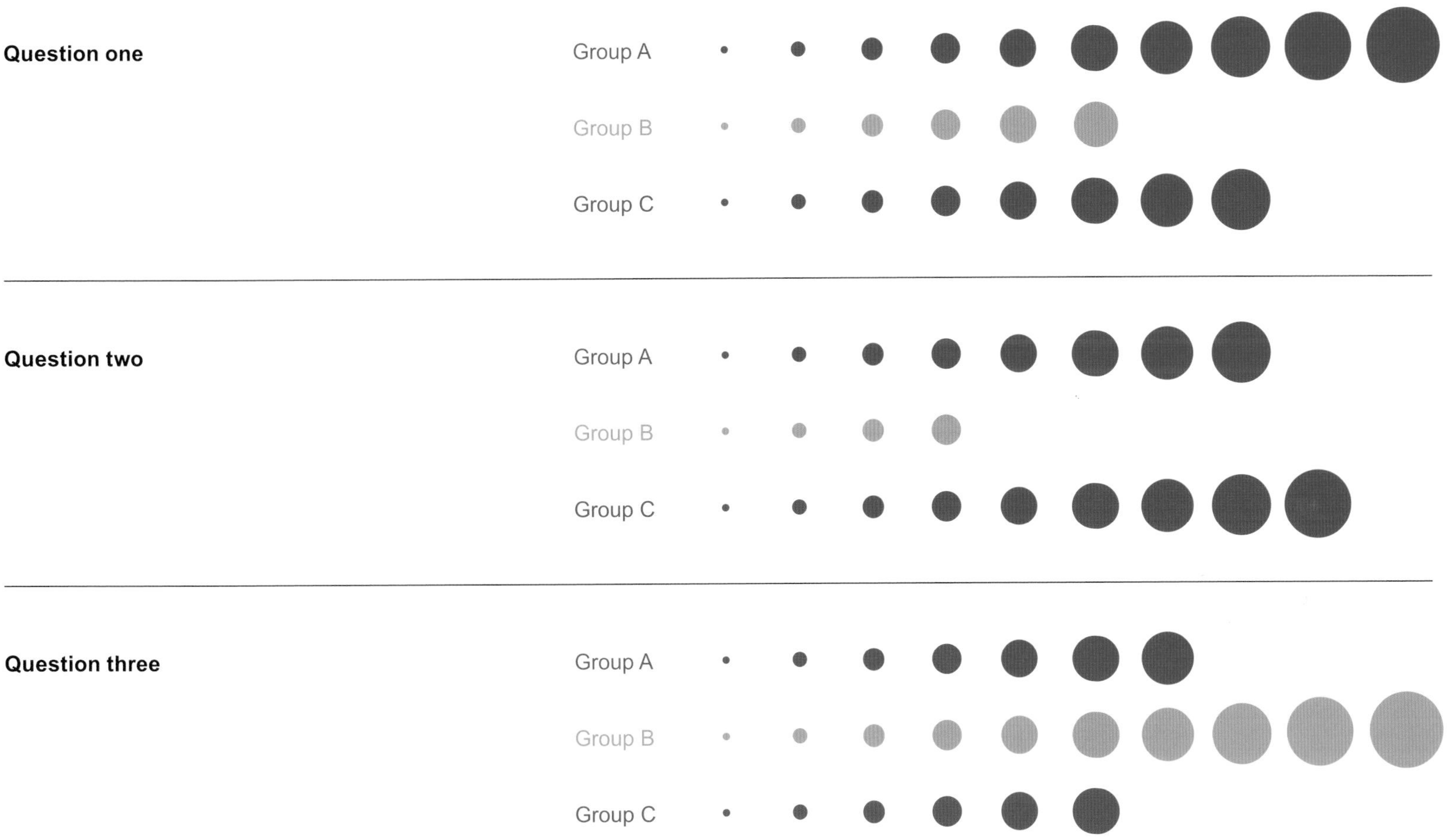

Groups of people have different attitudes to political, social and environmental issues, and answers to questions can differ widely. There has been some discussion as to how this kind of information should be presented. Some claim that percentage values are best and most accurately shown in tables. Graphs are not accurate enough and employed by image makers with axes to grind.

On the illustration above a system was devised by using dots within a square grid with ten percent increments. A full square represents 100%. This does not allow for figures like 7,6% or 11,5% but it gives a quick overall picture. At a glance it is evident that answers given by members of Group B differ dramatically from the other two. This is not so easy to show in a table.

The flow charts

Flow charts explain processes and can help to visualize connections between the parts in a product or in a system. Some are made strictly for insiders, others are made so that outsiders can follow a process and grasp connections. They can express both linear and circular motions.

There are many variations and we can only touch on the subject in this book. People working in the electronic industry are usually well acquainted with them but they have proved to be useful in other lines of activity. They are often to be seen in economic literature and are an essential tool in explaining management and organizational structures.

One variant is "Ishikawa diagrams" which show cause and effect. (Worth checking out if a situation calls for it).

Designers who are in a position to present a project to an organization are often met with scepticism. Explanations in the shape of flow charts can ease communication and have a good "understanding effect". In my opinion, the use of flow charts should be taught as an obligatory subject in engineering and design schools.

If a project has many participants it is good for everybody to know what the situation is and what the next steps are. Flow charts have only short captions and titles and cannot describe a process fully. This can be viewed as a weakness, but in web communication it is possible to make titles into links and hence elaborate on the matter in question. Reports can be downloaded as PDF documents and be studied carefully.

As for the graphic handling of a flow chart, a certain amount of sobriety and reticence is often called for. An overworked diagram with lots of colours, shades and diverse shapes can have an effect opposite of that intended. A flow chart is usually a down to earth thing.

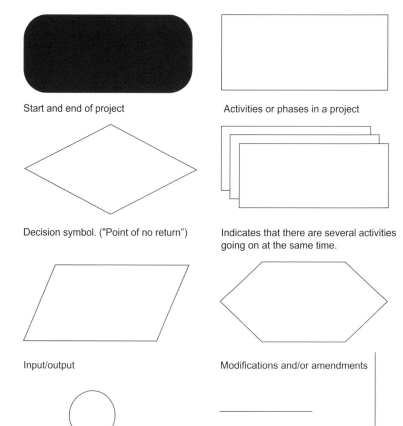

Start and end of project

Activities or phases in a project

Decision symbol. ("Point of no return")

Indicates that there are several activities going on at the same time.

Input/output

Modifications and/or amendments

The circle tells the reader that the chart does not end here.(It continues in the next column or on the next page).

Horizontal lines indicate connections. Vertical lines show the flow in the chart and connect the phases.

From British Standard BS 4050:1973 These have been in circulation for some time and must regarded as standards. They are widely understood by people who have more than two years of technical training. Other (more or less fanciful) symbols may have emerged. Most of them can easily be avoided (unless they are essential to what you want to show.)

Conceptual Design Development

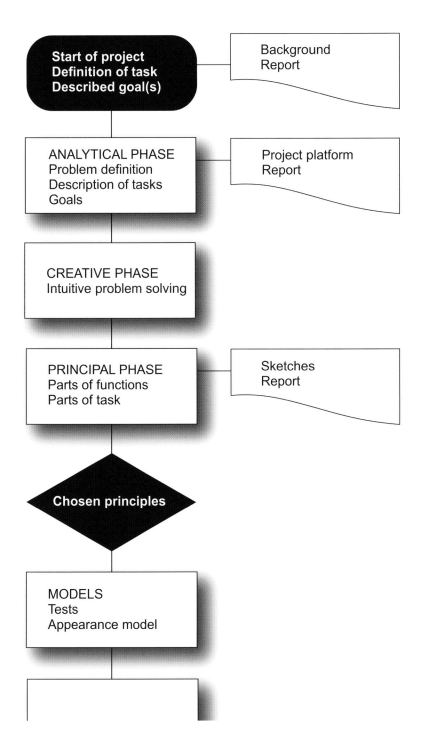

| Start of project
Definition of task
Described goal(s) | Background
Report |

| ANALYTICAL PHASE
Problem definition
Description of tasks
Goals | Project platform
Report |

CREATIVE PHASE
Intuitive problem solving

| PRINCIPAL PHASE
Parts of functions
Parts of task | Sketches
Report |

Chosen principles

MODELS
Tests
Appearance model

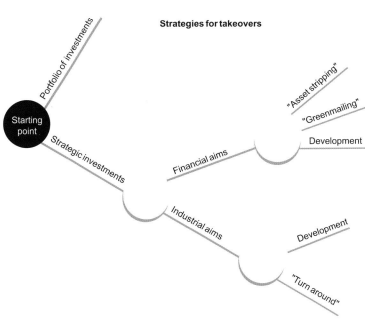

Strategies for takeovers

On the left is shown a section of a project with many steps. It does not give a true account of what goes on in the designer's head (which is not always as linear as the graph might lead you to believe). Still, it gives an outline of the methodology employed.

Above:
There are sometimes different ways to get to Rome.
(Done by the author for an article about mergers/takeovers for the journal "Practical economics".)

Unless otherwise mentioned, the diagrams in this chapter were produced "manually" using CorelDraw.

Diagrams in action

	A	B	C	D	E	F	G
1		January	February	March	April	May	June
2	Aluminium	6789	3789	5678	6789	5432	1987
3	Plastics	4830	6789	6789	2789	1873	6900
4	Glass	1987	987	1987	987	1435	1001

How a furniture manufacturer kept track of their storage of materials. Here are the figures from the worksheet. The categories (the months) are placed in the columns. The figures are in the rows.

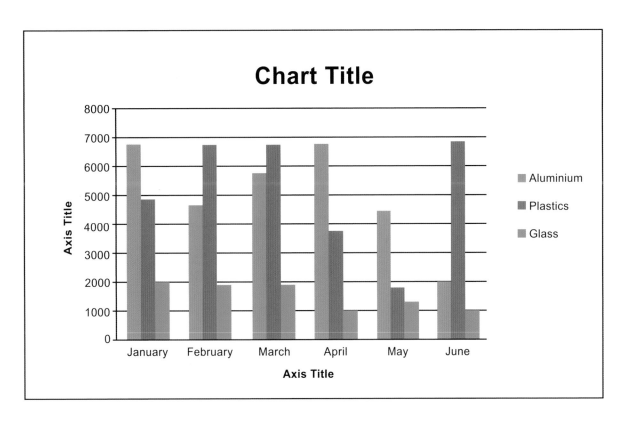

By employing the various options displayed in the INSERT Chart Menu in MS Excel we chose a historical bar chart from the selection and the result is shown here.
We shall now see how we can introduce design improvements to this graph.

Note:
This chapter is the only part of the book where only office software has been used for illustrations.
Recent versions of MS Office programs (2007 and later) have "Layout galleries" (under DESIGN) which speeds up the formatting.
Corel and Lotus also make programs where graphs can be based on spreadsheets, but their market shares must be described as small.

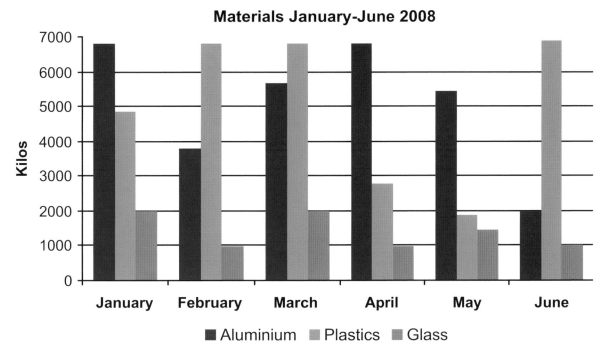

Materials January-June 2008

By trial-and-error in the commands both the appearance and readability has improved. In this sample the grid-lines against a white background helps to get to the values on the y-axis. The distance between the groups is equal to the width of one bar. New colour coding has been intro-duced: Cold (blue), warm (red) and grey. The spacing of the typography has been improved by right-clicking on the type and go to the FONT - Character Spacing - Condensed menu.

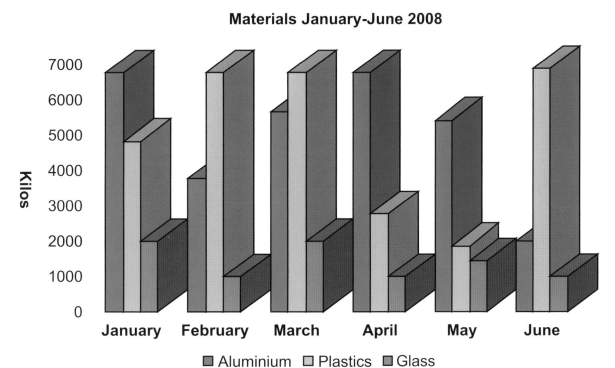

Materials January-June 2008

Here a three-dimensional effect has been emulated. The gridlines have been deleted. In this graph the emphasis is on comparisons, rather than accurate readings of quantities.

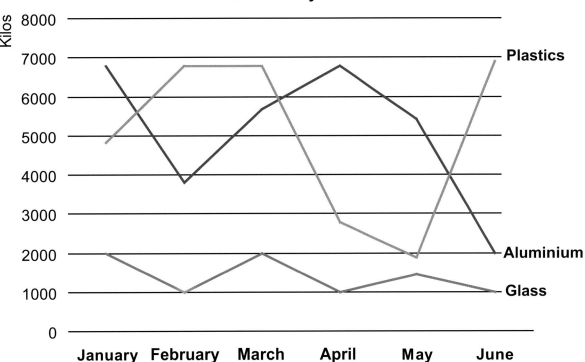

Materials January-June 2008

Kilos

Plastics
Aluminium
Glass

8000
7000
6000
5000
4000
3000
2000
1000
0

January   February   March   April   May   June

This line graph was based on the same figures and worksheet as the bar charts. The INSERT menu offers several choices but a 2D line graph that shows the variations over time seems to be the obvious choice.

The legend (the names of the materials) was made separately with the Text Box Tool. By right-clicking on the various elements in the graph it is possible to do adjustments in the Format Data Series menu. It is hard to argue against the speed with which these diagrams were made. The time spent formatting was relatively short compared to the efforts of making them from scratch in a drawing program.

Once all the formatting has been done, it is possible to store these in the DESIGN – Save as template menu. You then have a model which can be useful next time a job comes up.

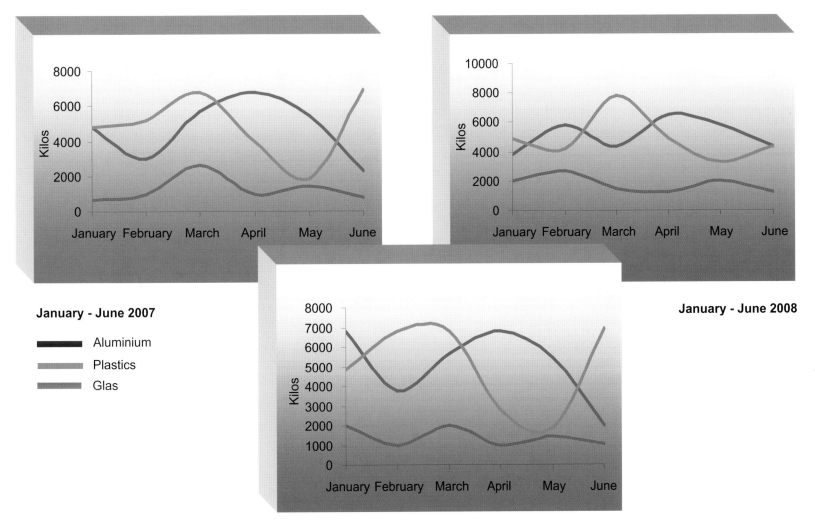

January - June 2007

—— Aluminium

—— Plastics

—— Glas

January - June 2008

January - June 2009

Anyone concerned with logistics knows that there should always be sufficient material in the storehouse to secure flow in the production. It is also important to make the right purchases when prices are favourable. Having too much in store can easily generate a negative cash flow

This decision making is not easy and is often based on prediction and hunches.

A diagram like the one above (based on past records) could help to graphically explain what variations to expect. This triple line graph was produced with the drawing tools available in MS Excel. There are a lot of things this program cannot do. (See chapter on software on page 41). Still, a diagram like this can be produced quickly prior to a business meeting and be shown in a digital presentation.

We are now leaving our furniture manufacturer. Hopefully, we have investigated some of the possibilities of using quantitative worksheets in a context which is close to a real life business situation.

These pages were made using Microsoft's 2007 Office applications.
The 2010 version introduced some new features which improved speed and functionality.
The basic visualization possibilities are roughly the same in the 2003, 2007 and 2010 versions of this program.

The first contact one has with a private or public organization can often be a bewildering and frustrating experience. This is not due to lack of information. It is the absence of an "information architecture" which makes life difficult for outsiders.

The illustration on the right is an example of building such a structure. The family tree makes it unnecessary to verbally explain the relationships between cousins and their respective grandfathers. During the renaissance these were often used by "good families".

One contemporary improvement is that one can press a few buttons on the telephone in order to be put through to the right person or department. Printed matter can to some extend guide you, but brochures have a habit of quickly going out of date. This is an area where the Internet has obvious functional advantages compared to other media.

One reason why organization charts do not tell you what you need to know is that they are made solely for internal purposes. Applicants to universities and larger organizations need to know where and to whom to send their application. Who answers what? What are the procedures? What are the "bureaucratic channels" one can use? This is more relevant that knowing who the chairman of a corporation is or having the names of the board of governors at a school.

Organization charts can be made in several office program packages. These are usually hierarchical and two-dimensional in structure. They start at the top and move down, sometimes ending with the assistant to the assistant manager. They are produced quickly and all one has to do is to type in names and titles. Here the advantages stop. The file formats do not usually comply with the requirements for printing and web communication. The effect of this is that they have to be redrawn (which does not save any time at all).

There are programs made specifically for "business graphics" that offer a fair amount of choices but, in many situations

Johannes Andrei: Affinity tree
Woodcut 1473

it is better to employ a graphic designer and have them done in accordance to the specific requirements.

Hierarchical, linear organizations do exist but more contemporary management philosophies advocate cell structures and groupings that are organized laterally. There is also a tendency to put together project groups for specific tasks. The participants are chosen according to their competence rather than the position they might have in the corporate structure. These groupings should then perform as autonomous units within the larger structure. This calls for another type of diagram than traditional organization charts. I shall ask the readers to return to pages 13 and 16. The combinations of shapes might give some ideas on how to organize visualizations that make sense in this area.

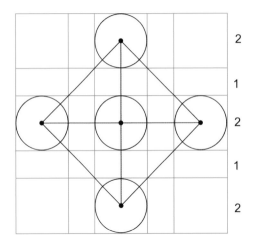

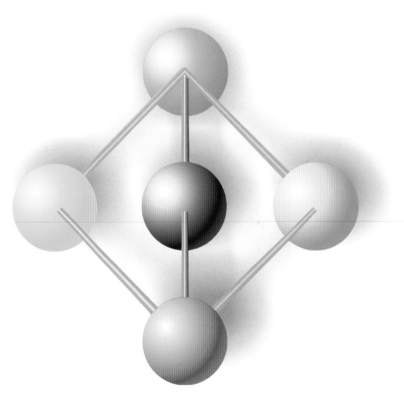

This is a model inspired by biology and physics. The connected elements are first organized in a flat grid and then presented with a 2-point perspective, giving the impression of being holistic. Colour coding and type can be added (not shown here).

This was done with the modelling options available in CorelDraw.

97

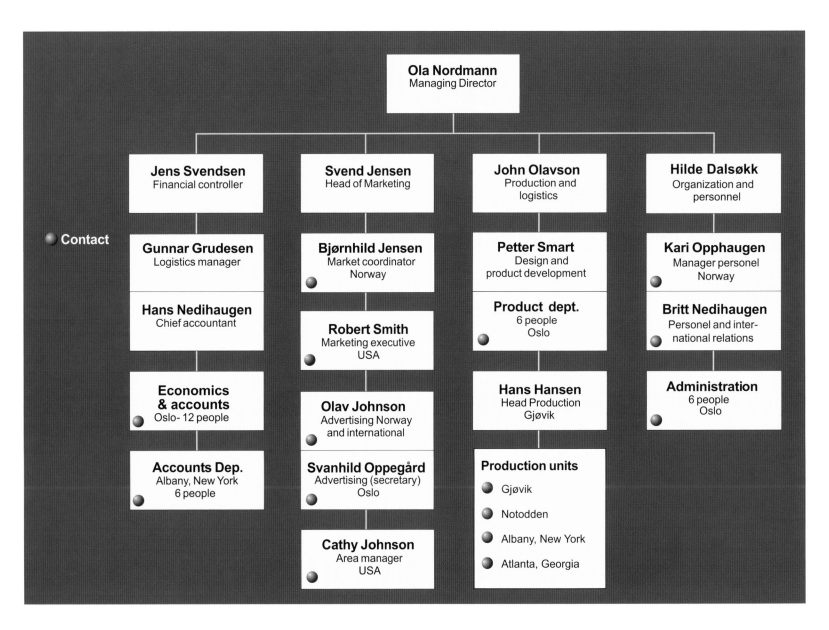

Web page designed by the author for a company that shall remain anonymous. The names employed are fictitious but their positions are real. It is a Norwegian company with considerable activity in USA.

This was made for external communication only. The real organization setup differs considerably from that shown on the website. The four columns are supposed to guide outsiders into those areas of the company's operations that are of specific interest to them. It took some persuasion to convince the client that this presentation was the right way to go.

The blue balls are links to e-mail addresses and phone numbers. It should also be clear that some members of the organization should not be disturbed by phone calls during office hours.

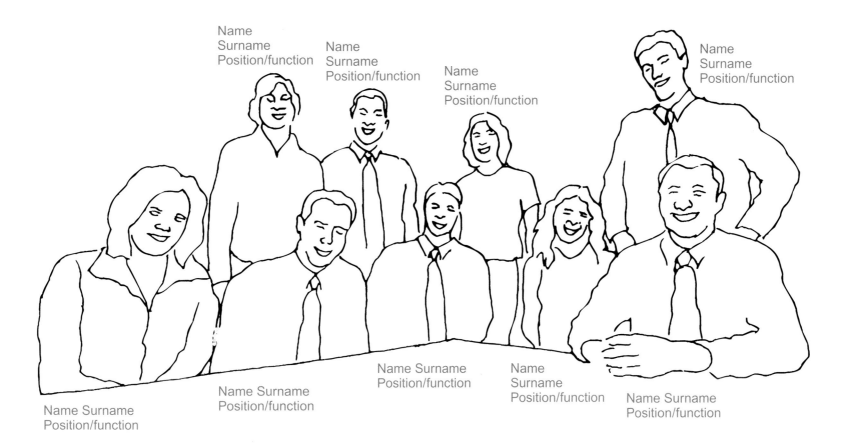

Name Surname
Position/function

Name Surname
Position/function

Name
Surname
Position/function

Name
Surname
Position/function

Name
Surname
Position/function

Name Surname
Position/function

Name Surname
Position/function

Name
Surname
Position/function

Name Surname
Position/function

Sketch for a webpage

Organizations are often "faceless". By connecting a face to a name, contacts can be more direct.

For a smaller, service-oriented group or firm, an investment in a page design like this could pay good dividends.

There are links connected to each person. (The blue type in the sketch).

The staging of a group photograph like this must be done with care. The lighting of the faces and the bodies require a studio setup and a photographer who knows what he is doing.

In this case, with a group of nine it is inevitable that the placement of people divides "leaders" from "supporters".

Still, with five people sitting and four standing one gets a good overall layout within the picture frame.

Very few companies can live off one national market alone. Not all people spend their entire life in the place where they were born. Keeping track of developments is a challenge for statisticians, social scientists and government officials. Needless to say, diagrams can help us to get a better understanding of movements and tendencies.

The choice of three Scandinavian countries is not dictated by the fact that the author lives in one of them (Norway). The following factors have determined the choice:
• They are geographically close
• They are (traditionally) Lutheran-Protestant societies
• The three languages are different but come from the same language tree (North Germanic)
• They are not too different in size
• As markets all three countries must be labelled "small".
• BNP per capita in the three countries do not show any dramatic differences.
• Statistics are reliable
(Any comparison between Switzerland and Russia will suffer from a serious lack of congruity)

Many foreign companies have failed in what they thought was one market. They have not taken into account the three countries' different histories, assets and prerequisites. Denmark has some rich and fertile farmland. Norway has little arable land and must be considered poor. Although both Danish and Norwegian manufacturers can boast some product successes, only Sweden has fostered manufacturing industries that operate on a large, international scale. Norway is a major supplier of oil, gas, aluminium and other commodities whilst export of manufactured, finished goods accounts for less than 12% of the total volume of exports.

Norway's largest export market is Great Britain. In Denmark Germany comes first. Sweden has USA, with Germany second. There is a fair amount of trade between the neighbouring countries. A remarkable development is that Denmark has a surplus compared to Sweden. Still, Sweden remains the "big brother" both in Scandinavia and internationally.

Statistically, movements between the three countries are only registered by citizensship. We do not have any reliable information about what people do. Still, one may assume that movements between countries are conditioned by job opportunities. Denmark is the oldest member of EU. As a consequence, Danish immigration to Norway (a non-EU country) has subsided. Over the last ten years, there has been a remarkable increase in Swedes living in Norway. That Sweden, with its nine million people and the largest industry in Scandinavia has more immigration than the other two, does not come as a surprise.

Immigration/emigration between two countries is a two-way flow. With three components we have a 3 x 2 situation. This cannot be explained by using any of the standard diagrams shown in the previous chapter. There are no "ready made" solutions. Shown here, are some attempts which (hopefully) will work.

Emigration and immigration

Three countries and six movements.
This was organized as a "motorway" in
accordance with the countries position
on the map. Norwegians travel south to
Denmark, go east to Sweden etc. The
hexagons are arranged allowing two
"roads" to travel out.

To attach scales (0-35.000) to this
graph is difficult. To compensate, the
exact figures appear at the end of each
road.

The flags are unconventional. Still,
the colours and shapes should secure
easy recognition, at least to a European audience.

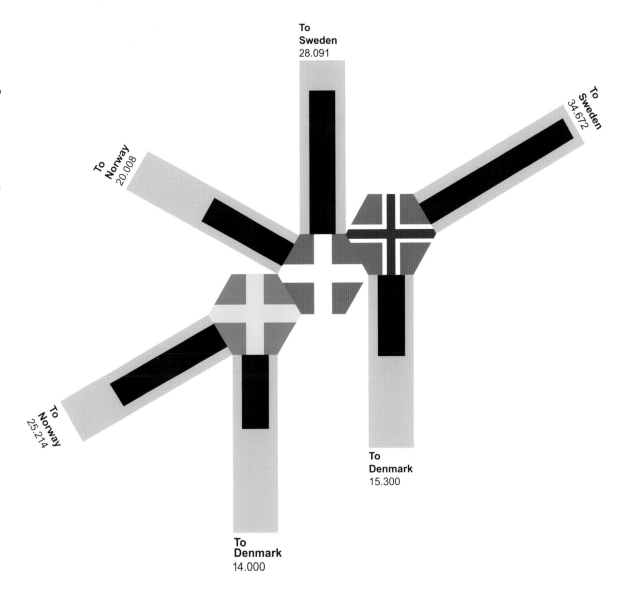

To
Sweden
28.091

To
Sweden
34.672

To
Norway
20.008

To
Norway
25.214

To
Denmark
15.300

To
Denmark
14.000

Emigration and immigration (2)

An isometric presentation has the advantage of showing three sides of a cube. See page 34 where axiometry is explained.

Accurate reading from the scale is somewhat impaired, but on the other hand we get a good overall picture of the flow to and from the three countries

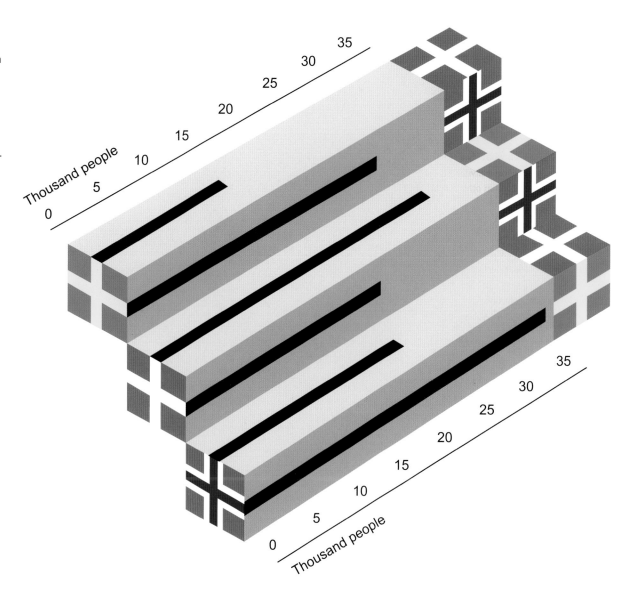

Scandinavian exports

When dealing with large quantities, isometric cubes are a natural choice. As the three countries do not have a common currency, the example shown is in Norwegian kroner (NOK). Each cube represents 10 million NOK (App. 1,25 billion Euros, 1.51 billion US $) The statistics are based on what crosses the national borders. The activities of Scandinavian companies in other parts of the world are not accounted for. The presentation shows that there is a fair amount of trade between the three. This trade is, however, small compared to what goes to USA and EU countries. The trade with Asia and East European countries is growing, but not yet substantial. The "Viking spirit" still prevails!

Both the demographic and trade figures are from 2003 (and made official in June 2004).
Many thanks to:
Statistiska Centralbyrån (Stockholm)
Danmarks Statistikk (Copenhagen)
Statistisk Sentralbyrå (Oslo)

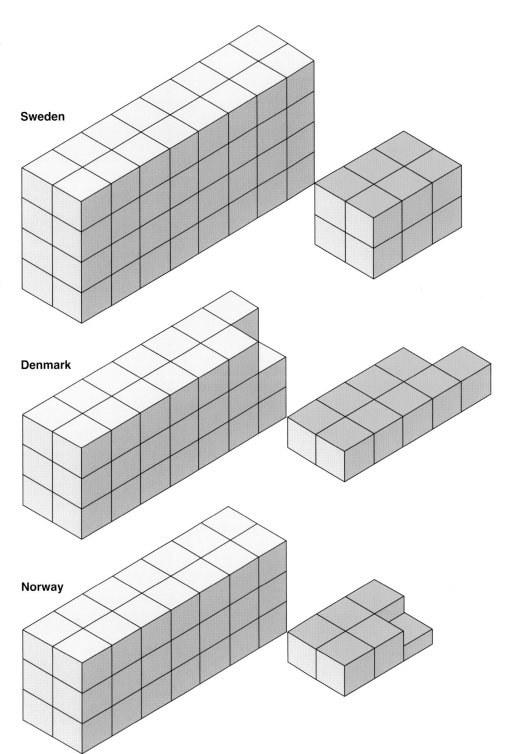

Sweden

Denmark

Norway

10
billion
NOK

Exports
outside
Scandinavia

Exports to
neighbouring
countries

Demography:
The changing face of society

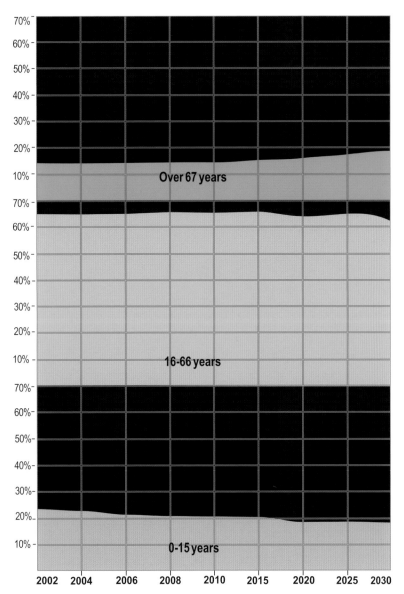

The illustration on the left shows the population of Norway divided in three age groups. It is a triple profile diagram with a common x-axis.

Statistics in this area are based on a combination of factual figures and predictions. These predictions come from macroeconomic models that are comprised of basis factors. Here are some:

• The fertility rate amongst women will remain at the present level (1.8 child per woman).

• People live longer
In 1950 only 8% of Norway's population was over 67 years of age.
One reckons that nearly half the population of Britain will be 50 plus after year 2020. Italy with its population of app. 58 millions will soon have to import qualified labour to keep the wheels turning. Too many companies are too eager to get rid of "oldies" too soon. This mentality will have to change.

• The workforce will be mobile.
The effects of an expanded EU are already showing.

• Immigration of non-Europeans to most West European countries appears to be growing.
The immigrants are usually in the age group 16-66. This will affect the ratio young/old in the countries they emigrate to.

• One assumes that there will be growth in both production and consumption in the years 2006-2030.

There are, of course, things that we today do not know enough about. These could be natural catastrophes, ethnic and political conflicts, financial crises and other occurrences which could affect the prediction models. What most

European countries have and will experience is a society which is different from what it was before 1970.

Norway is a country with a small population (4.8 mill.) spread out over an area which is long enough to cover the European continent. It is rich in resources, but the manufacturing industries have been dwindling. There has been a move towards "service" industries. No society can experience real economic growth when its members are too busy serving each other coffee or wine. This is a challenge that many European countries will have to face. It is more important to focus on growth in new industries than to worry about too many senior citizens collecting their pensions.

As for the makeup of the population, Norway experienced massive emigration to America in the years 1880-1925. In 1970 only 1.8% of the population was of foreign extraction. The diagrams on the right clearly show the changes.

The immigration from European countries has previously been topped by Danes and Brits. Since the early 1990s immigration from Britain has waned. The number of Swedes who seek job opportunities in Norway is remarkable. Like in most West European countries, the Norwegian building industry has benefited from a mobile and (mostly) competent Polish workforce.

Immigrants from Pakistan and Vietnam have been in Norway longer than any of the other non-European groups.

Note that statisticians have different definitions of "foreign". There are several categories. There is a growing group where only one of a person's parents is a first generation immigrant. For the sake of simplicity, the graphs are based on which passport the members hold.

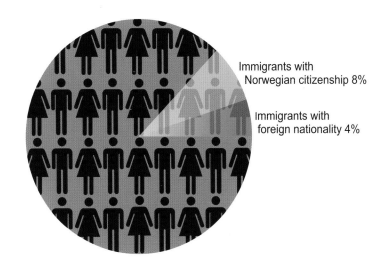

Immigrants with Norwegian citizenship 8%

Immigrants with foreign nationality 4%

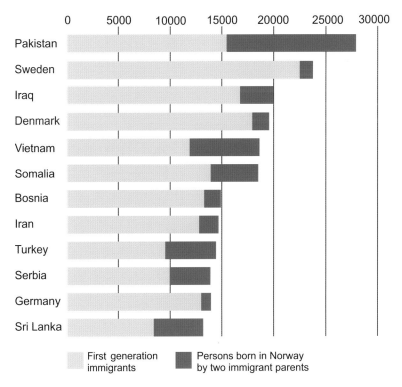

First generation immigrants

Persons born in Norway by two immigrant parents

The twelve larges groups of immigrants to Norway (2006)

Federal Bureau of Statistics (Oslo)

This is a (fictitious) Norwegian public company producing office furniture. Like all public companies they must produce audited accounts published in an annual report. The financial results speak for themselves, but there is also a need to get inside the more operational aspects of the company's activities.

Potential investors would often like to know more about which products and markets that show potential. Also where the expectations must be considered low. Annual reports sometimes give sparse information about this.

Unioffice is not one of the giants and has a small domestic market to operate in. Through active product development and careful analysis of the user's need their products have achieved a good position in a sophisticated and demanding market. It was never the ambition to compete on price. It is important for them to know when new office buildings and complexes come up. This calls for extensive market research and "presence" in the right spots.

Sales abroad are organized through subsidiary companies, part-owned operations, wholesalers, retailers and agents. This can, for outsiders, appear somewhat confusing.

There will always be considerations about what a company should publicise. There might be information of a more sensitive nature that should be kept inside the company's walls. Still, it is important that the people involved are properly informed at the appropriate times. This could be a cultural asset which should not be ignored.

unioffice

Market research

Advertising

Marketing Mix

Personal sales

Analysis of users' expectations

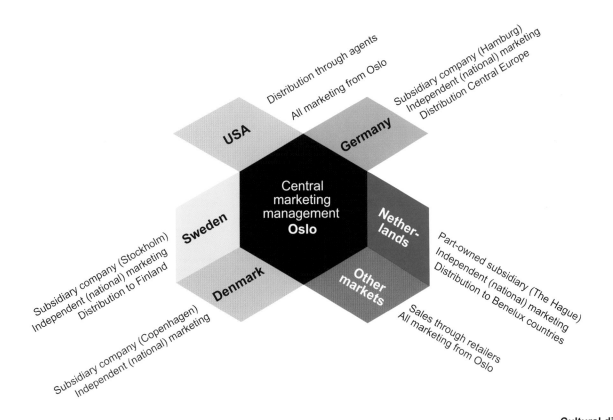

Distribution through agents
All marketing from Oslo

USA

Subsidiary company (Hamburg)
Independent (national) marketing
Distribution Central Europe

Germany

Central marketing management **Oslo**

Sweden

Nether-lands

Subsidiary company (Stockholm)
Independent (national) marketing
Distribution to Finland

Denmark

Other markets

Part-owned subsidiary (The Hague)
Independent (national) marketing
Distribution to Benelux countries

Subsidiary company (Copenhagen)
Independent (national) marketing

Sales through retailers
All marketing from Oslo

This is a difficult one. Explaining this verbally to an outsider would probably cause more confusion than understanding. The six non-Norwegian operations are organized differently and have different responsibilities. Their relationships to the central administration also differ.
The choice of a hexagon, and the use of 30° angles was a natural one. We are now approaching the borderland between "comprehension" and "information overload". Hopefully, we are on the right side of it.

Cultural distance

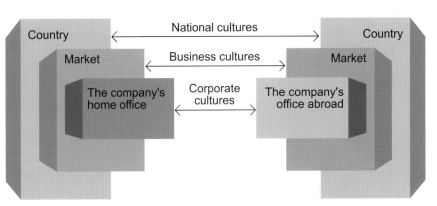

Country — National cultures — Country

Market — Business cultures — Market

The company's home office — Corporate cultures — The company's office abroad

This model could apply to many companies that have extensive operations abroad.

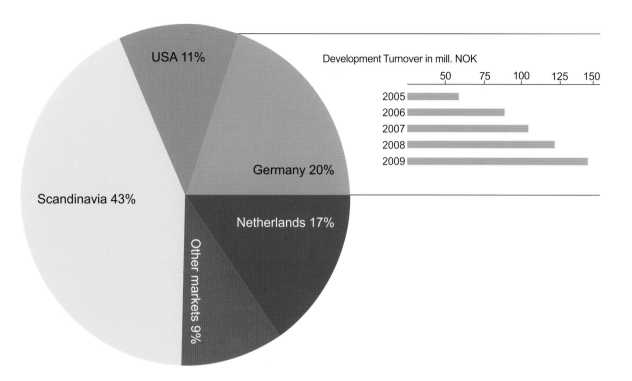

Development Turnover in mill. NOK

	50	75	100	125	150
2005					
2006					
2007					
2008					
2009					

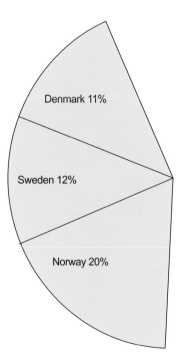

In this instance "Scandinavia" is treated as one market (although it is not). This in order to avoid too many segments in the total pie. Necessary details are shown separately.

The markets that have potential for growth are emphasized by using primary colours. An added bar chart shows developments in the German market.

By mixing a bar chart with a pie chart we can get both a comparison of volumes and a measure of acceptance of one of the company's products.

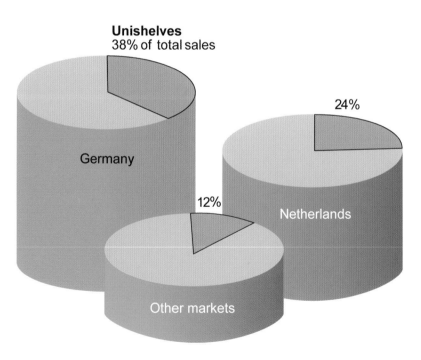

Unishelves
38% of total sales

CONCORDE office chairs, 5013 sold items

BOBBY polyester stackable chairs, 7120 sold items

COMFORTINUSE office chairs, 4220 sold items

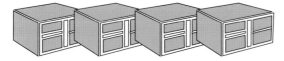

UNISHELVES cabinets, 4376 sold items

UNITABLE modular table system, 3040 sold items

This is a practical application of Neurath's isotypes presented on pages 63 and 64.
The drawings are simplified, but the shapes are recognizable and can take reduction in size well. Each figure represents app. 1000 sold items.

The colour coding links to those shown on the sector diagram.

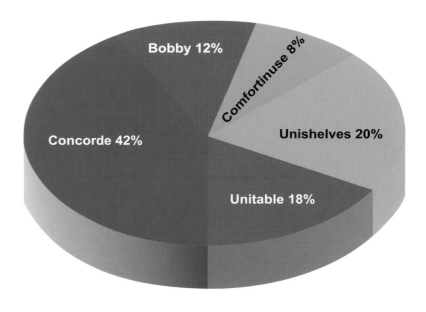

The company's total sales divided in product groups.

There are a multitude of stages one has to go through, in order to make a (saleable) product. In this chapter we shall deal with methods and procedures that are viable in the earlier stages of product development.

The flow chart as a tool has been dealt with in a previous chapter (see page 88).

Engineers, designers and inventors are often in possession of useful ideas, but too often these ideas are confined to the creator's heads: They are not communicated in a convincing and attractive manner. History has taught us that innovators are often met with little interest and lack of understanding; The story about the man who invented an electrostatic powder copying machine but could not find a manufacturer for it, is true. The company he founded is now known as The Xerox Corporation.

Needless to say, diagrams are one tool which might help to ease the understanding process. Radical ideas and "unconventional" procedures are sometimes easier to digest if they are seen in a context already familiar to the audience. In many instances, it might be wise to introduce the innovations gradually in comprehensible steps. "The shock of the new" would then be easier to cope with.

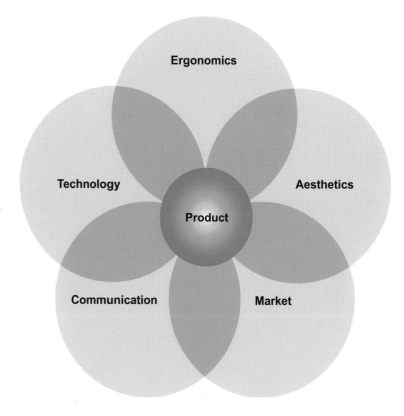

Factors that influence the design of a product
As for organising the parts of this design, there are several possibilities. In this instance a pentagon was used as basis.

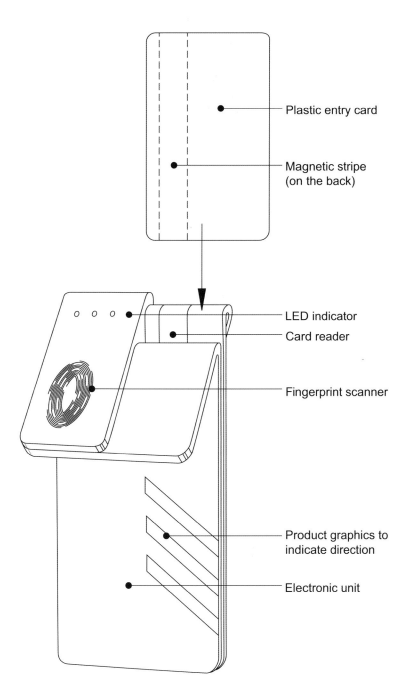

Plastic entry card

Magnetic stripe
(on the back)

LED indicator

Card reader

Fingerprint scanner

Product graphics to
indicate direction

Electronic unit

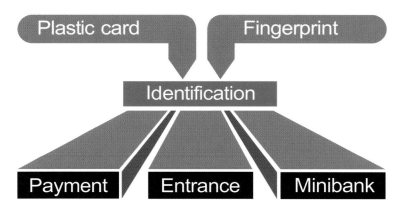

Plastic card

Fingerprint

Identification

Payment

Entrance

Minibank

Electronic unit for entrance control
The aim of the exercise is to focus
on a problem area and find possible
solutions. There is a growing demand
for identification of users: Illegal entries
to buildings, illegal immigration and
false credit cards are problems many
societies have to battle with.

The finger print is one of man's most
reliable identification marks.
In this design the user's fingerprint is
scanned by touching the apparatus.
In addition, the plastic card with
the magnetic stripe gives a further
(synchronized) control. This will
make code numbers superfluous and
the results of the actions will show on
a display.

Project: Conceptual Design
Development
Institute of Industrial Design, Oslo
3rd year of study
Student: Christian Rugaard
Tutor: Jan Gauguin

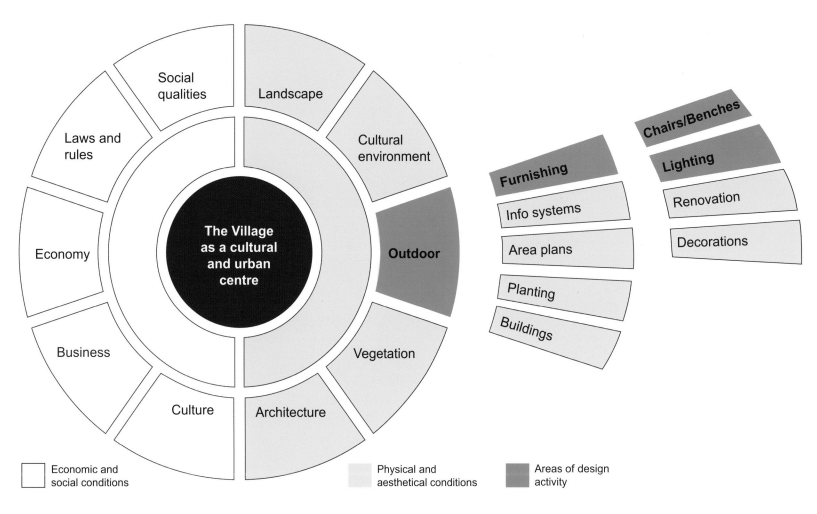

Economic and social conditions

Physical and aesthetical conditions

Areas of design activity

Social qualities · Landscape · Laws and rules · Cultural environment · Economy · Outdoor · Business · Vegetation · Culture · Architecture

The Village as a cultural and urban centre

Furnishing · Info systems · Area plans · Planting · Buildings

Chairs/Benches · Lighting · Renovation · Decorations

From the general to the specific

No architect, designer or town planner can "create" a village centre.

In a diagram like this it is important to point out areas where things can be done and sectors that have to be left untouched.

In this case the student has seen her project in a larger context and carefully studied some of the factors guiding her towards design activities and solutions. As her field of study is industrial design, she has naturally focused her interest on objects that can be improved.

The geometry should be easy to follow: All elements relate to the central (black) circle. We move gradually from left to right. (The direction in which we read).

The colour coding should (hopefully) distinguish the circles as well as the segments containing type.

When talking to an audience it would be natural to introduce parts of a design like this in sequence. This is can easily be done in PowerPoint, by showing objects separately on the screen as you go along.

Project: Conceptual Design Development
Student: Eva Widenoja
Tutor: Jan Gauguin
3rd year of study
Institute of Industrial Design (Oslo)

Diagrams don't simply happen. Neither are they contained in software packages. Solutions must derive from a careful analysis of the information at hand. We can break up the process into comprehensible stages:

The prerequisites

You must understand the material you are dealing with. If anything is not clear, seek help. You cannot expect statisticians, economists, pharmacists, engineers and corporate personnel to be trained communicators. On the other hand, you must assume that they know their own business. Don't be afraid of asking questions, even if they appear naïve.

You must understand the audience

Readers of business papers and management literature are trained to read and interpret diagrams. Engineers and technicians should have no trouble in dealing with a simple flow chart.
There are other audiences that are not so skilled, and not so easy to define: Pedagogical literature is one area where it would be wise to look into the school's curriculum and contact personnel before any direction is taken. There are different levels of "diagrammatic literacy".

You must know the possibilities and limitations of the medium to be used

Designing for a newspaper column is different from making a PowerPoint presentation. Animations done in Flash require a different approach to material for publications. The graphic devices you employ must suit the situation.

Stage 1: Analysing the contents

The material submitted to you usually contains articles, documents, tables and printout from spreadsheets. In some cases also diagrams (e.g. last year's annual report).
Once the material is gathered and analysed it should reveal any apparent possibilities.
Beware that diagrams are not always the solution. In some instances words, captions, figures, tabular matter and pictorial presentations do the job better. Not all statistics lend themselves to diagrams. The messages are simply too trivial to be worth any special graphic presentation. One should concentrate on what could function as "eye-openers" to the audience.
One must not be afraid of dramatizing "negative" trends: They can trigger appropriate actions necessary in rectifying a situation.
From a designer's point of view this stage in the process is the most challenging, but also the one that can lead to interesting solutions later on.

Stage 2: Finding means of communication

What are the information needs? It is not always apparent which type of diagram one should use. Trying out possibilities in a series of sketches might be a worthwhile exercise. (The examples shown on pages 68-88 in this book can serve as a "catalogue" to begin with).
Then, there are the components like line, areas, volumes, colour and typography to consider before things find their form. The work of the *Gestalt* psychologist in the 1920s still appears to be valid: (Figure/Ground Relationships, prägnanz, uniform connectedness, continuation, closure and similarity).

There are three characteristics of diagram perception one should pay specific attention to:
proximity, elements close to each other belong together;
similarity, elements that resemble each other belong together;
good continuation, lines that can be seen as continuous will be perceived as such.

Once the sizes and the directions have been found, a skeleton line drawing can be made on the computer. In a drawing program copies of these basic (skeleton) elements can be produced quickly and alternatives tried out. Speed of execution does not in itself automatically produce good results. Speed helps with trying out feasible solutions and weeding out those that are useless without wasting too much time. It is important not to "lock" things too early in the process.

One must always have the viewer's need for information in mind and find means to cover this adequately.

Stage 3: Evaluating the designs

Even on tight budgets and with severe time limits, it is mandatory to have the effectiveness of solutions tested. The client/editor you are working with will (in most cases) be the first to see the results. Your colleagues should in many instances provide useful comments. By converting the files to the PDF format they can easily be viewed on screen by a number of test persons.

Not all diagrams reach their audiences successfully. If interpretations are vague, faulty or do not create the necessary understanding, there are obvious reasons for trying something else. By determining what does not work as well as what might potentially work, you are in a better position to arrive at the right track. Negative feedback from an experimental piece of work when tested can be a positive exercise, if the gathered information helps to get the project in focus.

If you get the "aha" response from several people you have an indication that you have hit the target. Then, again, audiences differ.

Stage 4: Making diagrams work in print and on screen

We assume that you have finished most of the work mentioned in stage 2 and that it is time for a printout or a screen test. This is the phase where technical weaknesses are weeded out and reproduction problems are solved. Here are a few "don'ts":
• Hairlines should be avoided. They can cause problems in printing. Even 0,5 pt lines can show up too thin on a 72 dpi screen.
• Illustrations done in Microsoft programs usually won't print well. You can convert them to PDFs but in many cases you will have to redraw them in a program that works in "real" postscript. Microsoft use "True Image".
• Do not send drawings to a printer unless you are sure they have a program similar to what you are using.
Illustrator is widely used, but programs like CorelDraw or Freehand are not so common. Covert such files to EPS.
• You can use condensed bitmaps for presentations and on the web, but printers want them in TIFF with high resolution file size settings.
• Type can easily appear distorted or too small in screen view. Tight tracking can work well in print but can produce undesired results in web communication.
• Colour adjustments must comply with printing and web standards. Make sure that the bitmap files you are using for printing are in the CMYK mode. Do not be afraid of asking your supplier about how they would like to have the files sent to them. More about this in the chapter "About colour" on pages 26-31.

How to cope with PowerPoint presentations is explained fully on page 125. And, most important, your diagrams must work well within a total editorial and graphic framework. They must not be allowed to appear "alien" in conjunction with other elements in the layout. Too many similar looking diagrams in one and the same job can generate audience fatigue.
With a bit of patience and a sharp eye, you should get through this stage successfully too. See **Campbell/Dabbs** and **Johansson/Lundberg/Ryberg** on page 196.

Using GIS, GPS and PowerPoint

GIS has been used by by geographers for app. 40 years. It has been used primarily for making maps. Today, Geographic Information Systems (GIS) means the merging of cartography and database technology. Since the introduction of "desktop mapping", GIS can do a lot more:

• create information that was unavailable before;
• attach demographic data to defined areas;
• visualize changes over time;
• show cause-and-effect in a convincing manner;
• help decision makers in the planning of a new shopping centre.

The location of the shops will be determined after having analyzed and visualized the potential clientele in an area.

The starting point is usually a set of tables where all relevant data are stored. These tables are often plentiful, but do not give the viewer any "picture" of what they contain. When placed on a digital map the data can be visualized, compared, measured and analyzed.

In a "desktop mapping process" the basic layer contains the necessary geographic information covering a given area. The next layers can contain information about roads, forest, rivers, buildings etc. This layer-on-top-of-layer method has almost infinite possibilities of combinations. The layers can easily be manipulated and updated and information extracted in accordance with the communication needs and the strategy at hand.

Schools of architecture and urban planning, government planning units and sectors of industry have found these tools indispensable and use them to good advantage. Many are probably familiar with Al Gore and his worldwide campaign for drawing attention to environmental issues. Gore uses GIS and sophisticated software techniques extensively in his presentations.

There is a lot of software to choose from (see page 197). Prices and performance vary. Some programs have drawing tools in them that compare well with what you find in 2D programs like Illustrator or CorelDraw. Measured in bytes, many GIS renderings tend to be a bit on the heavy side. By converting them to PDF or PNG almost anyone can view them on their screens. For printing, however, high resolution TIFFs are recommended.

The general public is being acquanted with Google's use of GIS both on the web and on mobile devices.

So far, graphic designers and their clients/publishers have not paid too much attention to GIS. Guides and travel books are one sector where this technology could be used to an advantage. The reasons for this lack of interest might be a fear of dealing with calculations and not having the relevant software experience. Then, designers should possess "visual communication skills" that other professional groups do not have. It is about time that GIS is added to our repertoire.

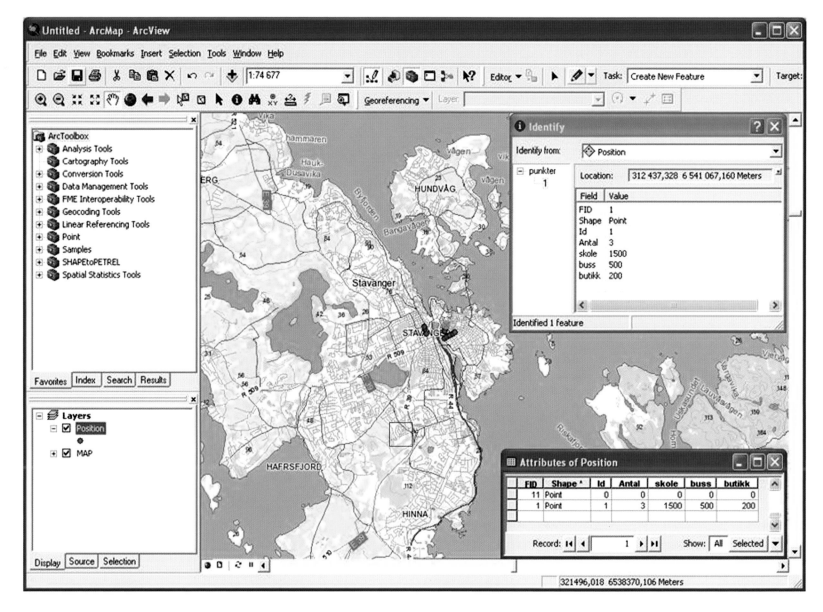

This screenshot shows the city of Stavanger, Norway with buildings, roads etc. On the right hand corner of the map there is an "identify box" giving info about distances to schools, buss stations and shops.

Based on this information it is possible to analyze and make decisions about where schools should be placed in relation to the population density and accessibility in a given area. Also the planning of bus routes and road structures are decided based on this information.

(Printed with the kind permission of GIS partner AS, Stavanger, Norway)

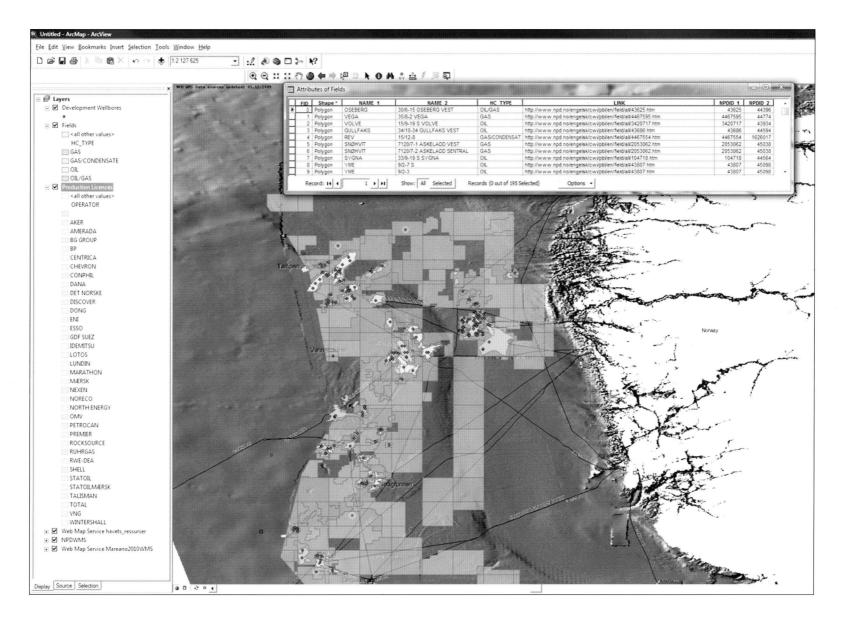

This illustration visualizes different activities in the vicinity of the Norwegian west coast.

It deals with a diverse amount of data:
Development Wellbores
Fields and Production Licenses
(The colour codes signify oil, gas and companies).

The license data gives names of the oil companies operating in the area.

In addition there are three WMS services (WMS is short for Web Map Service). These can give data about the spawning grounds for fish, the ocean floor and subsurface installations.

Other types of specialized information can be added (but not shown on the screen shot here).

Important in this context, is that one can predict possible conflicts between oil exploitation activities and maritime interests. When planning subsea installations, the topology of the ocean floor must be surveyed in detail.

The software used to produce the map above and the preceding illustration was ArcView from Esri Corp.
More about WMS and other services available at
http://en.wikipedia.org/wiki/Web_Map_Service
http://en.wikipedia.org/wiki/MapServer

(Printed with the kind permission of GIS partner AS, Stavanger, Norway)

Shown here are some of the graphic presentation methods one can employ in GIS communication.
Dot maps - Pie Charts - Fields - Circular quantities - 3D Mountain views.

Excellent and instructional videos can be viewed on www.esri.com.

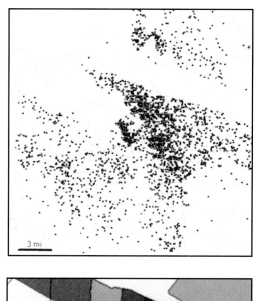

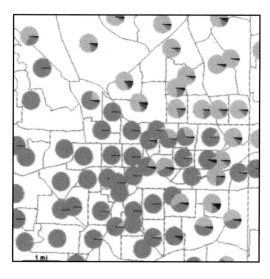

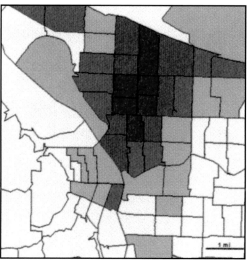

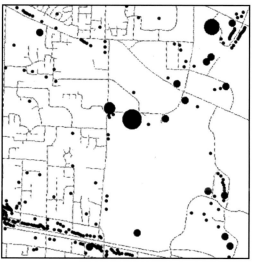

What is GPS (Global Positioning System) and what can it do?

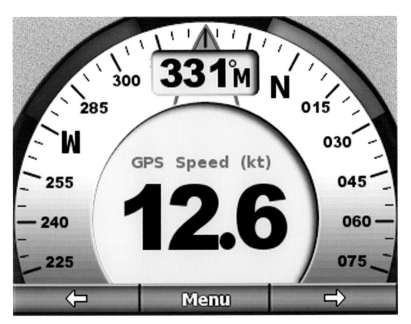

Display for marine autopilot   Day modus (top) and night modus

It is positioned in orbit and attached to the American satellite navigation system Navstar GPS. The administration is located in Colorado Springs, USA. It was first used by the USA defence in 1995 and soon thereafter became available to the general public.

It operates from a height of app. 20 000 km and consists of somewhere between 24 and 32 satellites distributed on six circular "roads". These satellites move around the globe twice per day and send signalled information to the earth. For the best results you must have contact with several of these satellites at the same time.

The GPS receiver receives this information and employs a three-point cross check in order to calculate the user's exact position.

GPS works under all weather conditions anywhere in the world. It is operational 24 hours a day provided the user has a (relatively) free view of the sky.

The GPS technology has proved to be effective in such areas as: maritime navigation, in combination with electronic maps; the administration of trailer transport in combination with telecommunication and the monitoring and control of public transport and taxis in large cities. It has also proven to be indispensable in the running of today's airports.

There is an equivalent European system (named Galileo) which is due to be launched in 2014. It promises to be more accurate (for civilian use) than the American system. It wil give you directions inside a building and be accurate to within three feet. Time will show.

Using maps, diagrams and "street pilots" to show you the way

Some car models come with navigation equipment attached to the cars and installed by the manufacturer. One usually has to pay extra for this added benefit. The current trend is to buy them separately and mount them on the dashboard. A GPS monitor does not weigh much and can easily be moved from one car to another. When you are not driving you can detach some of these devices from the car and walk around with it in your pocket.

Some manufacturers of mobile phones now offer GPS facilities attached to them. The GPS not only shows you where you are, but tells you where and when you should drive off from a main road plus gives data about distance, average speed and time used on a given distance. It often has touch-screen display and can adjust the light on the display when lighting conditions are not favourable.

If you have sun filters on your windows, this can hinder signals from the satellite in getting through. There is not always an automatic update or change when you cross a country border. If you move into foreign territory you should also bring with you a paper map. On lengthy drives one should make sure that there is enough electricity in the equipment. Most equipment has a capacity of roughly 15 hours in a stand by position. In use, one loses power quickly. Maps must be constantly updated in order to achieve maximum performance. When driving in a city with many tall buildings, there is the risk of impaired performance and inaccurate readings.

Be aware that this is a field where yesteryear's products quickly become obsolete. Recent models now have PND (Personal Navigation Device). This can include information about places of interest, where the nearest petrol station is located and your position of height above sea level. A good GPS measurement of your current speed of travel is usually more accurate than that shown on the speedometer in your car. The list of PND advantages is likely to grow in the near future.

In spite of the limitations and shortcomings mentioned above, sales of GPS equipment now show staggering figures. Many drivers call them their best "friend". People who are fond of sailing and boating feel much safer when they are navigating in the dark or cannot see land.

Divided screen with chart and radar information

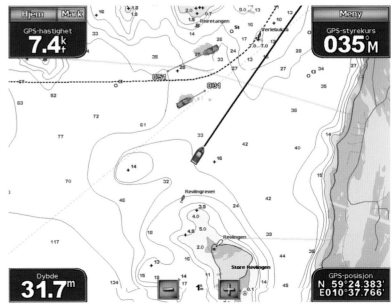

Chart with radar overlay

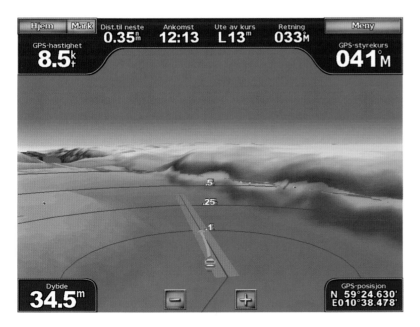

Auto guidance in 3D perspective

Three screen displays from a nautical guidance system.

This is a touchscreen device made to make your outdoor trips both exciting and educational.

It is tough and waterproof, and by pressing the buttons on the menu gives you (most of) the information you need.

Press, point, and then start walking.

Data projectors with improved resolution capable of projecting images on the screen with satisfactory sharpness and saturation are becoming standard features in many conference rooms and auditoriums. This equipment has come down in weight and price, too. By attaching a tablet PC to a laptop it is possible to do "on the spot" writing and drawings on a screen. Such a "digital blackboard" can work effectively in a classroom or in a discussion group.

However, it is not widely understood that a PowerPoint presentation is a medium that is *different* from the web and the printed page. Too many presentations fail to reach their audiences successfully. Therefore, a few guidelines seem necessary:

The files

MS PowerPoint has import filters for only a few file formats. These are TIFF, JPEG, EPS, PNG and Paitbrush Picture. Both bitmap and vector illustrations done in other file formats must be converted to any of these before they can be imported effectively from the Insert-Picture command. Bitmap images must always be in the RGB mode. The disadvantages with files in the TIFF format are that they have a tendency to be on the heavy side. A presentation containing many of these might make the total so heavy that you will have problems running your show from a laptop. In Photoshop you can save them as "Save for Web" and convert them to PNG-24 in ImageReady. These files will be compressed without too much loss of colour and definition. PNG (Portable Network Graphics) works well in electronic communication but should not be used for printing. They are lighter than native Photoshop files and should be imported in a size as close to the actual presentation size as possible.

JPEGs are also importable but this is a bitmap file format suited to the Internet. They can often come out a bit thin when enlarged on a big screen.

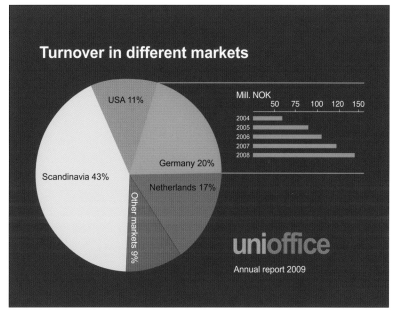

Dark background?

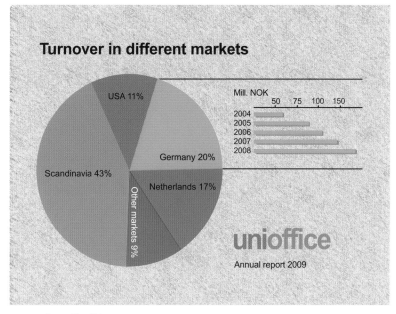

....or perhaps like this

The type

Some typefaces do not fare well in this medium. Under any circumstance, you must remember that in this medium type comes to the audience as reflected light (not as print on paper as one is often used to). Delicate serif faces like Times, Bodoni and Caslon are made for high-resolution offset printing on coated paper but get a rough treatment when shown on a screen in a room with dim lighting. "Robust" faces like Century Schoolbook and Georgia stand a better chance of survival.

Most sans serifs and Egyptians are generally suited because they do not have thin hairlines and thick/thin contrasts. One should avoid ultra thin, ultra thick and condensed faces as these have reduced legibility when viewed at an angle or from a far distance to the screen.

Sizes that are smaller than 20 pt. are usually unsuited for this medium. (The people who sit in the back of the auditorium will not be able to read titles or body copy that is too small).

PowerPoint has commandos for tracking and kerning. It is recommended to condense large titles a bit. How much depends on the typeface and the size you are using. This can be done by right-clicking on the type in the Slide Master and go to "Font" and then into the "Character Spacing" department.

The colours

Accurate colour management with percentage values is non-existent in this program. (They are usually to be found in more expensive programs). There are colour palettes that work on a hit-or-miss basis. One has to try them out on the projector to be used. After screen viewing, one might have to do the necessary adjustments in the file.

White is not a colour in RGB and is unsuited as a background. The "white" comes to the viewer as (unpleasant and harsh) reflected light from the screen. If you want a light background even the faintest grey or yellow is a better choice. In the "Background Styles" palette you can probably find a texture that is suitable and adjust the lightness using the transparency slider.

You might like to show everything on a dark background but this means working "up against the light". Photographs and other illustrations might need considerable adjustments. Still, things shown against a dark background can work well on a screen, but do not underestimate the amount of work this sometimes involves. (Read more about colour on page 26) Having manoeuvred around the pitfalls, we can concentrate on the structure and contents of our presentation.

An audiovisual presentation is primarily a presentation of you and what you have to say. The visual aids you employ can turn out to be smarter than you are. You must not allow this to happen. Be sure you have the technicalities under control and rehearse the show before you perform it. (If you do not have access to an auditorium, the "Slide Show" mode in the program gives a fair preview)

Phase 1: Establish the constants

Go to VIEW – Slide Master and create a template for all the slides in your presentation.The constants in the template are:

Margins (in SLIDE MASTER - Page Setup)

Hang lines

Go to VIEW and click on the "Fit to window" tab. In FORMAT find a (straight) line which you can draw on the Slide Master to indicate the top of the graphics you will later import. By using a hang line you avoid having your illustrations "jump" when shown in sequence.
(Don't forget to erase the hang line when the presentation is finished)

Typeface and sizes

A new document has a ready-made setup for this. This you can change at will. As mentioned earlier: Type sizes under 20 points you can easily dispose of.

Background and colour(s)

The program comes with a number of ready-made templates. Most of these are so busy and over-decorated that they will interfere with what you want to show. They can be modified and be made useful, but in most cases you will find that they do not comply with your specific needs.

As designers, we should be capable of creating backgrounds that suit the themes and the "mood" of our presentations. These can be created in both bitmap and vector programs and then be put in or imported into the Slide Master. These designs should be made to scale and cover the entire slide area. You have now solved the background/colour bit.

If you, somewhere in the presentation, want a single slide without this background, right-click on the edge of the slide and order "Format Background" in the menu. Go to "Fill" and order "Solid Fill" and order white in the colour menu. (Do not click the "Apply to all" button, just "Close".)

The footer

Go to VIEW – Presentation views – Slide Master. In the place-holders you type in necessary information about themes, authors and the date of gestation. It is always handy to have the slides automatically numbered (even if you want to swap them around later in the Slide Sorter menu).
A 12 pt. type size should be large enough for footers.

Your signature

Perhaps you would like to have your name, the theme of your lecture, or your company's logo on the Master Slide. Be aware that this can look tedious and pretentious when repeated on twenty slides or more. If you want to include any such elements, give them a discreet showing.

A presentation layout has constants and variables. To keep a good balance requires skills, imagination and taste. In any situation, the labour you invest in establishing the constants should earn good dividends.

Phase 2: Putting the presentation together

There are no two presentations that are similar enough to justify a step-by-step description of how this is done.

Should you get stuck, you can usually get good advice from the manual and the Help-menu. As for preparing the elements that go into the presentation, there are some valid working principles: The illustrations and photos you would like to use might come from very different source material. They could be large or small slides, illustration from books, drawings, excerpts from newspapers as well as digitally stored material. The pictorial material should be scanned and prepared to sizes you have established in the Master Slide. This will save time-consuming up-and-down scaling in PowerPoint. Portraits of people usually need cropping. In many cases you can confine the image to brows, eyes, nose, lips and chins.

Diagrams done in Excel can easily be imported by using copy/paste. There is a diagram module attached to PowerPoint but this author has never found out how it works. In any case, formatting possibilities are more developed and flexible in Excel.

Diagrams created in drawing programs (like Illustrator or CorelDraw) usually need "upscaling". Type must not appear too small on the screen. Backgrounds must be made transparent if imported into a slide that has a coloured or patterned background.

Photographs and drawings that are borrowed from published material should have an ownership tag attached to them. These you can place upside-down on the right side of the picture. This legal detail is often ignored or forgotten but it is necessary to pay attention to this if your presentation is for public viewing or put on the Internet.

A "wordy" presentation is a surefire formula for failure. Large amounts of copy must be pruned down to the absolute essential. A rule of thumb is that a single slide should contain no more than six lines. Each line should contain a maximum of eight words.

You can introduce titles and lines of type gradually as you speak. Go to Slide Sorter View and type Ctrl+A. This will activate all the slides. You can employ all the possibilities available in the ANIMATION menu: Fly in, fade in/out, wipe and adjust timing between slow, medium and fast.

Phase 3: The performance

When speaking to an audience, it is important that the audience focuses on you. Talk to the audience, not to the screen.

Never start the show with the lights dimmed. If you have something to say prior to the slide show, keep the lights on and the projector OFF. Once the projector starts working do not let the slides stay on the screen too long. Try to keep an even pace, with talk and slides complementing each other. There are no limits to how many slides you can show, but you must keep in mind that there is a limit to what an audience can absorb in one lump.

You might like to show captions and images only and not talk at all. In such an instance you should use the animation/automation possibilities in the Slide Sorter menu to programme speed and flow.

If you want to answer questions from the audience, or for some other reason interrupt the show, it is better not to show anything on the screen. If you are in the Slide Show mode, press the key "B" for black and the spacebar to start up again.

Once the show is over, turn the lights on and thank the participants for their attention. (Again, do not forget to turn the projector off. Press the key "B" if the projector is outside your reach.)

There are many aspects and usages of PowerPoint that have not been mentioned here. In some instances, a presentation can be enhanced by adding a Flash sequence to it. This needs an ActiveX extension. (Press F1 to read about how this is done). You can also add sounds, speech and music to your performance.

Do not forget to save a few slides of your presentation in the PowerPoint template format. (Saves time and work next time a job comes up.)

Both the menus and the interface have changed compared to earlier versions of this program. Most of these changes have been improvements. If you have a presentation which was originally done in an earlier version you can save it under a new name, open it in the latest Office version and see how it comes out. Adjustments might have to be done, but the "old" presentation is by no means lost. You can also open the old version in "Word outline" give it a new name in the new version and apply the necessary formatting that are available in the new version. Microsoft's Help-menus are comprehensive and there are instructive demos to be viewed on their website. You might also like to subscribe to many of the excellent instructional videos provided by www.lynda.com.

Other presentation tools
Layout programs can also be used for presentations if the pages are converted to PDF. The advantage of having them done this way is that they can be shown "everywhere". The recipients only need to have Acrobat Reader installed on their PCs or MACs.

Layout programs (like the ubiquitous Adobe InDesign) do not have all the facilities found in PowerPoint, but if you are only going to talk and add some illustrations to your speech you can easily turn pages meant for print processing to a presentation device. These must, of course, be in the "landscape" format.

If you are going to show photographs only, you could consider doing your entire presentation in Photoshop PDF. (Go to FILE – Automation – PDF presentation). You can then convert everything to PDF and show your pictures in full screen with Acrobat Reader. The program menu has timing, sequence and editing possibilities similar to those found in PowerPoint. This could save you a lot of work provided you have your pictures stacked up in an orderly manner in an Adobe Bridge collection.

Considerations not to be overlooked
Is the presentation going to be shown once only to a limited audience? If it is going to be distributed to a wider audience in different locations it is possible to format it for the web and send it over the Internet. Most web browsers can handle this and the recipients need not have the Microsoft Office suite installed on their machines.

Will you be using a MAC or a PC? The technology gap between the two platforms could cause problems.

Should I ask someone to have a look at it? In many instances it would be wise to have comments from your client or colleagues before showing the presentation to an audience. This can easily be done by sending them a PDF and ask them to attach comments/corrections using the "Commenting Tools" found in Acrobat Reader.

If you are not fully satisfied with how your photographic images appear on the screen, there are adjustment possibilities in the menu for "Picture Tools".

The abuse of PowerPoint

In certain academic and scientific areas there has been some resistance against presenting pictures and graphs as scientific evidence. Many felt that explanatory graphics were unnecessary crutches, not suited for those versed in analysis. Today's presentations are a radical departure from previous practices.

However, Edward Tufte (see page 55) attracted considerable international attention with his 32 page pamphlet "The Cognitive Style of PowerPoint" first published in 2003.

He raises a number of uncomfortable issues and takes a critical view of the widespread use of the medium in business, government and education. Rounding it all off with this crashing statement: "Power corrupts — PowerPoint corrupts absolutely".

It is true that "shorthand" verbal statements accompanied by coloured bullets have limited cognitive value. That this device automatically turns audiences into morons, is an exaggeration.

The word "PowerPoint" is often used as a generic term for all kinds of presentation software. Apple, Lotus, OpenOffice and Harvard Graphics also produce programs in this area. Presentation possibilities are also to be found in Adobe's multipurpose Acrobat Premium package. Adobe's Presenter can be shown on any Flash player. Newcomers like Sliderocket and 280 slides might attract Internet users. Critics of Microsoft now have yet another argument in their repertoire.

So far, very little empirical research has been carried out and commentators have taken divergent position related to the effectiveness of this medium.

All media can be abused: Internet is a marvellous invention and has made the old IBM slogan "Information at your fingertips" a reality. The Internet can also be used for racist propaganda, child pornography and fraudulent economic transactions.

It is the presenter that is in charge of the medium, the medium never was the message. Does Mr. Tufte believe that presentations were better in the "old" days when overheads and 35 mm slides were the tools in use?
(See page 196 **Farkas** and page 197 **Tufte**)

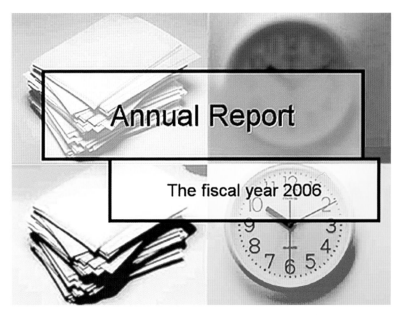

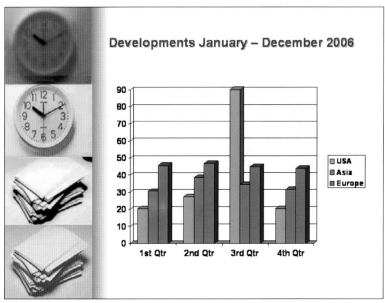

These are two slides from a "ready-made" template provided by the software manufacturer. The accounts department provides the figures and the secretary types them in. You have a presentation done in double-quick time — and the graphic designer can take the day off (if the company ever employed one).

Designer's Gallery

Diagrams as part of a total information system
The thirteen computerized kiosks are connected by fibre optic cables to a central server room and guide visitors (interactively) through the Campus. An LCD touch screen is the heart of the system. Each kiosk tells users:
• where they are
• how to get to any building
• where to park
• directory information
• event information
• specifics on accessibility

There are three ways to activate the kiosk:
• touch the anodized aluminium map
• touch the LCD screen itself
• push one of the buttons

While the aluminium map works like a conventional, static map, it is also interactive. A grid of infrared beams floats above the map; when the grid is broken by a pointed finger, the LCD screen is activated and gives information on the item to which the finger points.
The LCD screen is menu-driven and offers wayfinding information, an events calendar and much more. To secure optimal reading of maps and diagrams, a psychologist was added to the design team.
For the technophobic, a "help desk" button activates a handfree telephone that connects to a live person. Further technical details are available at www.cloudgehshan.com

Client:
"i-site" information kiosk for the John Hopkins University Campus, Baltimore, Maryland, USA

Designers:
Cloud Gehshan Associates, Philadelphia

132

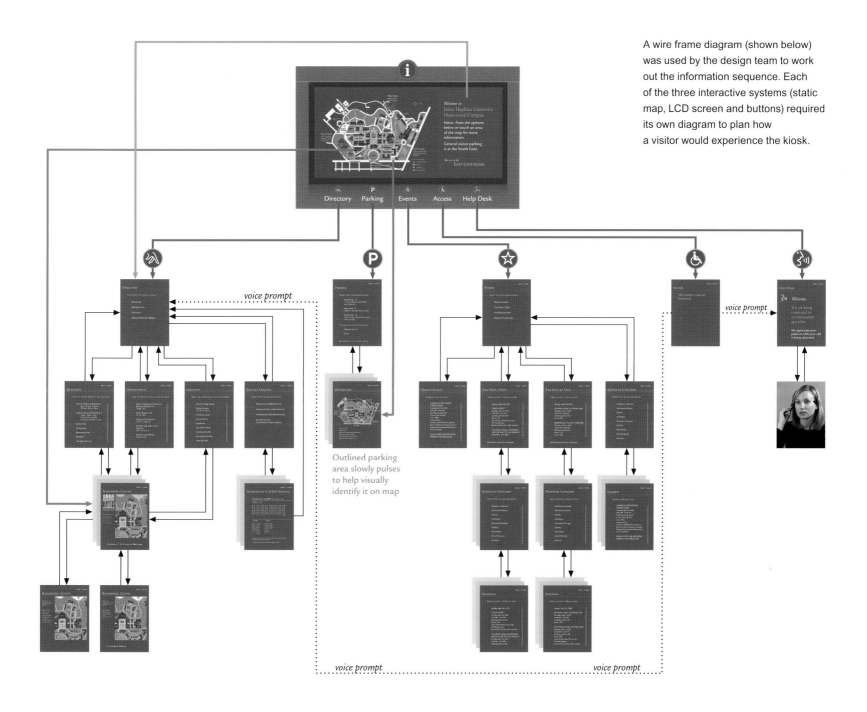

A wire frame diagram (shown below) was used by the design team to work out the information sequence. Each of the three interactive systems (static map, LCD screen and buttons) required its own diagram to plan how a visitor would experience the kiosk.

voice prompt

Outlined parking area slowly pulses to help visually identify it on map

voice prompt

voice prompt

voice prompt

The anodized aluminium map shows all buildings, visitor parking and kiosk locations.

The map always faces the same direction of the viewer (2 different orientations were drawn: north up and south up.)

Buildings are flat shapes, except for one "landmark" building at the top of the main quadrangle.

Static Map **Buttons** **LCD Screen**

Each kiosk offers directions to each building on campus. Diagrama show the best pedestrian route without any stairs; this route is not necessarily the shortest route, and each one was "walked" to check for potential obstacles.

The Dutch Cultural Council

advises the government how to spend money on culture in The Netherlands. In their annual report they give an insight in what they have investigated and put forward as advise to the government.

Each year they ask interesting designers or design groups to design the report.

They ask the designers to come up with their "own story", not necessarily graphs and tables. Because this was the first annual report we ever did, that was exactly what we wanted to do — make graphs and tables. Our "own story" became a set of 40 graphs about the state of culture in The Netherlands.

This graph shows the number of book titles published per million citizens in 12 European countries in the year 1992. Each country is given a colour code.

Client:
Raad voor Cultuur / Cultural Council
Den Haag / The Hague
The Netherlands

Designers:
De Designpolitie
Amsterdam, The Netherlands

16 > AANTAL GEPUBLICEERDE BOEKTITELS PER MILJOEN INWONERS > 1992

Space Syntax

is a multidisciplinary, highly skilled group of companies with offices in London, Sydney, Brussels, Tokyo, Stockholm, Durban, Boston and most recently Bucharest. Senior members of staff are qualified, practicing architects, planners, urban designers, transport specialists and software developers with many years of professional experience. Other members of the consulting staff are qualified and experienced in subjects including architecture, town planning, transportation, planning, urban design, work place design, knowledge management and software development. Space Syntax provides a unique, evidence based approach to the planning and design of buildings and cities. They focus on the creation of environments which are socially and economically successful. They work closely with local and national government departments, property developers, investors, architects, engineers and planners.

They use world-leading technologies to generate knowledge and make proposals. Their analyses and ideas empower people and help them make key decisions about the world around them.

Through groundbreaking research and international practice, Space Syntax have pioneered the use of new computer modelling technologies that forecast the essential characteristics of urban and building sustainability. These include movement patterns (pedestrians, vehicles and cycles), natural surveillance and land use viability. Their analysis has been accepted as objective evidence in planning inquiries and their evidence-seeking ethos has influenced design thinking and policy drafting throughout the world. The extensive use of diagrams has proved to be an indispensable tool in this process.
(More on www.spacesyntax.com)

This axial map of London shows the Space Syntax model of the city and represents the levels of global spatial integration in the pedestrian movement network. The global integration values are based on a calculation of mean 'depth' from each line to all other lines of the system. Depth in this analysis means the number of changes in direction from one line to another line along the shortest route. Red lines represent high spatial integration to blue for lowest spatial integration.
The concentration of red lines in the centre represents the heart of the city which with its intensified grid accommodates a wide range of activities and pedestrian movement.

Passenger routes observed in Victoria Station, London 2001

The research aims to investigate the effects of refurbishment in complex buildings on pedestrian movement patterns and to develop a model for forecasting the likely effects of proposed refurbishment works. The illustration comes from one of three case studies where the interaction between refurbishment and pedestrian movement is critical to business performance.

In particular, the research has aimed to:

• establish patterns of movement at different times of the day during a weekday and weekend, both before and during the closure;

• analyse the dispersal patterns of pedestrians to and from the station and surrounding area;

• establish patterns of stationary pedestrian activity;

• analyse movement into station retail facilities;

• assess the degree to which changes in spatial layout can be implicated in changes to the patterns of pedestrian movement and customer behaviour.

Thus far the research has found that customer flows can be robustly forecast on the basis of spatial analysis, as can areas of informal stationary activity.

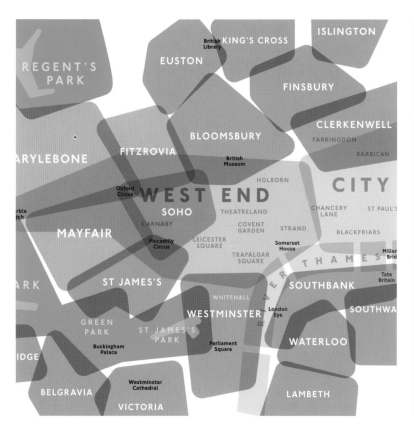

Legible London:
Improving pedestrian wayfinding in the Capital

London is a vast city of complex structures, many dating back to medieval times, with few long vistas but a myriad of destinations and attractive neighbourhoods. With more than 27 million visitors a year, walkability is important. It's well known that in the tube map, London has one of the best wayfinding diagrams in the world, but walking has been less well served. Over 40% of people have been using the tube map for walking too!

The idea of Legible London is to provide better support for the millions who walk every day – more than half of all journeys in the capital. Applied Information Group's 2005 Wayfinding study identified no fewer than 32 separate pedestrian signage systems in central London, resulting in visual noise rather than reliable, coordinated information. Legible London aims to provide that coordination: across neighbourhoods and borough boundaries, connecting up with the other transport modes, and delivering information not just in the street, but in all the ways people use to find their way around.

Diagrams were an important element of the Legible London design process, from demonstrating concepts and relationships, shown in the network of London's villages and neighbourhoods above, to the visual aggregation of data in the Walking the Tube study, shown on the following page.

Legible London
Client: Westminster City Council, New West End Company, Transport for London, The Crown Estate, Greater London Authority
Designers: Applied Information Group, London, UK

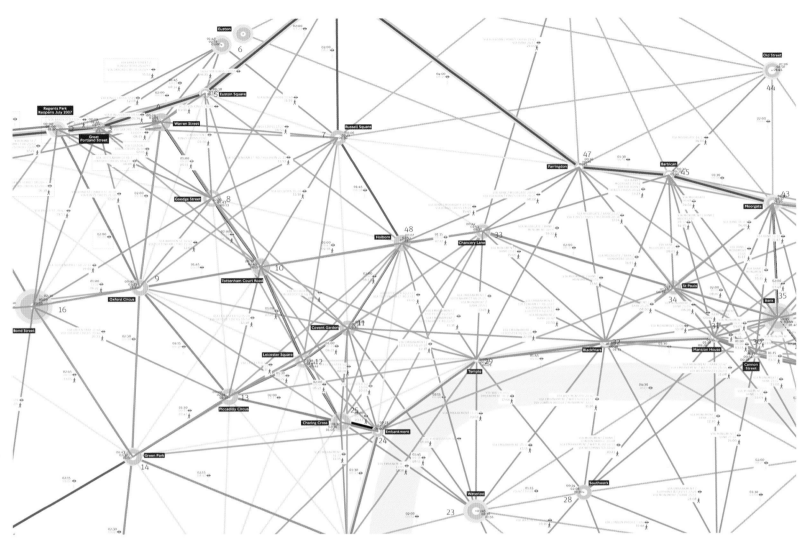

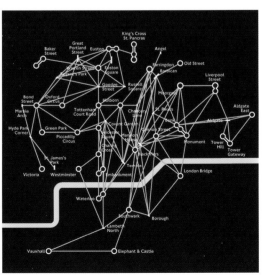

Walking the Tube Study

This study, which formed a basis of the reasons for Legible London, showed that 109 journeys in central London are quicker to walk from door-to-door than to take the Underground.

The study measured the time to get to the station platform plus the time for waiting and travelling on the tube, compared to the time to walk along the pavements at the average speed. This data was recorded in the diagram shown above and presented in the modified tube map shown left, with all yellow routes representing journeys where it was quicker to walk.

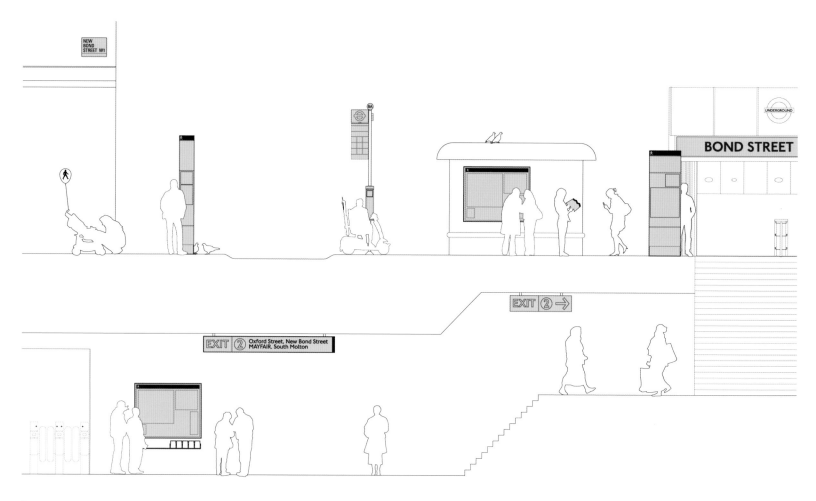

Seamless journeys

Legible London rationalises the addressing and directional language across transport and city streets, meaning information is consistent throughout journeys and areas can be more easily linked to one another.

The 'seamless journey' is the first principle of the Legible London system. It is the biggest challenge, with information, in most cities in the world, failing to be 'joined-up' and often tackled in an ad-hoc manner.

The drawing above demonstrates all the points in a journey, from tube station to street level destination, where the pedestrian receives information about where they are or where they want to go.

The diagram to the right illustrates how a journey is made in stages, moving between the 'steppingstones' of villages and neighbourhoods that make up central London.

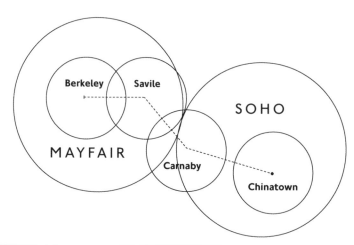

West End Prototype

A prototype of the Legible London system was installed in London's famous West End by AIG with product partners Lacock Gullam. The careful design process built upon principles of universal access and cognitive science, and resulted in an array of heads-up mapping available at key junctions in the street, at transport arrival points (tube stations and bus shelters) and in people's pockets on printed maps. An agreed set of landmarks and area names peppered the system.

The prototype was independently evaluated and surveys suggested journey time savings of 16% and a universal improvement in people's confidence to navigate on foot.

The diagram to the right, which shows the location of some of the on-street information points, was used not only for demonstrating the extent of the scheme to the client, but also in the production stages of the project; in planning locations and phasing sign installation. See **Fendley** page 196.

Photo copyright © 2007 Philip Vile / Applied Information Group

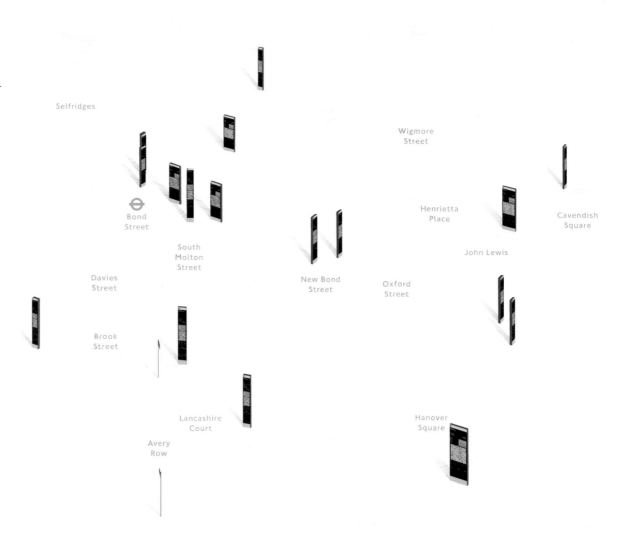

Selfridges

Wigmore Street

Bond Street

Henrietta Place

Cavendish Square

Davies Street

South Molton Street

John Lewis

New Bond Street

Oxford Street

Brook Street

Lancashire Court

Hanover Square

Avery Row

Quickmap

presents city and transport information at the intermediate level between diagrams and maps for quick and easy journey planning.

Transport diagrams often distort geography to simplify complex systems and city street maps often suffer from information overload. Neither is ideal for journey planning.

Presently, London has the iconic Tube Map which covers half of the Capital and The London Connections diagram of tubes and trains. Each is spatially inaccurate and different in scale. There are also five large scale bus maps, different in scale and composition. Coordination is badly needed. By identifying places and centres in geographic approximation and removing hinterland details, Quickmap integrates transport information at the city level, at a readable scale and from the perspective of the traveller.

Daytime buses, tubes and trains

142

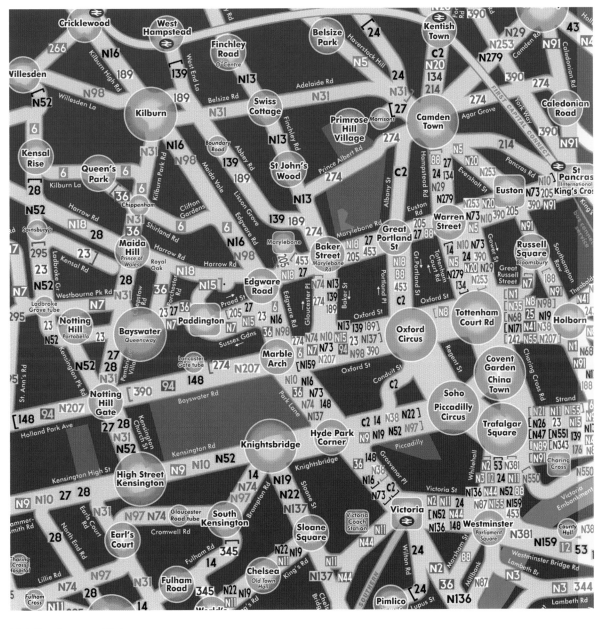

Nighttime buses and trains

Quickmaps cover the whole of London in a variety of formats supplemented with information on interchanges, fare zones, post codes, street names and some landmarks.

A combined bus frequency between centres is graphically indicated by road width where a wide road means many buses. And in the latest version of the London all-on-one map, coloured nodes help with faster and easier recall of places and centres.

Publications include London by bus, London all-on-one, London tube and walk, London Travel Planner and London Night Travel Planner. All are based on a similar scale and same spatial structure of London's places and centres.

Designed in CorelDraw for guide-books, interactive transport map-movies and publications

Quickmap, information designers and publishers London and Luton, UK

The National World War 1 Museum at Liberty Memorial
Kansas City, USA
Year: 2006

Primary scale panels are monumental and bold to relate metaphorically to the scale of the war. Their graphics — diagrams, graphs and maps — provide an alternative way of understanding history and offer a dramatic contrast to the wealth of archival images, still and moving, in the exhibition environment around them.

The graphic space of the panels is inspired by the early 20th-century avant garde, which combined text, illustration, and photography on an infinite field. The type itself (Berthold Akzidenz Grotesk) dates from this period. Vignetted images float out of the depths of space, while diagrams hover in the foreground across them. The design works to visually pull the viewer into each theme. The message of each major topic is delivered through the diagram; the first read of each panel. The panels are conceived as a coherent narrative; by reading just the primary text visitors grasp a clear view of the war and America's role in it.

Ralph Appelbaum Associates
New York City, USA

Design team:
Ralph Appelbaum, Principal in Charge
Joshua Dudley, Scott Simeral, Project Directors
Josh Hartley, Graphic Designer
Fabio Gherardi, Graphic Designer
Aki Carpenter, Graphic Designer
Tana Green Exhibition Designer
Luka Kito, Exhibition Designer
Jande Wintrob, Exhibition Designer

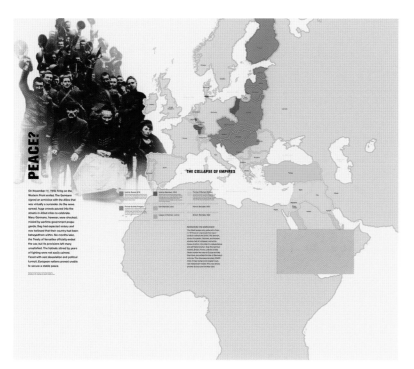

Top left
Diagram showing the breakup of
countries after the signing of the
Versailles Treaty.

Top right
Diagram showing British Merchant
ships sunk by German Submarines.

Bottom
Illustration showing the organization of
the United States Army by insignia.

The Braid
Ballymena Town Hall, Museum and
Arts Centre, Northern Ireland
Year: 2008

Set within a renovated Grade II listed
building, The Braid is the first newly
built museum to open in Northern
Ireland in 40 years. Running the full
length of the gallery is a stunning,
twenty-four-metre historical timeline,
placing Mid-Antrim events within
the wider scope of Northern Irish,
UK and European history. The
design of the timeline draws upon
Ballymena's history in the weaving
industry and uses various shades of
colour to represent local, national and
international milestones.

Ralph Appelbaum Associates
London, UK

Design team:
Phillip Tefft, Director of London
Operations
Vicci Ward, Head of Graphic Design
Simon Leach, Exhibition Designer
Daniel Warren, Exhibition and
Interactive Designer
Sarah Pollard, Exhibition Designer
Annabel Judd, Exhibition Designer
Mat Mason, Graphic Designer
Jennifer Blurton, Graphic Designer

Photos: Peter Mauss / ESTO

This is information design for Ilse Crawford and Jane Withers' "1% Water And Our Future" exhibition, which was on show at the Z33 Gallery in Hasselt, Belgium in the summer of 2008. The designers filled up the exhibition's first room with big 2D charts on the wall, and created 3D charts on the floor (out of water-related items like hoses, buckets, sponges), depicting a huge variety of facts about water and its use and abuse in the past, present and future. In addition, they produced a free, take-away newspaper with even more facts, plus a call-for-action with 20 simple ways to start saving water today.

Designers: karlssonwilker inc
New York City, USA

148

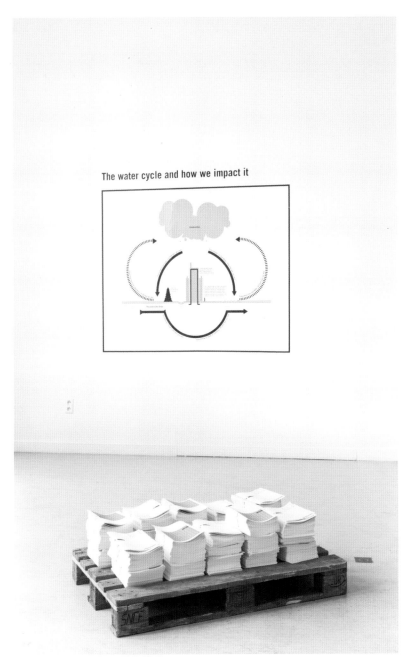

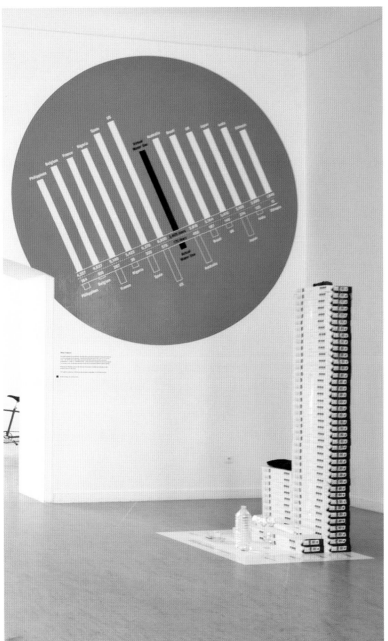

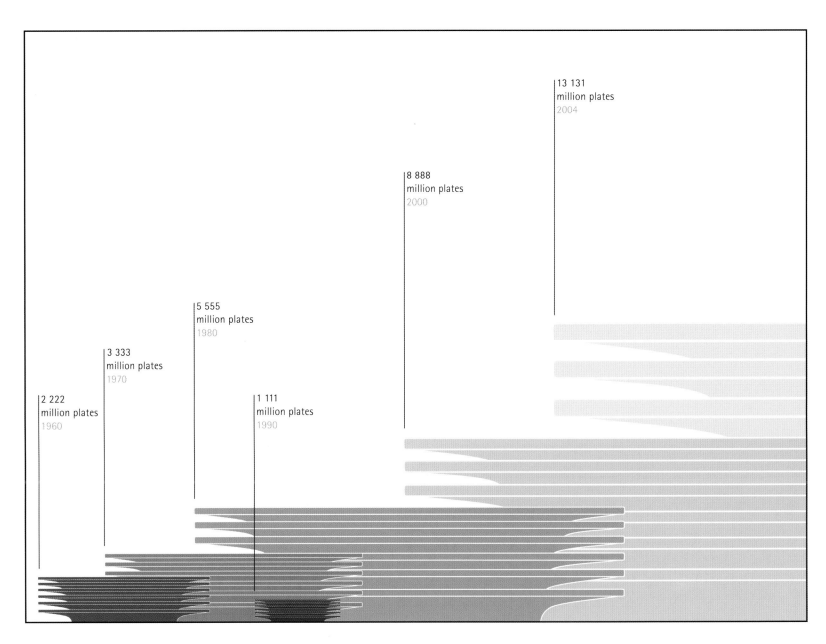

13 131
million plates
2004

8 888
million plates
2000

5 555
million plates
1980

3 333
million plates
1970

2 222
million plates
1960

1 111
million plates
1990

These two diagrams are part of an overall corporate design concept for bulthaup. The well known company *bulthaup* designs and produces exclusive living spaces such as kitchens and the objects that go into them.
The diagrams focus on the world of cooking: In this case plates and cups and the chronological development in sales and how they relate to the company's turnover.

Client: Bulthaup GmbH & Co KG
Aich, Germany

Designers:
Baumann & Baumann
Büro für Gestaltung
Schwäbisch Gmünd, Germany

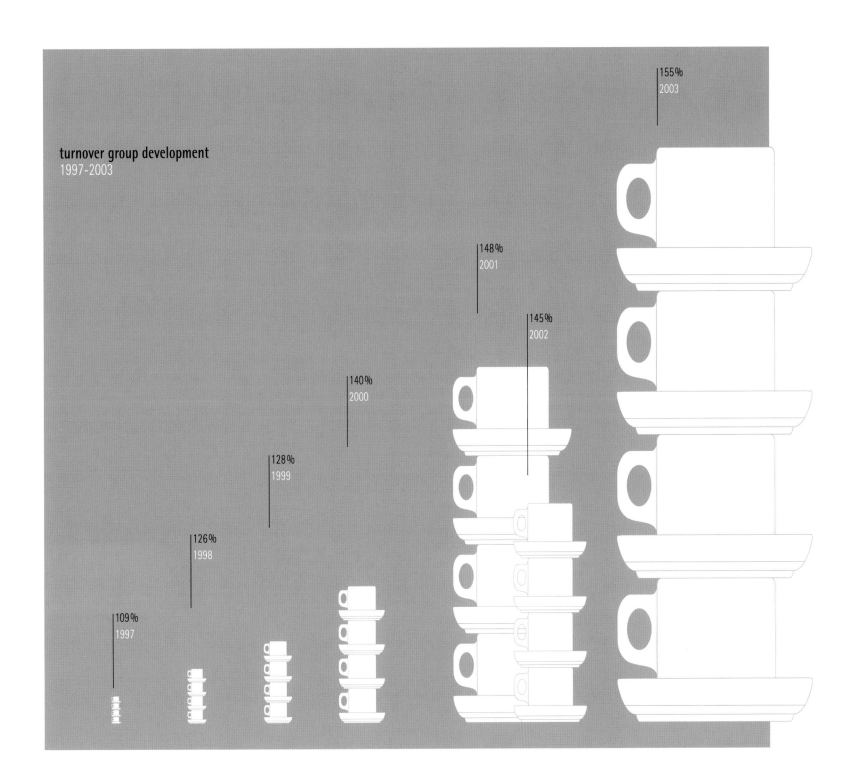

turnover group development
1997-2003

155%
2003

148%
2001

145%
2002

140%
2000

128%
1999

126%
1998

109%
1997

Super Cheap Auto

As the name suggests, Super Cheap Auto is not the shy retiring type. Much of their print and packaging is big and brash in both colour and design. Instead of trying to pare this back, Frost Design embraced the aesthetic and used it as the basis for the design. With all the visual prompts for the concept available at the Super Cheap Auto stores, We didn't need to look far for inspiration.

The theme for this report was about building and growth of the Super Cheap business within the DIY market place. They have continued to develop their business by expanding retail outlets and domination in the market place and also by adding a new camping brand called BCF.

Throughout the report, key financials are built from actual store products; spanners, oil bottles, spray cans, spark plug boxes and are used to create number sequences. Graphs, for example, are tool sets used in the building process, all photographed directly on the shop floor. The report in its approach exemplifies this DIY approach.

Client: Super Cheap Auto
Designers: Frost Design, Sydney, Australia
Creative Director: Vince Frost
Designer: Ray Parslow
Design Manager: Beverley Hall
Photographer: Ray Parslow

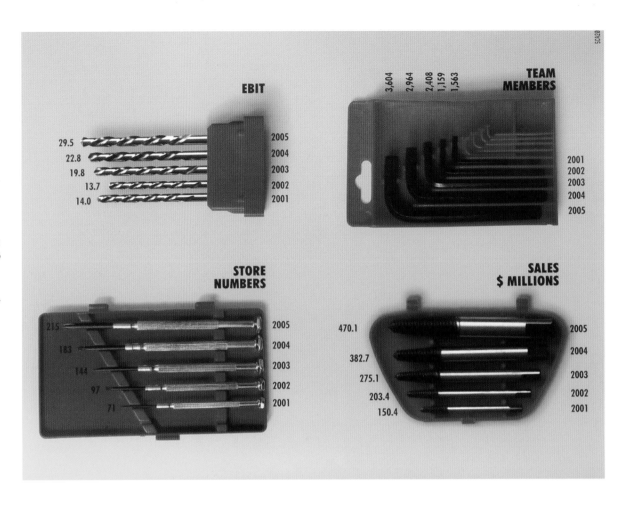

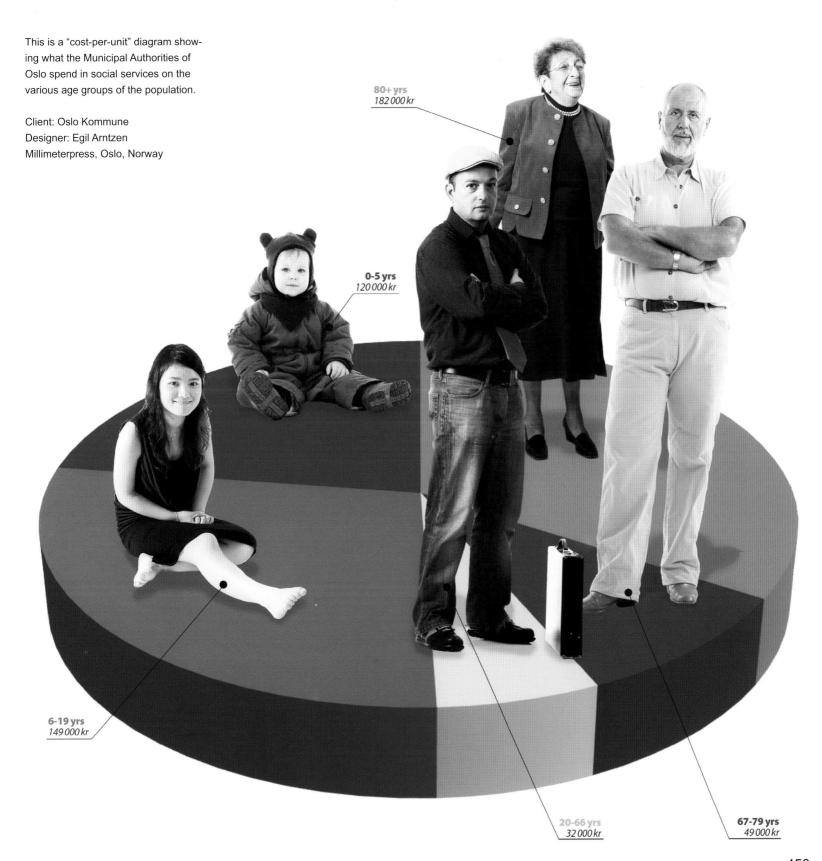

This is a "cost-per-unit" diagram showing what the Municipal Authorities of
Oslo spend in social services on the
various age groups of the population.

Client: Oslo Kommune
Designer: Egil Arntzen
Millimeterpress, Oslo, Norway

80+ yrs
182 000 kr

0-5 yrs
120 000 kr

6-19 yrs
149 000 kr

20-66 yrs
32 000 kr

67-79 yrs
49 000 kr

153

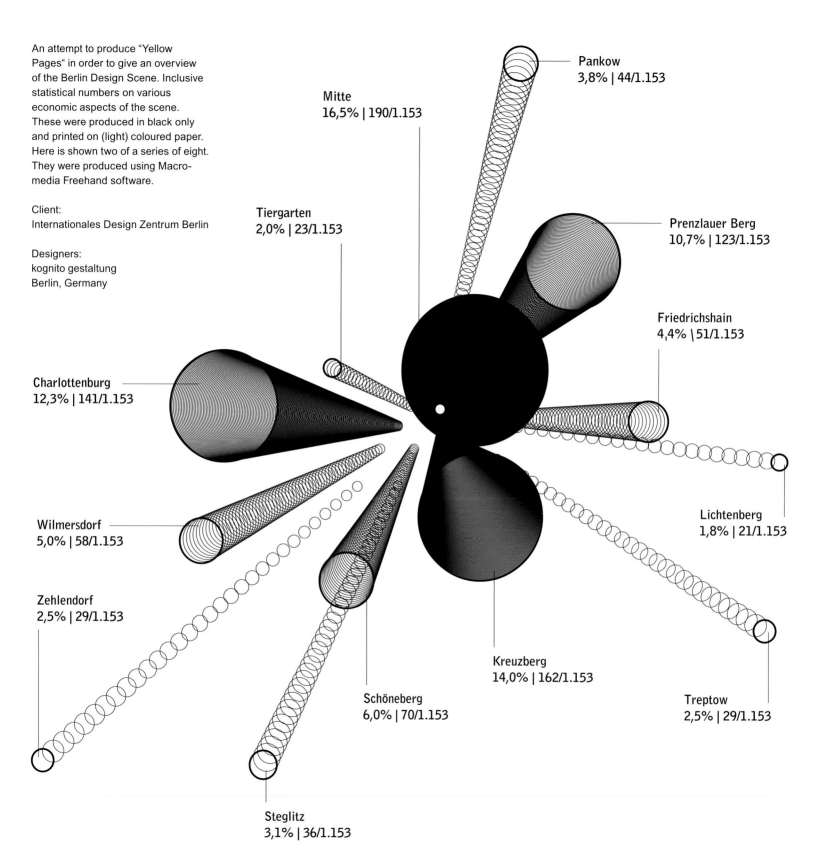

An attempt to produce "Yellow Pages" in order to give an overview of the Berlin Design Scene. Inclusive statistical numbers on various economic aspects of the scene. These were produced in black only and printed on (light) coloured paper. Here is shown two of a series of eight. They were produced using Macromedia Freehand software.

Client:
Internationales Design Zentrum Berlin

Designers:
kognito gestaltung
Berlin, Germany

Pankow
3,8% | 44/1.153

Mitte
16,5% | 190/1.153

Prenzlauer Berg
10,7% | 123/1.153

Tiergarten
2,0% | 23/1.153

Friedrichshain
4,4% \ 51/1.153

Charlottenburg
12,3% | 141/1.153

Wilmersdorf
5,0% | 58/1.153

Lichtenberg
1,8% | 21/1.153

Zehlendorf
2,5% | 29/1.153

Kreuzberg
14,0% | 162/1.153

Treptow
2,5% | 29/1.153

Schöneberg
6,0% | 70/1.153

Steglitz
3,1% | 36/1.153

154

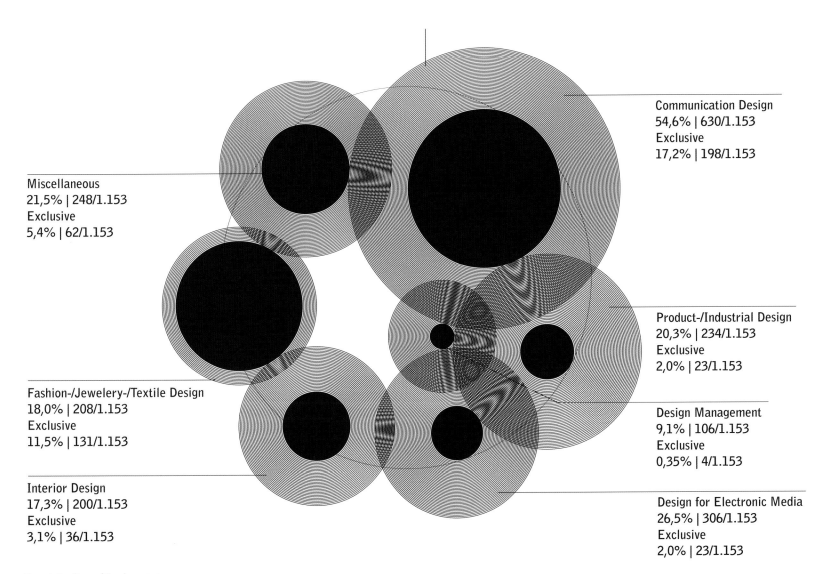

Communication Design
54,6% | 630/1.153
Exclusive
17,2% | 198/1.153

Miscellaneous
21,5% | 248/1.153
Exclusive
5,4% | 62/1.153

Product-/Industrial Design
20,3% | 234/1.153
Exclusive
2,0% | 23/1.153

Fashion-/Jewelery-/Textile Design
18,0% | 208/1.153
Exclusive
11,5% | 131/1.153

Design Management
9,1% | 106/1.153
Exclusive
0,35% | 4/1.153

Interior Design
17,3% | 200/1.153
Exclusive
3,1% | 36/1.153

Design for Electronic Media
26,5% | 306/1.153
Exclusive
2,0% | 23/1.153

Specialisation of the bureaus.
The black centre of the graphic sym-
bolizes the exclusive specialisation.
Because of multiple naming the sum is
more than 100 percent.

Our brief was to bring alive some facts and figures about investment in the arts in a publication produced by the organisation Arts & Business. This particular diagram which is part of a series, illustrates how regional investment compares across the UK. The overall aim of the publication is to communicate in a lively and engaging way the state of private investment funding, in particular, regional funding during 2005 to 2006.

The diagrams appeared in "Private Investment Benchmarking Survey 2005/06: Summary of Results". Software used was Macromedia Freehand and Quark Xpress

Client: Arts & Business

Art Direction: Paula Benson / Paul West
Design: Paula Benson / Andy Harvey
Design firm: Form, London, UK

Scotland
-10.6%
2004/05 £24.8m
2005/06 £22.2m

N.East
+52.6%
2004/05 £7.3m
2005/06 £11.1m

Yorkshire
-30.4%
2004/05 £8.8m
2005/06 £6.1m

W.Midlands
-39.2%
2004/05 £13.5m
2005/06 £8.2m

E.Midlands
+25.6%
2004/05 £2.9m
2005/06 £3.7m

N.West
-9.6%
2004/05 £10.9m
2005/06 £9.8m

N.Ireland
-28.4%
2004/05 £2.9m
2005/06 £2.1m

East
-35.3%
2004/05 £11m
2005/06 £7.1m

Wales
-27.9%
2004/05 £10.4m
2005/06 £7.5m

London
+3.5%
2004/05 £294.6m
2005/06 £304.9m

S.West
+56.5%
2004/05 £7.7m
2005/06 £12.1m

S.East
-1.8%
2004/05 £16.2m
2005/06 £15.9m

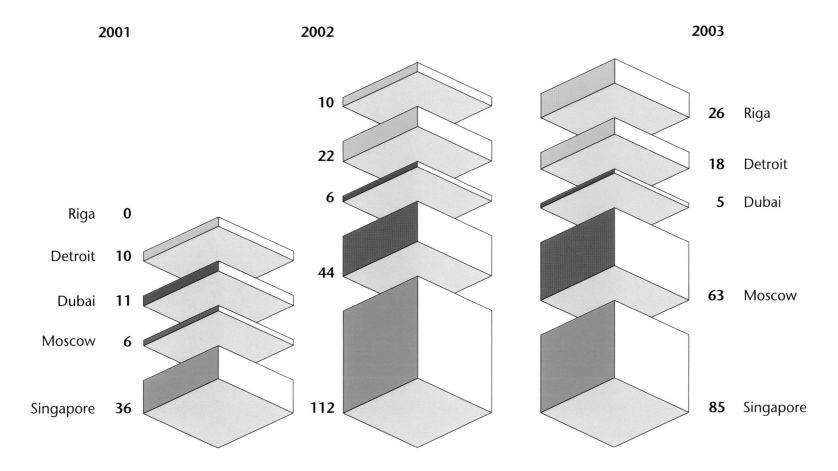

2001

Riga 0
Detroit 10
Dubai 11
Moscow 6
Singapore 36

2002

10
22
6
44
112

2003

26 Riga
18 Detroit
5 Dubai
63 Moscow
85 Singapore

As a government agency Zukunfts-agentur Brandenburg (Brandenburg Economic Development Board) has to produce an annual report detailing the organisation's activities around the world. The agency's main task is to attract investment into the Brandenburg region from local centers as far flung as Singapore, Moscow and Detroit.

The diagrams in the agency's annual report not only have to track the increase in activity along a timeline, but they also illustrate the contribution of its local centres around the world. The diagrams show that there is scope for a design beyond the humble bar chart, that can become an important element of a company's house style.

The diagrams were created using Adobe Illustrator.

Client: Zukunftsagentur Brandenburg
Designer: Thomas Manss
Thomas Manss & Company
Berlin, Germany

Traversing the city

People move intuitively. They amble,
hurry, drive, ride and walk. What do
they perceive? What guides them, what
is their orientation?

Moniteurs initiated the "Infotracks" project in conjunction with Designmai in
Berlin. It is a research into how people
move in the city and how they decide
which way they choose to go.

By mapping, comparing and analyzing
differently created data graphics,
a collection arose as well as a photographic collection of graphics and
typography seen in the urban space of
Berlin. As such it shows how symbols,
colours and structures shape a city and
what visual language the city speaks.
The web-based image archive follows
the routes from the Moniteurs office in
the city centre to the Designcity, where
the Designmai took place, in Kreuzberg. The locations of all photos are
marked on a map of Berlin. The
"visitor" retraces the various routes.
He focuses on various themes. He dis-
covers trails and paths along which he
moves every day.

The creation, integration and system-
atic conception of structures provides
scope for information and communication. With visionary methods and
new materials, the diversity of urban
information could be more clearly
structured. Identity, readability and
standardization in relation to social and
technological development are aspects
of this investigation.

Moniteurs
Kommunikationsdesign GmbH
Berlin, Germany
Designers: Heike Nehl, Isolde Frey
Sibylle Schlaich

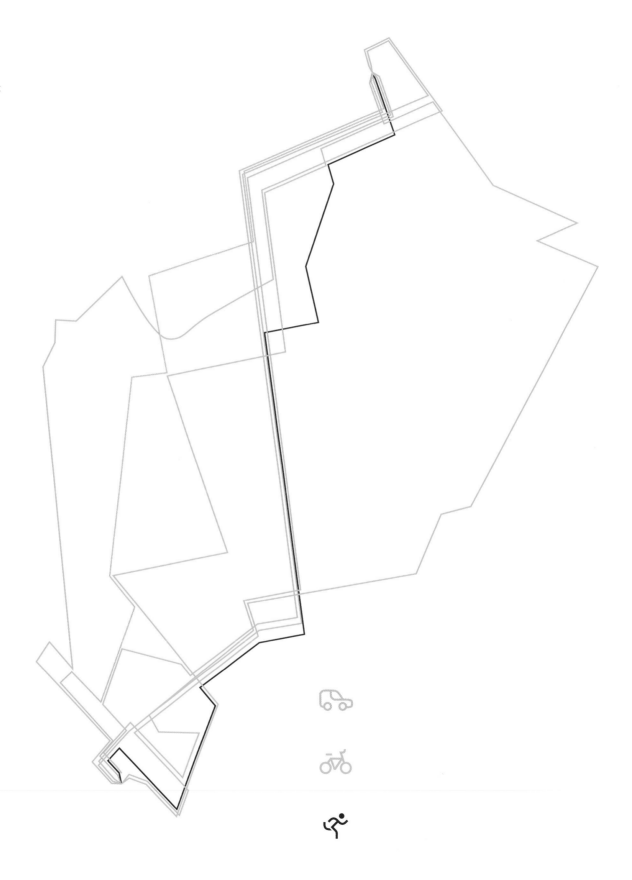

158

A Time zone Globe

The exercise was to show the time zones of the world but not as an ordinary map (like you always see them in an atlas). So I put them on a globe.
I put little alarmclocks in to show the time differences.
The illustration was produced using a combination of Cinema 4D, Photoshop and Illustrator.

Client: NRC Next
(a Dutch national newspaper)
Designer: Fokke Gerritsma
Amsterdam, Netherlands

Showing the buildup of the organization

The CIBG-organisation is part of the Ministry of Health and Welfare. It is made up of twelve units with diverse tasks visualized by the lines. The colour on the outside of the circle shows that some units are working in the same field of health care. With one exception that the gradient in the SBV-Z unit shows that tasks are overlapping. The inner circle is put on top of all the units to show that they are one organisation.
The graph appeared on the cover of an information leaflet.
The software used was Adobe Illustrator.

Client: CIBG
Designer/firm: Faydherbe/De Vringer, The Hague, Netherlands

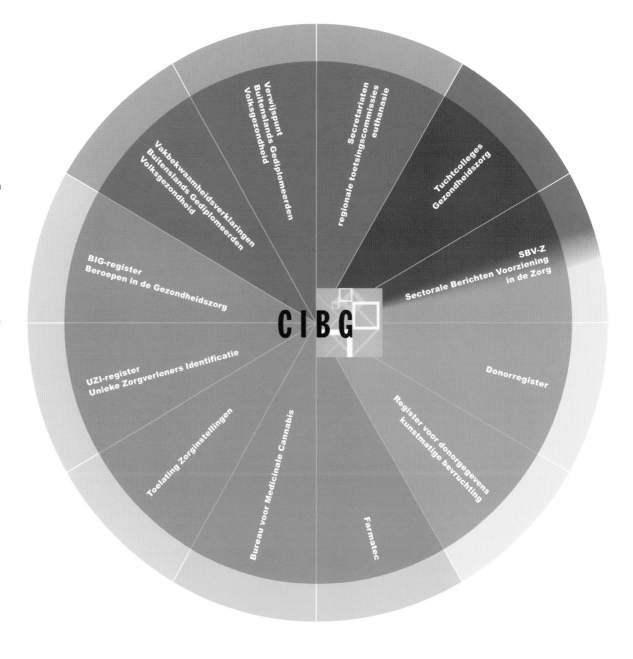

Beak shapes between Darwin's finches in relation to habitat and diet

Darwin's finches have beaks that are shaped according to the type of survival situations they face in their habitats.

The purpose of the diagram is two-fold. First is to compare the finches' physical beak features to tools, so the viewer can comprehend how they evolved to be able to forage the different types of foods available on the Galapagos Islands. At the same time, the diagram categorizes the finches into genuses and species, so that the viewers can see the range of speciation that occurred.

This diagram was illustrated for a personal project named "Evolution on the Galapagos Islands", a collaborative effort between Mia J. Chuang, Melissa Muller, Dante Carlos, Christina Schuett, and Henry de Leon.

It was created using Adobe Photoshop and Illustrator.

Client: Art Center College of Design
Designer: Mia J.Chuang
OtherPlane Inc., Vancouver, Canada

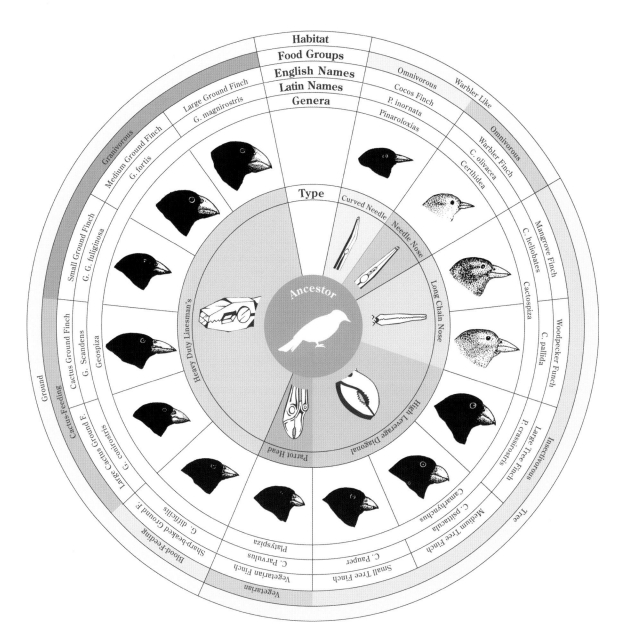

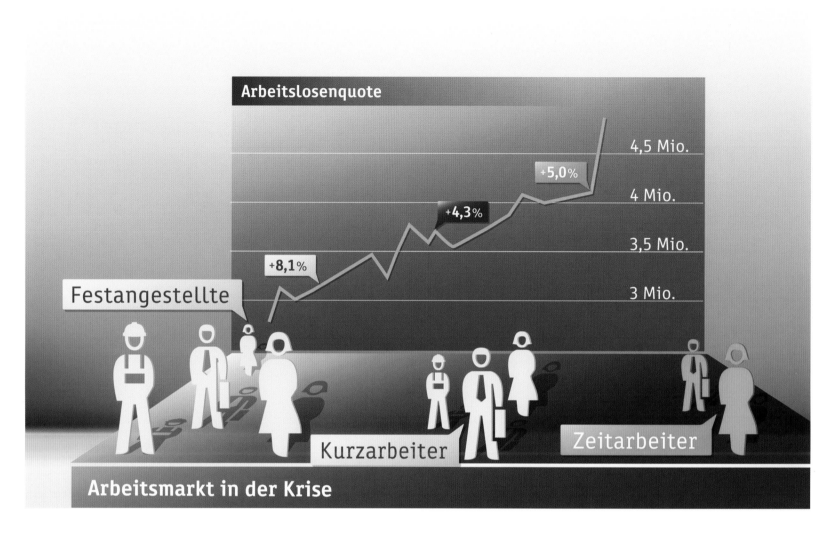

Arbeitslosenquote

4,5 Mio.

+5,0%

4 Mio.

+4,3%

3,5 Mio.

+8,1%

3 Mio.

Festangestellte

Kurzarbeiter

Zeitarbeiter

Arbeitsmarkt in der Krise

Redesigning the daily news

The 'heute' news programme is ZDF's flagship and something of an institution on German television. The internet more than anything else has changed young target group attitudes towards the media. ZDF has reacted to these changes by restructuring the news, from a new studio construction through to a thorough redesign of the news itself. Technical benchmarks have been set by updating the old studio technology, enabling a completely virtual studio design.

Edenspiekermann developed a new typeface family for the news that helps emphasize the independent nature of the revamped programme. The 'heute' typeface includes an extensive pictogram set with over 300 symbols, some of which are animated, for use in designing weather maps and other explanatory graphics.

Client: ZDF, Mainz, Germany
ZDF news program 'heute'
ZDF news program 'heute journal'

Designers:
Edenspiekermann AG, Berlin
Fabian Rottke, Creative Director
Ralph du Carrois, Type Designer
Erik Spiekermann, Managing Partner

The illustration shows the "Crisis in the job market"
"Festangestellte" (Permanently employed)
"Kurzarbeiter" (People who are employed for limited periods)
"Zeitarbeiter" (People who are hired to do temporary work)

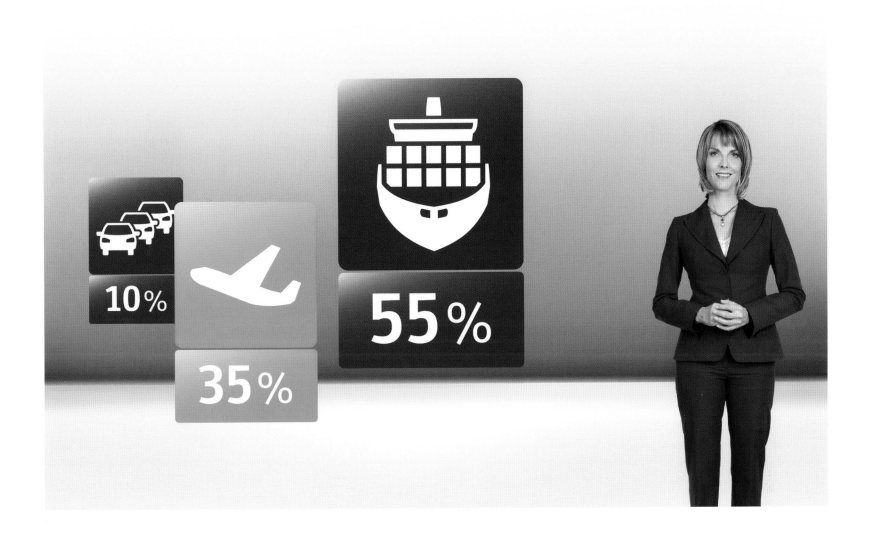

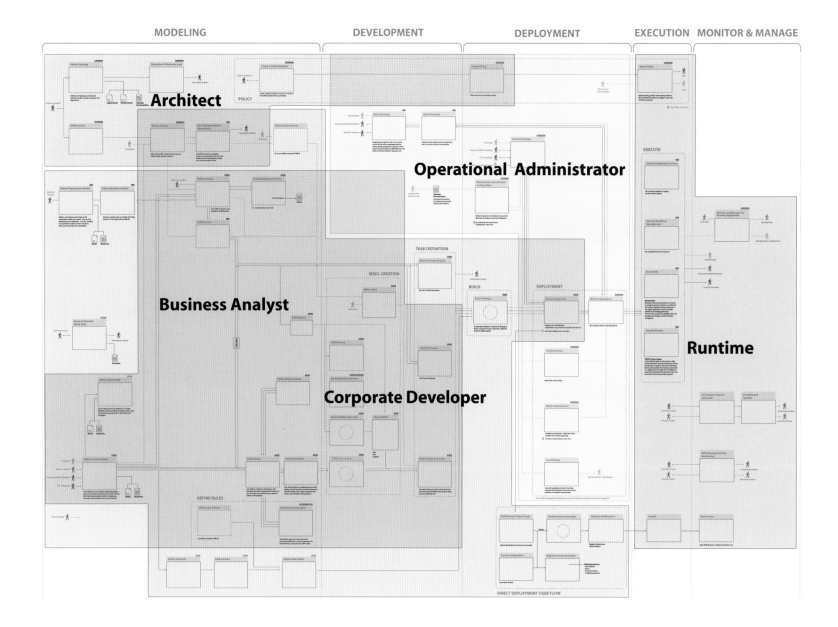

User Experience Map for Building TIBCO Infrastructure Applications

The design challenge was to define and solve the complex relationship of the TIBCO business objectives and technology implementation for their end users. The project goal was to visually define a series of abstract and technology concepts while keeping the end user's role in focus.

Enterprise software applications have grown exponentially more complicated because the solutions in question are somewhat intangible and can never be seen at once by any one person. The designer's role in this project is to interpret all the domain knowledge from a set of individuals into one view so all team members can grasp the high level concepts.

The map focuses on the user's experience for the creation and delivery of infrastructure applications across distributed and heterogeneous IT environments.

The map was designed to communicate the TIBCO products in the context of the TIBCO Personas during the different phases of the development process.

The original map size is 100" x 50" (250 cm x 125 cm). The map was designed using Adobe Illustrator.

Client: TIBCO Software Inc.
Art Direction: David Sciacero
Palo Alto, CA, USA / Gothenburg, Sweden

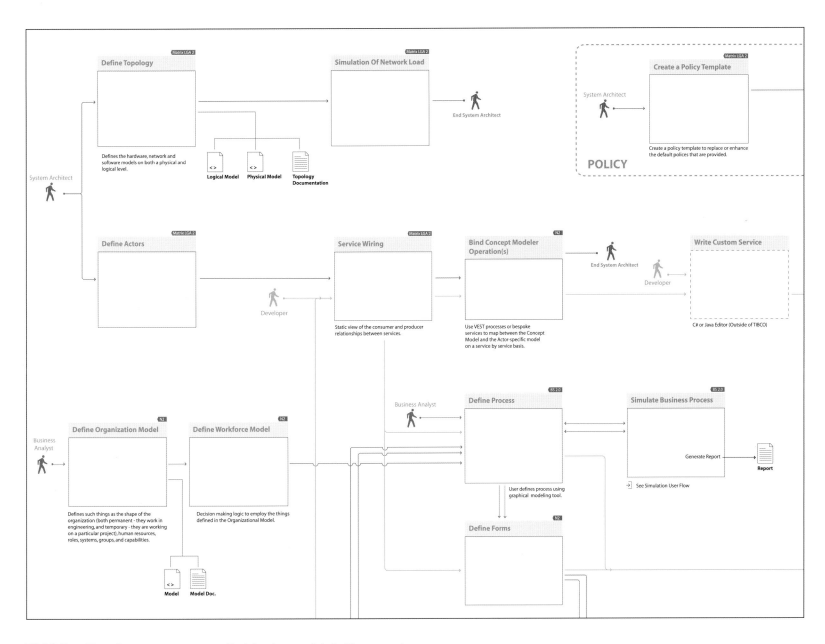

Define Topology
Matrix LGA 2

Defines the hardware, network and software models on both a physical and logical level.

Logical Model   **Physical Model**   **Topology Documentation**

Simulation Of Network Load

End System Architect

System Architect

Create a Policy Template
Matrix LGA 2

Create a policy template to replace or enhance the default polices that are provided.

POLICY

System Architect

Define Actors
Matrix LGA 2

Service Wiring
Matrix LGA 2

Static view of the consumer and producer relationships between services.

Developer

Bind Concept Modeler Operation(s)
N2

Use VEST processes or bespoke services to map between the Concept Model and the Actor-specific model on a service by service basis.

End System Architect

Developer

Write Custom Service
Matrix LGA 2

C# or Java Editor (Outside of TIBCO)

Business Analyst

Define Process
BS 2.0

User defines process using graphical modeling tool.

Simulate Business Process
BS 2.0

Generate Report

Report

→ See Simulation User Flow

Business Analyst

Define Organization Model
N2

Defines such things as the shape of the organization (both permanent - they work in engineering, and temporary - they are working on a particular project), human resources, roles, systems, groups, and capabilities.

Model   **Model Doc.**

Define Workforce Model
N2

Decision making logic to employ the things defined in the Organizational Model.

Define Forms
N2

TIBCO User Experience Map Detail

The map follows the different user flows through the development process across the product offerings. Each user role is represented by an icon and color. The viewer can follow the different user processes represented by each box.

Each box is associated with a supporting detailed user flow in another map. The different phases of development is represented by vertical columns.

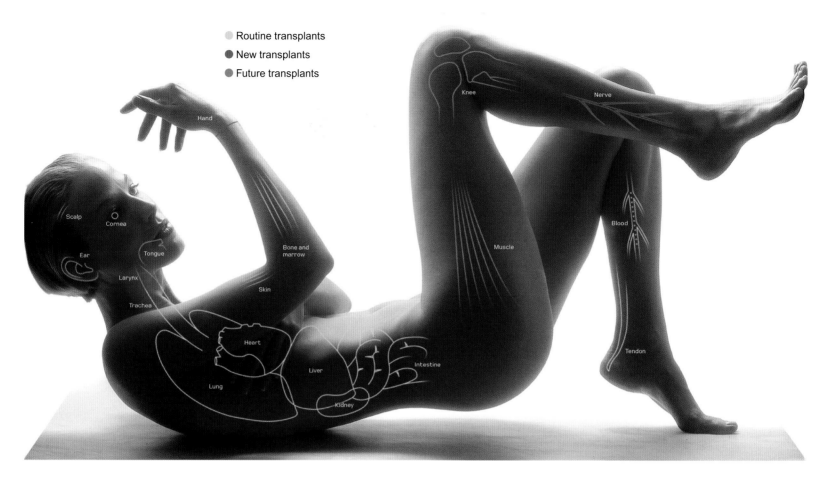

This was made for Popular Science Magazine to show current and future transplants of body parts for a feature called "Bodies by Design."

Graphics by John Grimwade
Designer: Chris Garcia
Photographer: Earl Ripling
New York City, USA.

**Number of Hiv infected people
per continent**

The illustration was used in "Infact",
a book to raise awareness about the
Aids epidemic in Asia (2008)
The image was produced by using
Post-it's, black paper and a camera.
Then prepared in Photoshop.

Client: Mainline, Amsterdam
Designer: Jeroen Disch,
Lava Graphic Design
Amsterdam, The Netherlands

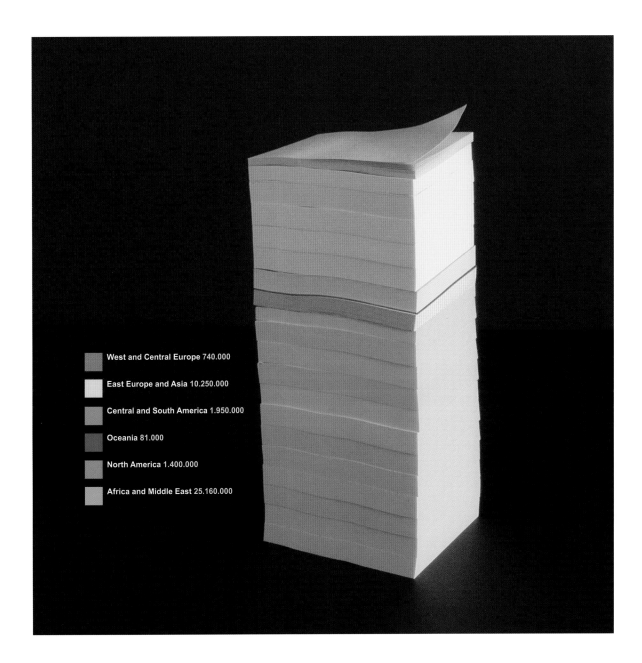

West and Central Europe 740.000

East Europe and Asia 10.250.000

Central and South America 1.950.000

Oceania 81.000

North America 1.400.000

Africa and Middle East 25.160.000

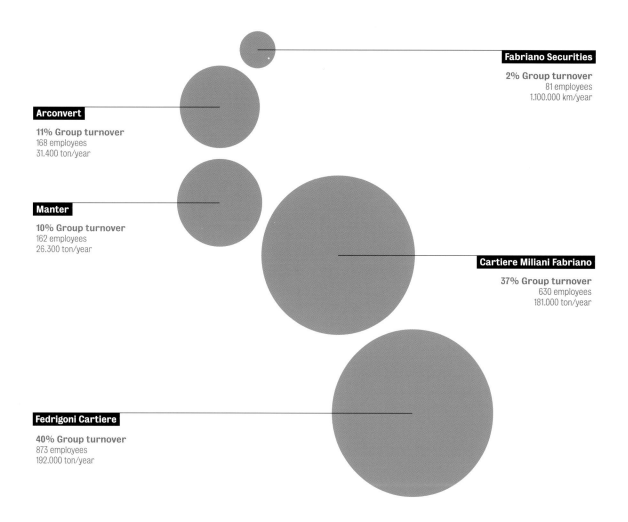

Fabriano Securities

2% Group turnover
81 employees
1.100.000 km/year

Arconvert

11% Group turnover
168 employees
31.400 ton/year

Manter

10% Group turnover
162 employees
26.300 ton/year

Cartiere Miliani Fabriano

37% Group turnover
630 employees
181.000 ton/year

Fedrigoni Cartiere

40% Group turnover
873 employees
192.000 ton/year

Fedrigoni Group is an Italian conglomerate of highly specialised paper manufacturers with a portfolio ranging from papers for artists and fine printing to bank notes and labelling.
Because of the highly specialised nature of the business, the Group's corporate brochure introduced every subsidiary with its individual portfolio. The diagram above was not only designed to show all the Group members, but at the same time illustrate each company's share of the overall Group revenue.

The traditional way to depict this type of information is the pie chart. In this case the inspiration for the designs was taken from Fedrigoni's core business, the diagrams resemble the rollers of a printing machine.
The diagrams were created using Adobe Illustrator.

Client: Fedrigoni Group
Designers: Thomas Manss, Enrica Corzani
Thomas Manss & Company
London, UK

Bowers & Wilkins is a leading manufacturer of high end loudspeakers,
sound docks and car audio systems.
In the company's corporate brochure
diagrams provide detailed information
about the business.
From turnover and the geographical
share of revenue to an analysis of the
competition, the diagrams did not only
provide the essential information, they
were designed as an extension of the
world of Bowers & Wilkins. By using
loudspeaker components as the basis
for organization, pie and bar charts, the
diagrams turned anonymous facts and
figures into tailor-made illustrations.
The diagrams were created using
Adobe Illustrator and Photoshop.

Client: Bowers & Wilkins
Designer: Thomas Manss
Thomas Manss & Company
London, UK

USA

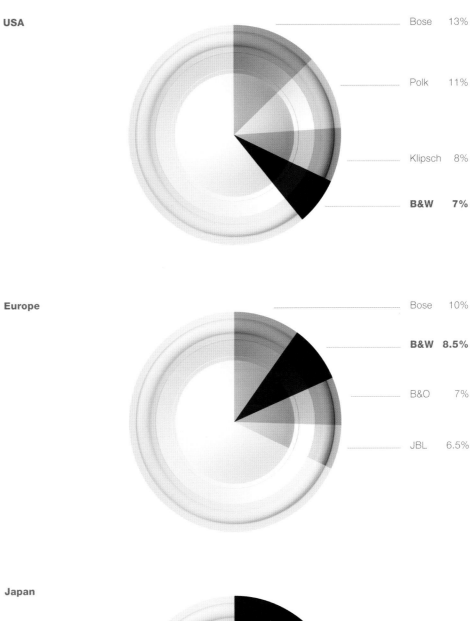

Bose 13%
Polk 11%
Klipsch 8%
B&W **7%**

Europe

Bose 10%
B&W **8.5%**
B&O 7%
JBL 6.5%

Japan

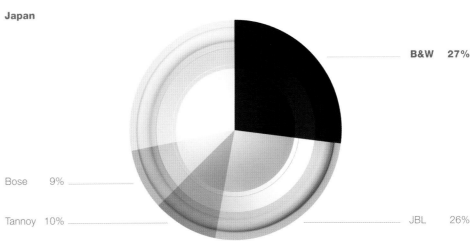

B&W **27%**
Bose 9%
Tannoy 10%
JBL 26%

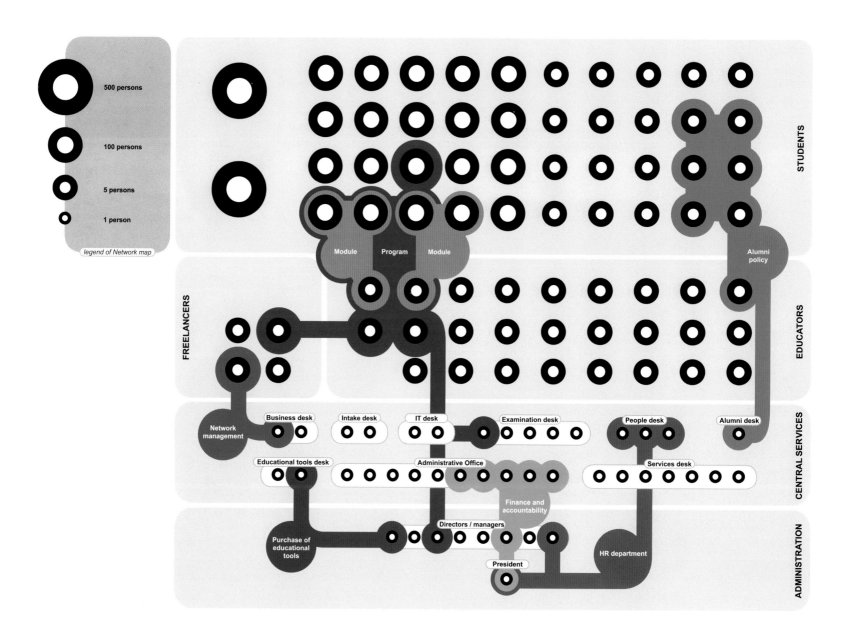

Legend:
500 persons
100 persons
5 persons
1 person

legend of Network map

STUDENTS

FREELANCERS

EDUCATORS

CENTRAL SERVICES

ADMINISTRATION

Module · Program · Module

Alumni policy

Network management

Business desk
Intake desk
IT desk
Examination desk
People desk
Alumni desk

Educational tools desk
Administrative Office
Services desk

Finance and accountability

Purchase of educational tools

Directors / managers

HR department

President

The Network School – a flexible organizational chart

This project aims to visualize the dynamic interaction between student, teachers and staff in a school which is organized as a network organization. This organization chart, appeared in a book with A3-size maps visualizing the business plan for a futuristic school, titled De Netwerkschool ('The Network School').
Software used: Adobe Indesign.

Designer: Carien Franken
Dutch information visualization company De Argumentenfabriek (The Argumentation Factory),
Amsterdam, The Netherlands

The Credit Crisis

Stock ascending **Descending**

100% 75% 50% 25% | 25% 50% 75% 100%

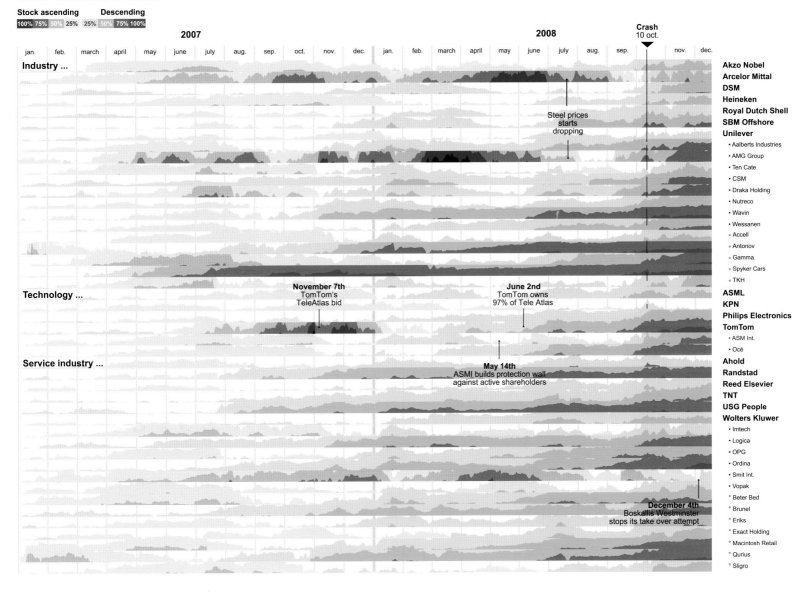

2007

jan. feb. march april may june july aug. sep. oct. nov. dec. jan. feb. march april may june july aug. sep. nov. dec.

2008

Crash
10 oct.

Industry ...

Steel prices starts dropping

Technology ...

November 7th
TomTom's TeleAtlas bid

June 2nd
TomTom owns 97% of Tele Atlas

Service industry ...

May 14th
ASMI builds protection wall against active shareholders

December 4th
Boskalis Westminster stops its take over attempt

Akzo Nobel
Arcelor Mittal
DSM
Heineken
Royal Dutch Shell
SBM Offshore
Unilever
- Aalberts Industries
- AMG Group
- Ten Cate
- CSM
- Draka Holding
- Nutreco
- Wavin
- Wessanen
- Accell
- Antonov
- Gamma
- Spyker Cars
- TKH

ASML
KPN
Philips Electronics
TomTom
- ASM Int.
- Océ

Ahold
Randstad
Reed Elsevier
TNT
USG People
Wolters Kluwer
- Imtech
- Logica
- OPG
- Ordina
- Smit Int.
- Vopak
- Beter Bed
- Brunel
- Eriks
- Exact Holding
- Macintosh Retail
- Qurius
- Sligro

How the crisis of credit affected Dutch companies

At the end of 2008, after a long period of great losses at the Amsterdam Stock Exchange, the Dutch newspaper Het Financieele Dagblad (Amsterdam) wanted to visualize how the crisis of credit dramatically affected the main 73 Dutch funds.

All funds - without exception - turned red. More than 24000 data entries were combined in this colored chart. The graph is made up of grid lines drawn in Illustrator. Each set of lines is attached to companies listed in the right hand column. Inside each set of lines there is a scale (from +100 to -100) where the colours go from dark blue (growth) to dark red (shrink). This visualization method is known as "horizon graphing".
(Here is shown a section of the illustration that originally appeared on the front page of the newspaper)

Client: Het Financieele Dagblad

Designer: Frédérik Ruys, Vizualism
Utrecht, The Netherlands

Identifying applications shared by departments

Analysis of overlaps among corporate applications created for different divisions. The diagram identifies opportunities to reduce costs by eliminating duplicate development and maintenance efforts. Divisions are Hair (Cheveux), Skin (Peau), Life Science (Vivant) and Material Science (Matière).

Client: L'Oreal Recherche
Design: Paolo Sancis
Concept: Paul Kahn, Laurent Kling
Created by: Kahn+Associates
Paris, France
Software: Adobe Illustrator

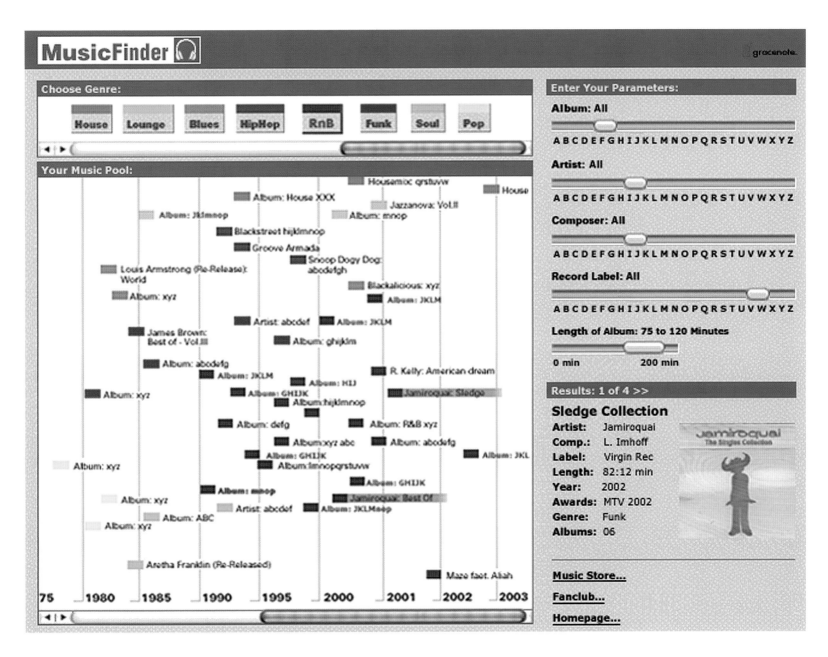

Music Finder

Prototype design of music meta-data visualization for desktop computers based on the University of Maryland's "Film-Finder" paradigm. One of a series of visual experiments produced with Adobe Photoshop in 2003. Published later in Aaron Marcus: "Integrated Information Systems," *Information Design Journal*, 17:1, 2009, pp. 4-21, p. 12.

Designers:
Aaron Marcus and Carmen Doerr
Aaron Marcus and Associates, Inc.
Berkeley, California,USA

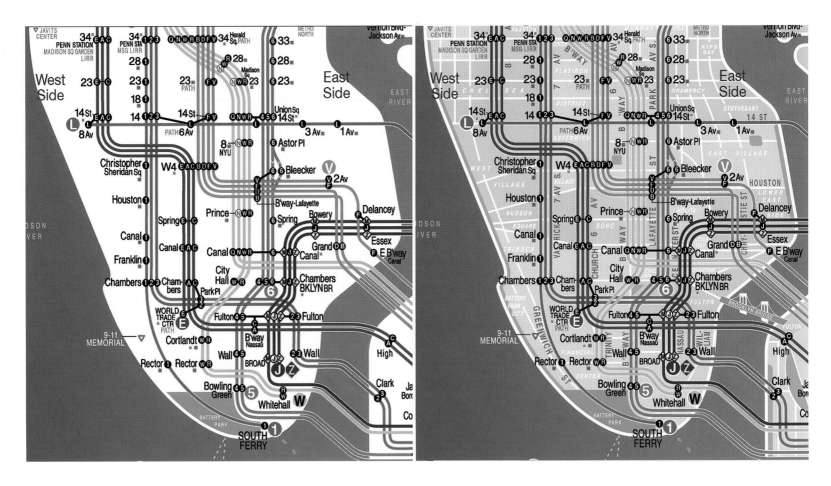

New Diagrams for the New York City subway system

The New York City subway has the biggest number of stations in the world (468), the second longest network and it's seventh in daily passenger numbers. There have been earlier diagrammatic maps created for the New York City Subway system, most notably the Salomon Map of 1958 and the Vignelli Map of 1972, (both inspired by the 1933 Beck Map of the London Underground. See page 48).

However, these attempts ultimately failed because they did not successfully match the station stops belowground with New York's numerical graph system of streets and avenues aboveground. So when, to take just one example, the Vignelli Map placed the 50th Street/Broadway station west of the 50th Street/8th Avenue station - when in fact is east - it created confusion for many riders. Since then (1979 to the present) New York has gone back to a geographic style subway map

with abbreviated lines that is rather cumbersome and confusing in its own right.

The KICK Map, was designed to address New York's unique issues by creating a diagram-style map that is geographically station-accurate. Small in size and simple to use, it clearly shows all the subway lines and transfer points. Larger in-station versions show streets, parks and color-coded neighbourhoods while maintaining system clarity.

Designer: Eddie Jabbour, Kick Design
New York City, USA

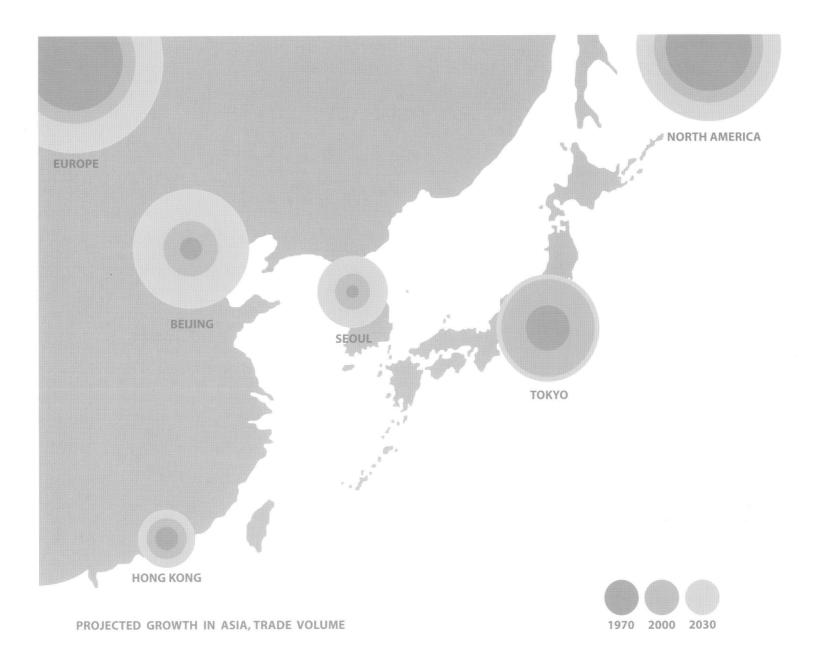

EUROPE

NORTH AMERICA

BEIJING

SEOUL

TOKYO

HONG KONG

PROJECTED GROWTH IN ASIA, TRADE VOLUME

1970   2000   2030

The diagram is part of a book about a new town in South Korea - Songdo City. Prepared for the general public, the book explains the master plan of the future city.

A series of diagrams, one per page, unfold the process of city planning, from broad social and economic context to specific urban planning conditions, street layouts, and ideas for public spaces. The first neighbourhoods of Songdo city are under construction, and the project has been the subject of debate in Korean and international press.

The diagram above captures dynamics of development of Asian regional centres. A dot, representing a geographical location on the map is oversized, showing the relative volume of trade. Superimposed circles represent past, present and projected trade volumes. More information about the project is available from www.studioradia.com and www.timerman.com

Client: KPF Architects
KPF book design team: James von Klemperer, Jisop Han, Richard Nemeth, Anne Timerman.
Design: TM/R Timerman Design, New York City, USA

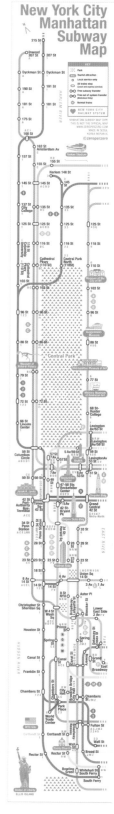

Exhibition at a gift shop

The designers wanted to show their producs more like "goods" than objects on show in a design exhibition.

This was done at the New York International Gift Fair at the Jacob K.Jarvis Convention Center on Manhattan, NYC in February 2010.

The space was small, but they used it economically.

The Manhattan Subway Map measures 95mm x 60mm (3.7inches x 2.3 inches) and is printed on box tape. The diagram of the peninsula is repeated 55 times which makes the total length of the tape 25 meters.

Designers: ZERO PER ZERO studio, Ji hwan Kim, Sol Jin.
Seoul, South Korea

Magazine cover

The illustration shows a section of the diagram the designers did for the Tokyo Railway System.

Issued in the spring of 2009

Software: Adobe Illustrator

Client: "Curve" Victoria, Australia

Designers: ZERO PER ZERO studio, Ji hwan Kim, Sol Jin. Seoul, South Korea

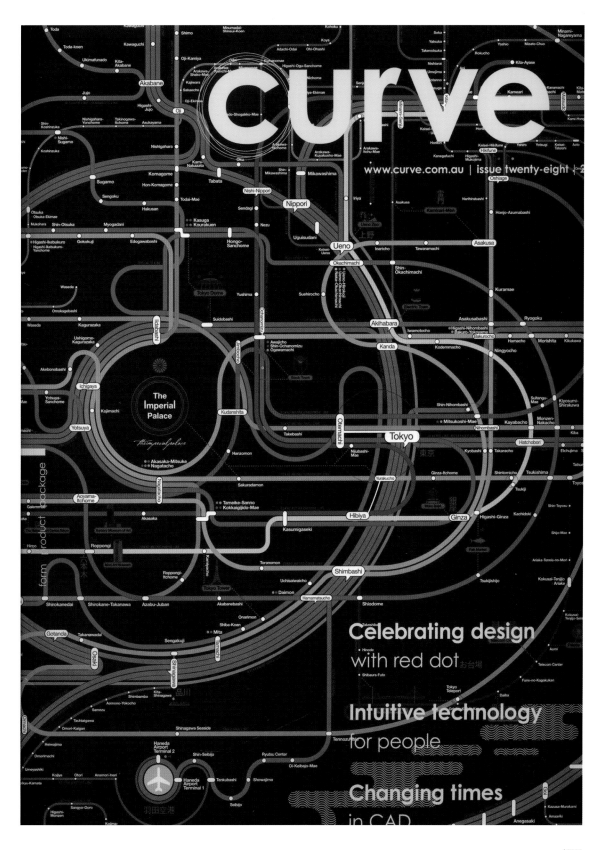

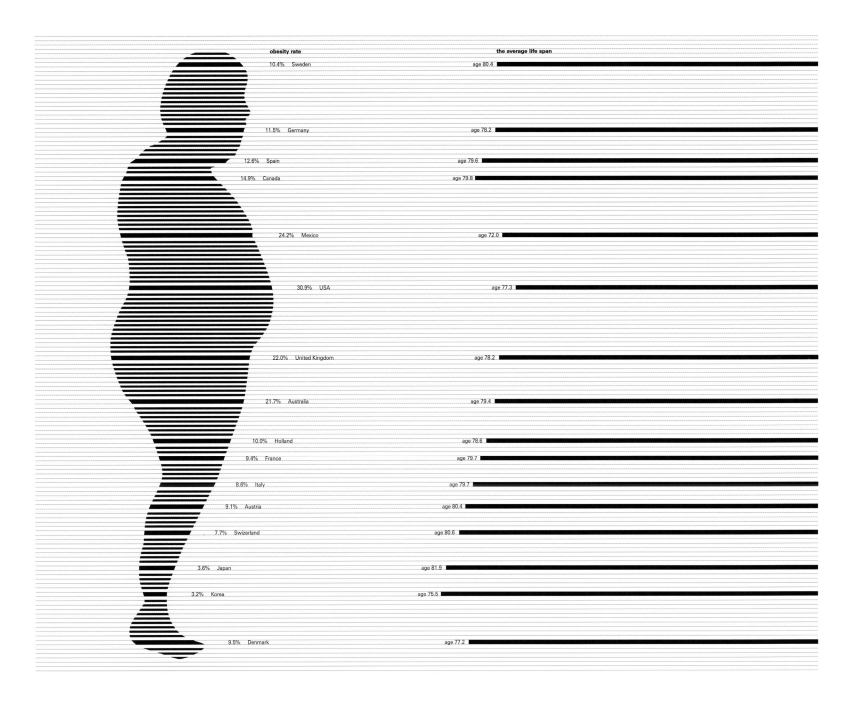

obesity rate

the average life span

10.4% Sweden	age 80.4	
11.5% Germany	age 78.2	
12.6% Spain	age 79.6	
14.9% Canada	age 79.8	
24.2% Mexico	age 72.0	
30.9% USA	age 77.3	
22.0% United Kingdom	age 78.2	
21.7% Australia	age 79.4	
10.0% Holland	age 78.6	
9.4% France	age 79.7	
8.6% Italy	age 79.7	
9.1% Austria	age 80.4	
7.7% Swizerland	age 80.6	
3.6% Japan	age 81.9	
3.2% Korea	age 75.5	
9.5% Denmark	age 77.2	

The diagram is one of about 80,
which were created by students of the
Musashino Art University in Tokyo
during a workshop.
This example shows the percent share
of corpulent people in different countries as well as their average life span.

Client:
Musashino Art University
Department of Science of Design
Tokyo, Japan

Workshop for design students
Guest Professors:
Barbara and Gerd Baumann
Baumann & Baumann
Schwäbisch Gmünd
Germany

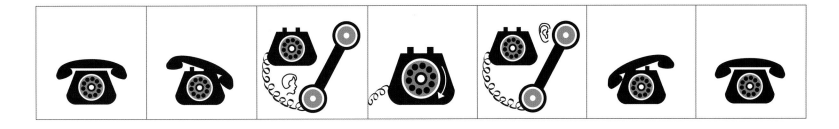

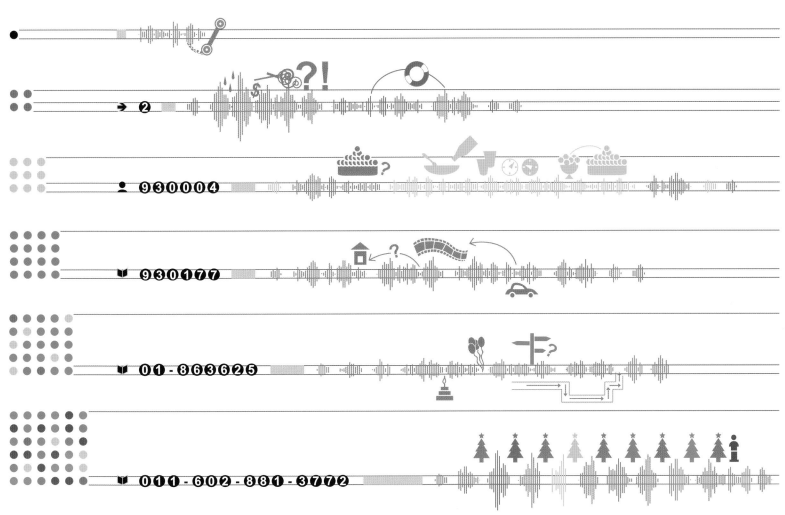

Teleconversations

This diagram is part of a series that represents different functions of a cellular phone. Just as the cell phone system divides areas on the map into cells, the device divides itself into multiple functions that match those of a telephone (through sound waves), letter (through text), and camera (through visuals). As a whole, the series aimed at showing the diversity of communications in the age of technology.
This representation aimed at paying homage to the telephone as a tool of communication on different levels:
a) various messages, b) sent across a multitude of locations, c) between people sharing different relationships.

Exercise done at Arizona State University, Tempe, Arizona, USA
Designer: Tina Sleiman

➜	speed dial	individual	●
●	memory	family	●
📖	phone book	extended family	●
❷	phone number	community	●
	waiting time	national contacts	●
|||||	sound	international contacts	●

179

UNSC/R - Mapping the United Nations Resolutions

UNSC/R: this is the abbreviation for the United Nations Security Council Resolutions. These documents represent the decisions of the UN's executive body.

This massive amount of data (more than 1700 documents) doesn't come in any organized form. The purpose of this project is to apply information design strategies to create visual maps of the Resolutions to help students in politics approach the subject of the UN. The graphic in the image is part of a series of experiments aimed to map the Resolutions.

Grey area: United Nations Security Council Resolution. The whole amount of Resolutions since the birth of the UN (1946).

Cyan area: resolutions regarding peacekeeping operations. Every Resolution coloured with cyan, is considered a document related to interventions of the UN personnel as observers or as agents of control. Those situations usually identify countries with falling dictatorships, civil or ethnic wars.

Red area: high tension situations involving UN peacekeepers. Many situations concerning the peacekeeping operations configure violent scenarios where the peacekeepers have to deal with non-predicted escalations of tension between civilians, rebels or invading armies.

MA 2009 self-initiated project,
at London College of Communication
Designer: Piero Zagami

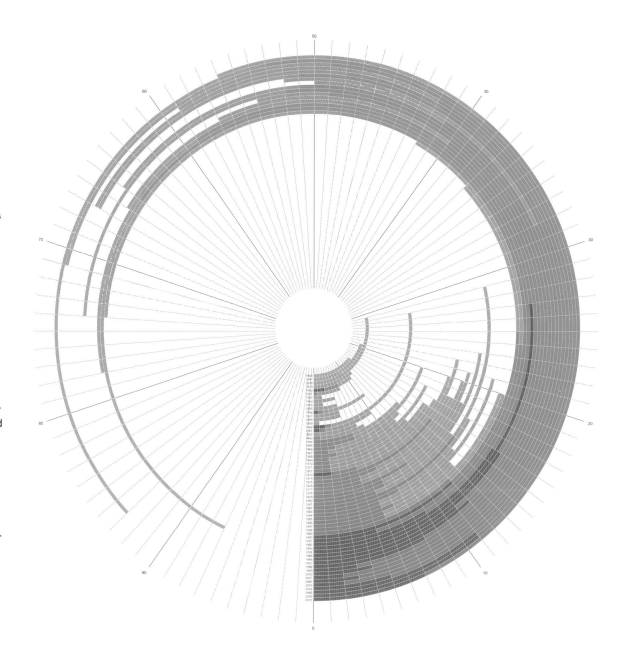

180

This diagram is part of an information design editorial on automobile accidents in the United States. This portion of the narrative shows the most common angles of impact between vehicles during automobile accidents, and correlates the angle type to the proportion of fatalities in both multi-vehicle and single-vehicle incidents.

Work done at University of Washington, Seattle, Washington, USA
Associate Professor Karen Cheng
Visual Communication Design Program
Division of Design, School of Art

Designer: Andrew S. Allen

Type of Impact

Impacts can occur in four different ways: frontal, side, rear and rollover. Although many impacts may occur in one accident, usually the first impact is the most damaging. From the collected data it is clear that frontal impacts are not only the most common but also very deadly. Most frontal and side impacts occur in multiple vehicle (MV) crashes while rollovers are more common among single vehicle (SV) crashes.

Fatality Rate
(per million registered vehicles)

31%   MV SV

MV = multiple vehicle crash
SV = single vehicle crash

FRONTAL IMPACT

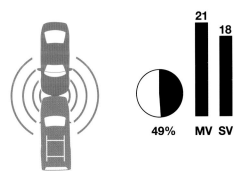

SIDE IMPACT

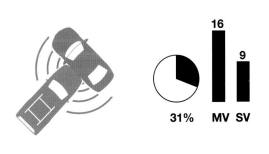

REAR IMPACT

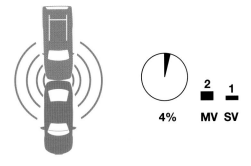

ROLLOVER

Eye colour and use of glasses

Eye colour

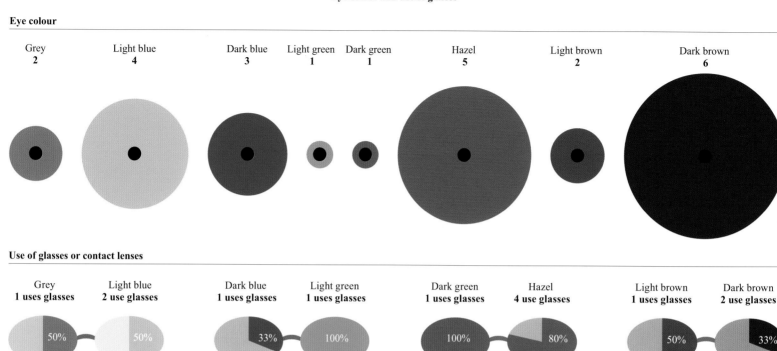

| Grey **2** | Light blue **4** | Dark blue **3** | Light green **1** | Dark green **1** | Hazel **5** | Light brown **2** | Dark brown **6** |

Use of glasses or contact lenses

| Grey **1 uses glasses** | Light blue **2 use glasses** | Dark blue **1 uses glasses** | Light green **1 uses glasses** | Dark green **1 uses glasses** | Hazel **4 use glasses** | Light brown **1 uses glasses** | Dark brown **2 use glasses** |
| 50% | 50% | 33% | 100% | 100% | 80% | 50% | 33% |

At what age people started to wear glasses

9   12 13 14   16 17 18 19   23   27   29

The brief was to create a graphical representation of information with data gathered within a target group of 24 people. In these diagrams the chosen subject was eye colour and use of glasses within the group. A further diagram shows at what age people started to wear glasses, according to gender and eye colour.

The majority of people surveyed had dark brown eyes, followed by hazel and then light blue.
At least one person in each group was wearing glasses or contact lenses.
A high percentage of those with dark blue and dark brown eyes have better eyesight than those with green eyes. Most people wearing glasses started between 12 and 19 years old, with a concentration between the age of 12 and 14. On 13 people wearing glasses or contact lenses, 9 were women and only 4 were men.

The diagrams have been produced using Adobe Illustrator, and they were part of a project requirement on the Visualisation of Statistical Information, during the course Grad Cert Design for Visual Communication 2009 at the London College of Communication. Designer: Grazia Trisciuoglio

Blur, Gig History

The image is part of a diagram that displays 20 years of concerts of the band Blur through a tube map-like aspect. Each tube line corresponds to a different year. The lines interchanges correspond to when the band played in the same venue several times throughout the years.

This project was included in a publication about the band and distributed freely in their gigs in London (June-July 2009) to the fans of the band.

Agency: Stylorouge
Art Direction: Sarah Foley
Designer: Piero Zagami
London, UK

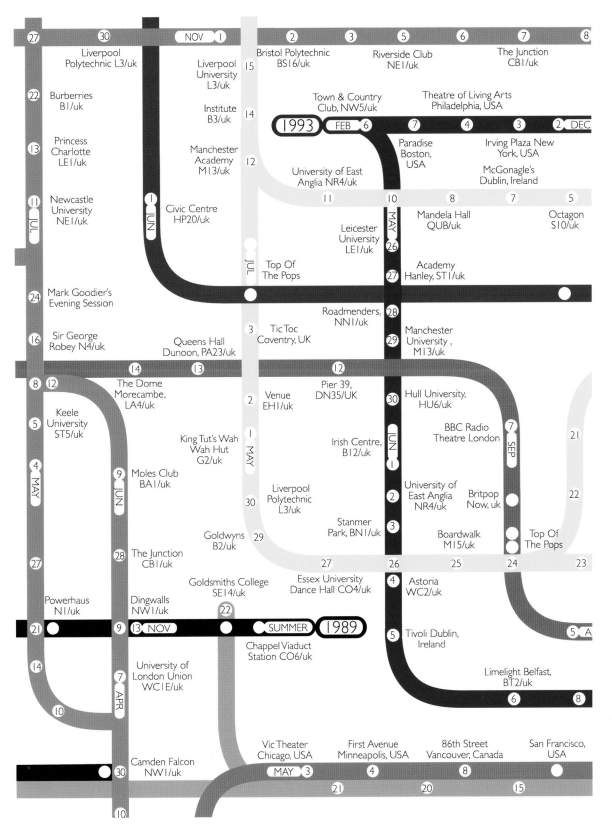

Networks at Heathrow Airport

Since the opening of Heathrow Airport in 1948 the number of flights has increased by 5% each year. To date, Heathrow Airport supports half a million flights and approximately 70 million passengers per year*

Pollution and noise are two of the major concerns of unease and distress for local residents, of which this is a study and visual representation of the latter.
This study is focused on uncovering the noise created by the vast network hub that is Heathrow Airport, specifically looking at the sources which create that noise, by breaking down the noises into visual and interactive formats.

This was achieved by recording noise levels at different locations in and around the airport building\boundaries. The information recorded was then presented in a visual format in order to communicate the levels of noise.

* UK Civil Aviation Authority, statistics 2008.

Self generated project done at London College of Communication
Designer: Ian Carr, Bath, UK

Noise Rings (illustration)
One ring portrays noise levels recorded at a location in and around Heathrow Airport.
A complete circle represents two minutes.
This is the average time gap between two planes landing.*
The colour change represents the change in noise level.

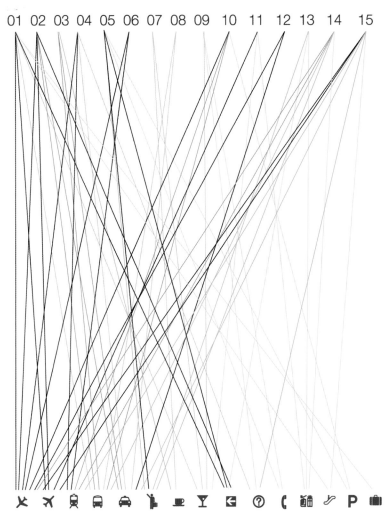

Location

01 02 03 04 05 06 07 08 09 10 11 12 13 14 15

Noise Density
Each column portrays noise levels
recorded at locations in and around
Heathrow Airport. Each line represents
when the noise level reached above
the average of 57 dB.*

Noise Matrix
The matrix displays the link between
each location and the type of sound
recorded over two minuets. This is the
average time gap between two planes
landing.

Visualizing Gender Stereotypes

is a personal research into gender stereotypes focusing on how children become aware of these and how they receive stereotyped messages through visual communication. The info design outcome is a book, which illustrates the findings collected during a workshop conducted in an Italian summer school with 42 children.

Valentina D'Efilippo: "I chose this topic because we are all daily influenced – positively or negatively – by stereotypes. Because of the complex nature of the field of stereotypes, this project aims not to provide any conclusions to this issue. As an infographic designer I merely want to show the children's point of view. I am interested in the potential of graphic design to visualize sociological and psychological areas; I believe that, although we may be unable to resolve the impact of gender stereotypes, at least we can publicize it, as knowing a problem is the first vital step towards its solution."

Software: Adobe Illustrator

Designer: Valentina D'Efilippo,
Design for Visual Communication,
London College of Communication,
2007.

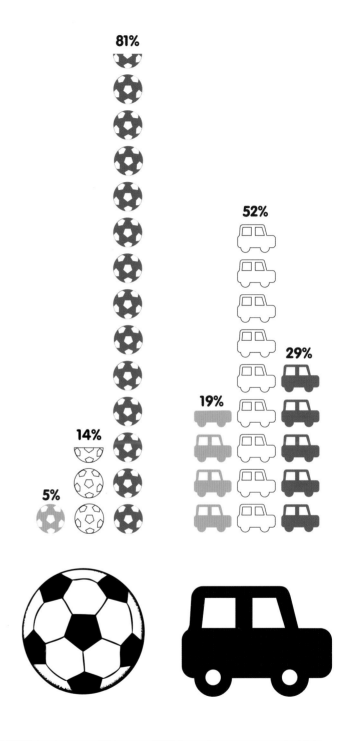

186

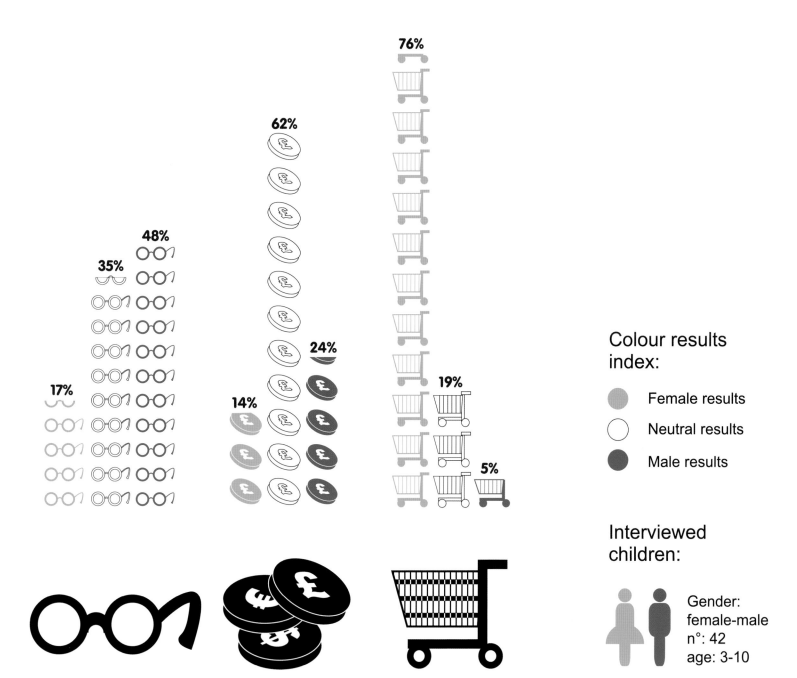

48%

35%

17%

62%

24%

14%

76%

19%

5%

Colour results index:

Female results

Neutral results

Male results

Interviewed children:

Gender:
female-male
n°: 42
age: 3-10

Information Design for Analysis and Advocacy

Communication design students need to develop the skills necessary to research, analyze, develop and present visual information. Specifically, these skills include the ability to:
- research and assemble a comprehensive set of data;
- transform data into clear and persuasive information graphics;
- discuss, analyze and evaluate good and bad information design.

The vehicle for student exploration is an analysis of energy issues in the United States and abroad. Initially, students work in small groups to research specific energy topics. Then, students work individually to develop a series of comparative charts, tables, graphs and diagrams.
The final data graphics are organized into a editorial information design narrative (a series of three two-page spreads).
Software used was Adobe Illustrator.

Work done at University of Washington, Seattle, Washington, USA
Associate Professor Karen Cheng, Visual Communication Design Program, Division of Design, School of Art

This diagram is part of an information design editorial on the generation of electricity in the United States and abroad. This portion of the narrative describes and analyzes the development of renewal forms of energy (such as solar, wind, geothermal, biomass and hydroelectric energy).

Designer: Sean Douglass

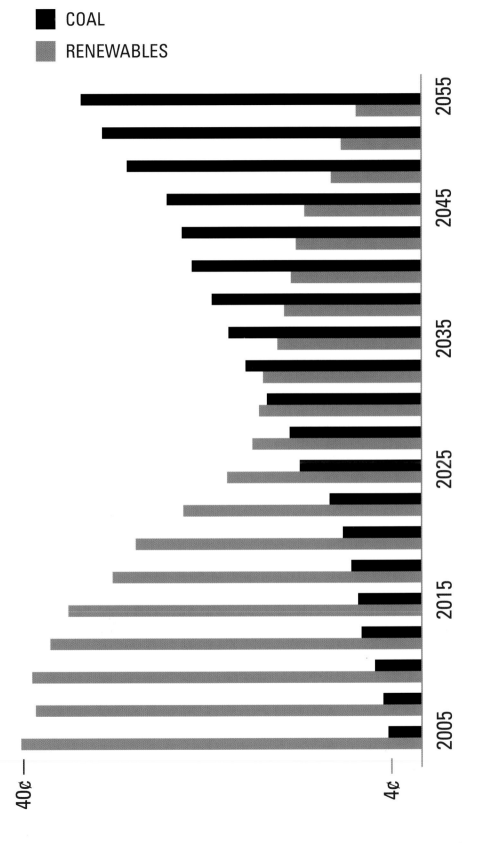

COAL
RENEWABLES

40¢
4¢

2005
2015
2025
2035
2045
2055

 **E85 STATIONS**
% Selling E85

 **HYBRID CARS**
% New Car Production

 **CONSUMPTION**
% Total Car Fuels

 **PRODUCTION**
% World Production

 **CAR OWNERS**
% of Population

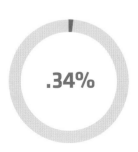 .34%

 18%

 5%

 29%

 77%

 96%

 67%

 40%

 45%

 15%

This diagram is part of an information design editorial on ethanol (E85), an alternative fuel to petroleum. The diagram compares aspects of fuel consumption in the United States (top row) vs. Brazil.
Brazil has one of the largest and most successful biofuels programs in the world.

Designer: Nivi Ramesh

The ComplexCity Project
explores major cities around the world focusing on how their urban sprawls have evolved over time. Using the patterns formed by roads in each city, Korean born designer Lee Jang Sub creates complex graphic configurations, combining the idea of natural and manmade systems. In the process he finds a concealed aesthetic within the convoluted pattern of urban networks. He started with his hometown Seoul, and has already completed Paris, Rome, and Moscow. The first image illustrates the intricate urban pattern of Moscow, while the second is representative of Rome.
This was a personal project which was later utilized for a range of wall decorations by the Spanish company Granada Design.
First, the streets were redrawn in Illustrator, and then vector sources were utilized in order to make organic patterns.

"Picking up on the inherent similarity between transportation systems in cities and the morphology of leaves and trees, is Lee Jang Sub's ComplexCity series of works. These elaborate mappings of roads and highways mimic the venation patterns in leaves and the rhizomatous configurations of tree branches, creating delicate organic filigree structures in a range of different mediums, including light."

Designer: Lee Jang Sub
Seoul, Korea

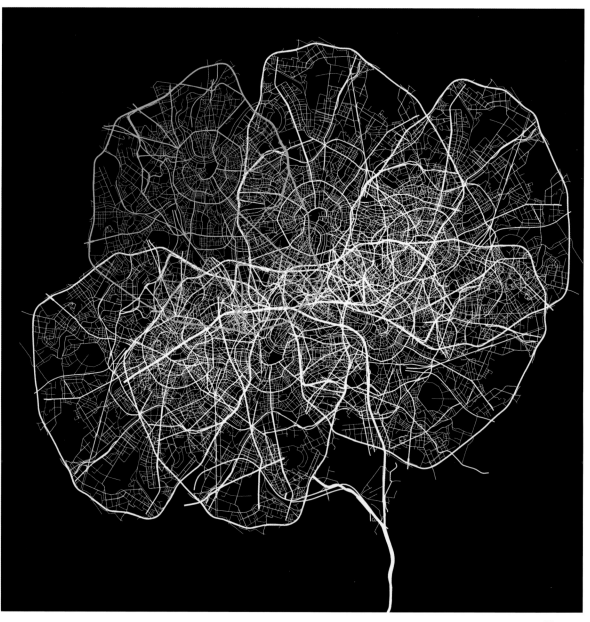

Moscow

190

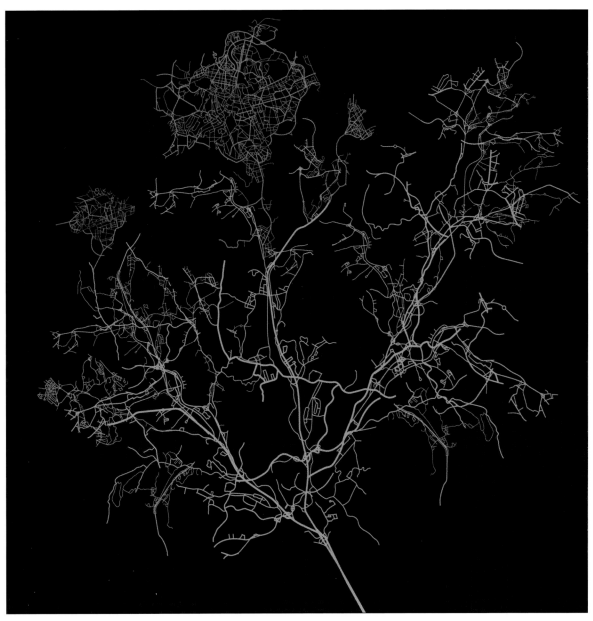

Rome

Subject: Dreams

The project was given to Final Year students on the BA(Hons) GMD Information Design course. The aim was for students to explore the subject of '"Dreams". It was an open brief in that students could interpret it from their own viewpoint.

In this example, the project explained the typical stages of sleep and why we dream. It explored the different levels of sleep looking at brain waves, the stages of sleep, cycles, REMs and other patterns.

These were interpreted diagrammatically in three dimensions as a series of ingenious pop-up diagrams.

There were numerous pages to this book which were all meticulously cut by hand taking hundreds of hours. Additionally using Adobe Illustrator software.

Student name: Kyung Hwa Lee
Faculty of Design
BA(Hons) Graphic & Media Design,
Information Design pathway
London College of Communication, UK

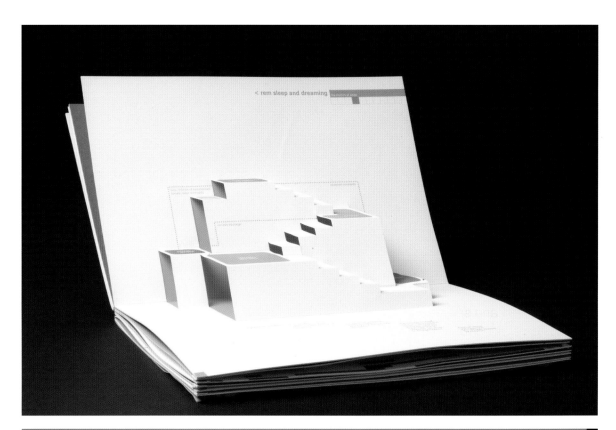

An Epilogue

Information design: The state of affairs (and the making of this book)

This book is partly the result of a research project intended to map out the origin, the sources and the possibilities within an area of humanistic activity. The working title became "Diagrams" which to many people's ears could sound like a narrow field within the graphic design spectrum.

There is no shortage of "how-to" books on the market. (Go to amazon.com. Type in words like "Branding" or "Colour" in the search field and see how many titles you get). By adding the subtitle "Making Information Accessible through Design" the scope widens considerably. I could have have been tempted to call the work "Creating Understanding" but the complexity of the world we live in is too daunting for such an attempt to be feasible.

We are all in dept to designers like Anton Stankowski (1906-1998) and Will Burtin (1908-1972) who devoted much of their activity to visualizing complex subject matter. As a student I was well aware of their efforts, but they belonged to a different generation and had to operate in what we now call "manual times".

Emerging of new media such as Geographic Positioning Systems, electronic guides, smartphones and various presentation devices are not only being developed fast, but will require visual communication skills to an extent that we per today do not know enough about. "Smart electronics" might not turn out to be so smart in the hands of amateurs.

As for previous books with diagrams as the core subject, Lockwood (1948) and Boundford (2000) left many things unexplained and untouched. The activities of Edward Tufte are described on pages 55 and 130.

When collecting specimens for the "Designer's Gallery" section of the book I quickly discovered that offices who concentrate on information design are (relatively) few and far between. There is good work being produced in New York, London, Amsterdam and Berlin, but results from the "outskirts" could have had a better and wider representation. The design press (both on paper and the web) is not too eager to show results from projects and investigations. One exception is the Journal of Information Design (www.benjamins.nl) This journal and their data collections is an indispensable international forum for discourse, critique and presentation of projects.

Some design schools have good courses; some touch the subject only superficially, and some do not treat information design at all. In the "Designer's Gallery" you will find work done by students who are aiming for an MA degree in the subject. This is a hopeful sign for the future.

No designer/author is infallible. Guiding hands and minds are needed. I am particularly thankful to Jan-Erik Kristiansen (Federal Bureau of Statistics, Oslo) who showed me the paths through the sometimes bewildering landscape of statistics. Designer/author Peter Wildbur (Tonbridge, UK) and author/publisher Robin Kinross (London) provided corrective comments and led me to interesting source material. Aaron Marcus (Berkeley, CA, USA) took an interest in the project at an early stage and contributed in many ways.

A special thanks to Frederik Ruys (Utrecht, The Netherlands), who took a critical look at the pages before we sent the book to production.

I am also thankful to my former employer the Oslo School of Architecture and Design for giving me the time and encouragement to start research on this project back in 2003. The readers have probably already gathered that this book was made possible through extensive international correspondence. I would like to thank all the "Internet friends" I have gathered in the process of making it. If you have any questions or comments, I shall be pleased to receive them. My email address is janjepga@online.no

Jan Gauguin   Oslo, September 2010

Acrobat (see Adobe Acrobat)

Adobe Acrobat

A program that creates "portable document format" (PDF) files. These files contain fonts, pictures and all the characteristics in the original postscript document and can be opened on any platform. A PDF file can be used both for proofs and as a base for printing. Proofs can travel easily over the Internet provided they are stored in a small file size. For printing the so-called "Press Quality" preset is recommended.
Adobe Acobat Professional is the program used for *creating* files, whilst Acobat Reader can be downloaded from Adobe's website free of charge. PDF files can also be created in Microsoft's office applications.

Adobe Presenter

A software application that can be used together with a Flash player. An alternative to Microsoft's Power-Point.

Audience

in this context means an assembly of spectators or readers who receive the information and interprets it. Those you can reach through publications, on the Internet or in audiovisual presentations.

CD (Compact Disc)

A digital storage technology originally developed by Philips and Sony Corp. on which data is stored by means of tiny pits burned into the disc's surface.

CD-ROM (Compact Disc Read Only Memory) is the most widely used disc for storing and distributing digital data.

It is not rewritable. It has a capacity of app. 650Mb but this can vary from one manufacturer to another. Most computers sold now have a recorder/player for CD-ROMs on them.
The technology is not foolproof and the medium itself must be labelled "fragile". When working on a project it is wise to store the data *both* on one's hard disc and on CD ROM until the job is finished.

Colour bar

A device printed on the edge of proofs which enables the repro house or printer to check the fidelity of colour separations and the accuracy of printing.

CorelDraw (see Vector graphics)

A vector based drawing program from Corel Inc.,Ottawa, Canada. CorelDraw was the most widely used drawing program for PC users in the 1990s but is now facing tough competition from Adobe and this company's "Creative Suite".
Corel offers fonts, clipart, textures and stock photograps as part of their package.

ClearType

is the name of a Microsoft Windows technology to improve the appearance of text on certain types of computer display screens, especially LCD flat-panel monitors. It is a form of subpixel rendering for text. It was introduced with Windows XP and has since been refined in newer Windows editions.

CMYK

Abbreviation for the standard four printing colours cyan, magenta, yellow and black. Black is represented by the letter "K" for the "key" plate.

Demography

The scientific study of human population, their changes, movement, size, distribution and structure.

Densitometer

A precision instrument used to measure the optical density and other properties of colour and light in transparencies, printing film, reflection copy and computer monitors.
Indispensable as a tool for calibrating display devices so that they conform to a set of standards, particularly where colour is concerned.

dpi

abbreviation for "dots per inches"

Freehand (see Vector graphics)

A vector drawing program program produced by Macromedia. No longer in use because Macromedia was bought by Adobe.

GIF (.gif)

Graphic Interchange Format files are used for line images transmitted over the Internet. Is gradually being replaced by PNG.

Hexachrome

A printing process developed by Pantone Inc. based on six inks rather than the four CMYK. Orange and green are the extra colours.

Illustrator (see Vector graphics)

Interface

The point of interconnection between two entities.
The point of interconnection between two systems or subsystems.

ISO

International Standards Organization is a Swiss-based body responsible for defining many elements concerning photography, film speeds, colour management, www protocols and other matters.

JPEG (.jpg)

The abbreviation stands for Joint Photographic Expert Group. A popular file format which is often used for transmitting images on the Internet. The user can define the degree of compression on a scale from "high" to "low". In layouts for printing low-resolution JPEG files are often mounted in as substitute for the real bitmap files in order to keep the number of bytes in the document down. A JPEG image is usually thin and should not be used for high quality printing. JPEG should never be used for enlargements like blow-ups or posters.

LAB (Lab colour)

is the internal colour model used by Photoshop when converting from one colour mode to another.

Leading
The word has its origin from the days of metal typesetting. Strips of lead were placed between lines of type to increase the space between them. In electronic applications, the leading can be user-defined and stored in a menu. Example: Type size: 12 pt, Leading: 4pt which gives 12/14 pt.

lpi
Abbreviation for "lines per inch".

PMS
is short for PANTONE MATCHING SYSTEMS. A series of guides and swatch books used to determine colour values. In communication with printers and other suppliers they are useful in order to secure consistency and accuracy in colour reproduction.

MAC
is short for an Apple Macintosh computer. The MAC was the first machine to utilize the GUI (the graphic user interface) in 1984. A revolutionary technology first developed by Xerox Corporation's Palo Alto Research Centre. Xerox decided not to launch their own computer but concentrate on their core business, making photocopying machine. Steven Jobs' firm Apple Computer Inc. managed successfully to produce a machine that revolutionized the entire graphic industry in the late 1980s. The MAC uses an operating system (MAC OSX) and a technology which is totally different from what is found on a PC. A MAC is also a "personal computer" but never called a PC.

Macromedia
A software manufacturer which merged with Adobe in 2006.

Master Page (see Templates)

PC
is an IBM personal computer, first launched by International Business Machines in 1981. It is now a generic term for any computer which is IBM compatible and can run on the "Windows" operating system.

PDF (see Adobe Acrobat)

Postscript
The most widely used page description programming language used in the graphic industry.
First launched by Adobe in 1985 and the fundament for Desktop Publishing developed by Paul Breinard the same year.
The standard today is Postscript Premium (Version 3).

PNG (.png)
is an acronym for Portable Network Graphics, a file format often called "ping". It provides 10-30 percent "lossless" compression compared to TIFF and PSD. It is suitable for the Internet and for electronic display (like in PowerPoint), but is not recommended for printing. It cannot produce colour separations.

Polygon
A closed plane figure bounded by straight lines. The number of lines and angles may vary.

QuarkXpress
A publishing program manufactured by Quark Inc. The most popular layout program amongst MAC users since the late 1980s. Is now facing heavy competition from Adobe's InDesign.

Structure
The mode of construction or organisation which enables parts to appear as a whole.

Template
(also called Master Page) contains attributes that will be common to all the pages in a document or a presentation. These can be number of columns, page numbers, type styles etc. In many programs, templates can be stored and used for future jobs.

Texture
The surface characteristics of a particular area or body.

TIFF (.tif)
Acronym for Tagged Image File Format. A standard and popular file format for scanned, high-resolution bitmap images and colour separations. Used for both colour and greyscale images. TIFF is a so-called "Open Standard" and can be imported into both layout programs and office applications.
The files are ideal for printing but tend to be a bit heavy for screen projection and the Internet. See PDF, PNG, JPEG and PDF, which offer various degrees of compression.

Vector graphics
Images made up of mathematically defined shapes, lines, curves and fills. These can be displayed at any size or resolution without loss of quality.
2D vector graphics programs that are most used by designers are CorelDraw and Illustrator.
Most 3D CAD programs also have vector graphics facilities.

Windows
An application developed by Microsoft. The latest version (Windows 7) is a successor to XP and Vista and was lauched in November 2009.

X-height
The height of lower case letters such as "x" with no ascenders or descenders.

Recommended reading:
Alastair Campbell
"The Designer's Lexicon"
ISBN 0-304-35505-4

Literature

Albers, Josef
"Interaction of color"
Revised and expanded edition 2006
ISBN 0300115954

Bertin, Jacques
"Semiologie graphique"
Edition Gauthiers Villars, Paris 1947
(First edition)
"Semiology of Graphics" The
University of Winsconsin Press 1983
ISBN 0801 8987
Reprint (French only) 2005
ISBN 978-2713220272

Campbell, Alastair
"The Designer's Lexicon"
London 2000 ISBN 0-304-35505-4

Campbell, Alastair
"The Digital Designer's Jargon Buster"
London 2005 ISBN 1904705359

Campbell, Alastair & **Dabbs**, Alastair
"The Digital Designer's Bible"
Lewes, East Sussex, UK 2004
ISBN 1-904705-27-8

Critchlow, Keith
"Order in Space"
London 2000 ISBN 0500340331

Dansk Design Center
"Finding the Way"
Text in Danish and English
ISBN 87-87385-78-3

The complete guide to Digital Graphic
Design (New Edition)
Thames & Hudson (2005)
ISBN 978-0500285602

Elam, Kimberly
"Geometry of Design"
ISBN 1-56898-249-6

Elam, Kimberly
"Grid Systems – Principles of organizing type" ISBN 1-56898-249-6

ESRI: The ESRI Guide to GIS analysis
Volume 1 1999 ISBN 1-879102-06-4

Finkelstein, Ellen
"PowerPoint 2007"
McGraw-Hill 2007

Farkas, David K.
"Towards a better understanding of
PowerPoint deck design"
Information Design Journal, vol 14,
number 2, 2006, p.162-171

Fendley, Tim
"Traffic & Transport"
Information Design Journal
Volume 17, No.2, 2009

Fraser, Tom
Designer's Color Manual
London 2004 ISBN 081184210X

Fraser, Tom & **Banks**, Tom
"The complete Guide to Colour"
ISBN 1-904705-22-7

Frandsen, Jesper
"De(t) Gyldne Snit – I kunst, natur og
matematik"
Denmark 1991 ISBN 87-91246-01-6

Friendly, Michael
"Revisions of Minard" 1999. 12 pages.
(PDF document to be downloaded)
www.math.yorku.ca/SCS/Gallery/
minard/minard.pdf

Gage, John
"Colour and Culture, Practice and
Meaning from Antiquity to Abstraction"
Thames and Hudson, 1993

Garland, Ken
"Mr.Beck's Underground Map"
Capital Transport, London 1994

Gatter, Mark
"Getting it Right in Print: Digital
prepress for graphic designers"
2005 ISBN 081099206X

Gerster, Karl
"Programme entwerfen/Designing
programmes"
ISBN 978-3-03778-092-3 (German)
ISBN 978-3-03778-093-0 (English)

Golledge, Reginal (Ed.)
Wayfinding Behaviour
John Hopkins University Press, 1999

Gombrich, E.H
"The Image and the Eye"
Further studies in the psychology of
pictorial presentation
Oxford 1982 (Phaidon)

Graphis Diagram 2
New York 1996

Hartmann, Frank & **Bauer**, Erwin
"Otto Neurath: Visualisierungen"
ISBN 3851147049

Jelen, Bill
"Charts and graphs for Microsoft Office
Excel 2007"
ISBN 0-7897-3610-1

Johansson, K.,**Lundberg**, P.
& **Ryberg**, R.
"A Guide to Graphic Print Production"
2nd edition 2007
ISBN: 978-0-471-76138-9

Klee, Paul
"Das Bildnerische Denken/"The thinking
Eye"
(Different editions in several languages)

Klee, Paul
"Notebooks"
Basel 1970/London 1973/78

Maeda, John (Editor)
1. Fresh Dialogue 9: In/Visible: Graphic
Data Revealed, by AIGA New York
Chapter
ISBN 9781568988160

Mijksenaar, Paul
"Visual function: An introduction to
information Design"
1997 ISBN 156898118X

Mollerup, Per
"Wayshowing"
Lars Müller Publishing 2005
ISBN 3-03778-055-X

Neurath, Otto
"Gesammelte bildpädagogische
Schriften"
Vienna 1991 ISBN 3-209-00863-9

Neurath, Marie & **Kinross**, Robin
"The transformer - principles of making
Isotype charts"
London 2008
ISBN 978-0-907259-40-4

Playfair, William
"The Commercial and Political Atlas
and Statistical Breviary"
Cambridge University Press, 2005
ISBN 13-9780521855549

Pring, Roger
"www.colour"
London 2000 ISBN 304 356077

Roberts, Lucienne & **Thrift**, Julia
"The Designer and the Grid"
Rotovision 2002 ISBN 3-209-00863-9

Samara, Timothy
"Making and breaking the Grid"
Rockport, USA 2004
ISBN 1-56496-893-6

Tufte, Edward
"The visual display of quantitative
information"
Graphics Press, USA 1984/2001
ISBN 0961392142

Uddin, M.Saleh
"Axiometric and oblique drawing"
New York 1997 ISBN 0-07-065755-6

Vossoughian, Nader
"Mapping the modern city"
in Design Issues vol 22, No.3, summer
2006
MIT Press Journals

Vossoughian, Nader
"Otto Neurath - The Language of the
global Polls"
NAI Publishers 2008
ISBN 978-90-5662-350-0

Werner, Steve
"Wll it print?"
Article in InDesign magazine
April/May 2009

Wilkinson, L.
"The Grammar of Graphics"
Springer, New York 1999

Wurman, Richard Saul
"Information anxiety 2" what to do when
information does not tell you what you
need to know"
Hayden/Que 2000

Zwick, Carola
"Digital Colour"
ISBN 978-2-88479-026-0

Interesting websites:

Design & Technology
http://desktoppub.about.com/mbody.
htm
GATF Graphic Arts Technology
Foundation:
www.gatf.org
www.aiga.org
www.creativepro.com
www.pdfzone.com
www.strata.com
http://dx.sheridan.com/index.html

GIS software
www.geoplan.ufl.edu/software.html

GPS equipment
http://www.thegpsstore.com
www.magellangps.com
www.garmin.blogs.com

About diagrams
www.nigelholmes.com
www.visualmining.com/examples/index.
html
www.apple.com/no/keynote/charts.html
www.edwardtufte.com
Searchword: "Semiologie Graphique"
www.visualcomplexity.com
www.tableausoftware.com/flowingdata

About colour
www.colormatters.com/
entercolormatters.html
wwww.color.org
http://pantone.com
www.serve.com/apg/cgi-bin/colorpicker.
cgi
www.american.edu/guidelines/
hexcolors.html
www.serve.com/apg/cgi-bin/colorpicker.
cgi

Geometry
www.42explore.com/geomet.htm
www.studyworksonline.com/cda/
explorations/

Typography
www.microsoft.com/OpenType/OTSpec/
https://istore.adobe.com/type/browser/
C/C_otfpro.html
www.fonts.com

Presentation techniques
www-businessonline.com
http://presentationsoft.about.com
www.masterviews.com/powerpoint_for_
learning.htm
http://presentationsoft.about.com/od/
firststeps/p/lose_audience.htm
www.fusioncharts.com

Instruction videos
www.lynda.com
www.layersmagazine.com

Organizations
Information Design Association
www.infodesign.org.uk
ICOGRADA
www.icograda.org

Statistical literacy
www.statlit.org

Contributors/contacts

USA and Canada

Anne & Eugene Timerman
TMR Design
2109 Broadway #3157
New York, NY10023, USA
www.timerman.com
anne@timerman.com

Ralph Appelbaum Associates
RAA NY
88 Pine Street
New York, NY 10005, USA
www.raany.com
frontdesk@raany.com

Cloud Gehshan Associates
400 Market Street, Suite 300
Philadelphia, PA 19106, USA
www.cloudgehshan.com
rbogart@cloudgehshan.com

karlssonwilker inc
536 6th Avenue
New York City 10011, USA
www.karlssonwilker.com
nicolejacek@me.com

Aaron Marcus and Associates, Inc.
(AM+A)
1196 Euclid Avenue, Suite 1F
Berkeley, California 94708-1640, USA
Aaron.Marcus@AMandA.com
www.AMandA.com

Kick Design
(212) 683-3665
347 5th Ave
New York, NY, USA
Att: Eddie Jabour
www.kickdesign.com
mail@kickdesign.com

John Grimwade
Information Graphics
630 First Avenue #18L
New York, NY 10016, USA
www.johngrimwade.com
jg@johngrimwade.com

Mia J.Chuang
OtherPlane Inc.
4473 West 9th Ave,
Vancouver, BC, V6R 2C9, Canada
www.otherplane.org
mia@otherplane.org

Associate Professor Karen Cheng
School of Art
University of Washington
Box 353440
Seattle, WA 98195-3440
www.design.washington.edu
kcheng@uw.edu

TIBCO Software Inc.
David Sciacero
7621 Via Del Reposo
Scottsdale, AZ 85285, USA
sciacero@yahoo.com
www.tibco.com

Europe

Applied Information Group
26–27 Great Sutton Street
Clerkenwell
London EC1V 0DS, UK
www.appliedinformationgroup.com
info@aiglondon.com

Baumann & Baumann
Büro für Gestaltung
Bahnhofstrasse
73625 Schwäbisch Gmund
Germany
www.baumannandbaumann.com
info@baumannandbaumann.com

Becky Johnson - Designer.
Form®: Design and Art Direction
47 Tabernacle Street,
London EC2A 4AA, UK
becky@form.uk.com

De Designpolitie
Graaf Florisstraat 1a
1091 TD Amsterdam
The Netherlands
www.designpolitie.nl
info@designpolitie.nl
Att: Pepijn Zurburg

EdenSpiekermann Berlin
Friederichstrasse 126
10117 Berlin, Germany
www.edenspiekermann.com
n.haegeli@de.edenspiekermann.com

Space Syntax Limited
4 Huguenot Place
Heneage Street

London E1 5LN, UK
www.spacesyntax.com
i.ansaberga@spacesyntax.com

Faydherbe / De Vringer
2e Schuytstraat 76
2517 XH Den Haag,
The Netherlands
info@ben-wout.nl

Frédérik Ruys,
Vizualism
Bekkerstraat 117
3572 SG Utrecht
The Netherlands
www.vizualism .com
f.ruys@vizualism.com

Kognito Gestaltung
Wikingerufer 7
10555 Berlin-Tiergarten
Germany
www.kognito.de
write-to@kognito.de

Kahn+Associates
90, rue des Archives
75003 Paris, France
www.kahnplus.com
julia.moisand@kahnplus.com

Moniteurs
kommunikationsdesign gmbh
Ackerstraße 21/22
10115 Berlin, Germany
www.moniteurs.de
s.schlaich@moniteurs.de

Fokke Gerritsma
NRC Handelsblad
Marten Meesweg 35
3068 AV Rotterdam
The Netherlands
Gerritsma@nrc.nl

Piero Zagami
4 Bath Street, Flat 3, EC1V 9DX, UK
www.pierozagami.com
pierzag@gmail.com

Ian Carr / Print and New Media
flat 5, Hillside House
Frome, BA11 1LB, UK
info@iancarr.net
www.iancarr.net

Thomas Manss & Company
Sybelstraße 68
10629 Berlin, Germany
www.manss.com
jeannette@manss.com

Millimeterpress as
Kongens gate 3
N-0153 Oslo, Norway
Att: Egil Arntzen
egil@milli.no

Jeroen Disch
Lava Amsterdam
Silodam 1F, 1013 AL Amsterdam,
The Netherlands
www.lava.nl
jeroen@lava.nl

De Argumentenfabriek BV
W.G.-plein 478
1054 SH Amsterdam
The Netherlands
www.argumentenfabriek.nl
carienfranken@gmail.com

Australia and Asia

Frost Design
15 Foster Street Surrey Hills
NSW 2010 Sydney, Australia
http//frostdesign.com.au/
info@frostdesign.com

Lee Jang Sub
401, 327-5, Sangsu-dong, Mapo-gu,
Seoul, Korea 121-829
leejangsub@gmail.com
www.leejangsub.com

Tina Sleiman
Zayed University
P.O.Box: 19282
Dubai, UAE
tina.sleiman@gmail.com
tina.sleiman@zu.ac.ae

ZERO PER ZERO studio
Ji hwan Kim, Sol Jin)
#303, Jinyoung Bldg, 392-3,
Hapjeong-Dong, Mapo-Gu,
Seoul 121-886 South Korea
zeroperzero.studio@gmail.com
www.zeroperzero.com